Understanding Public Law

Public Law is concerned with the law governing the institutions of the state and the relationship between the state and the individual, and is a core subject for all students reading for a qualifying law degree. This concise, student-friendly guide will help equip students with an understanding of the key aspects of the UK's political and legal systems as well as building an understanding of the relationship between the different branches of the state such as the executive, legislature and judiciary.

Understanding Public Law provides a consideration of the main themes in a logical, progressive manner, highlighting the broader political and social contexts, and focusing on how and why the law has developed as it has.

Throughout the text, key terms are identified and explained from the outset, helping students new to the subject familiarize themselves with the vocabulary of public law; chapter outlines and summaries help to focus the reader on the key topics; and a set of self-test questions at the end of each chapter encourage students to consider and reflect on what has been learnt. Supported by a companion website offering opportunities for examination practice and revision, *Understanding Public Law* is the ideal introduction to this essential subject.

Hilaire Barnett, BA, LLM, was previously at Queen Mary College, University of London, and is the author of the best-selling textbook, *Constitutional and Administrative Law*, also published by Routledge-Cavendish.

Understanding Public Law

Hilaire Barnett

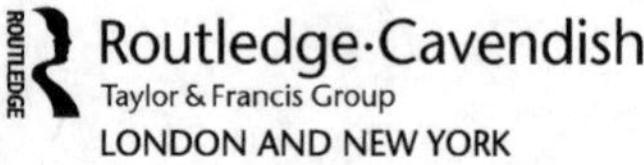

First edition published 2010
by Routledge-Cavendish
2 Park Square, Milton Park, Abingdon, Oxon OX14 4RN

Simultaneously published in the USA and Canada
by Routledge-Cavendish
270 Madison Avenue, New York, NY 10016

Routledge-Cavendish is an imprint of the Taylor & Francis Group, an informa business

Typeset in Times by
RefineCatch Limited, Bungay, Suffolk
Printed and bound in Great Britain by
TJ International Ltd, Padstow, Cornwall

British Library Cataloguing in Publication Data
A catalogue record for this book is available from the British Library

Library of Congress Cataloging-in-Publication Data
Barnett, Hilaire.
Understanding public law / Hilaire Barnett. — 1st ed.
p. cm.
1. Public law—Great Britain. 2. Civil rights—Great Britain.
I. Title.
KD3930.B373 2009
342.41—dc22 2009020043

ISBN10: 0–415–55254–0 (hbk)
ISBN13: 978–0–415–55254–7 (hbk)

ISBN10: 0–415–55255–9 (pbk)
ISBN13: 978–0–415–55255–4 (pbk)

ISBN10: 0–203–86581–2 (eBook)
ISBN13: 978–0–203–86581–1 (eBook)

Contents

Preface

Understanding Public Law provides a concise introduction to and explanation of constitutional law and administrative law, which together make up Public Law. In addition to acting as a starting point for study, it is hoped that *Understanding Public Law* will prove a useful resource for revision of the subject.

Unlike the majority of states around the world, the United Kingdom's Constitution is 'unwritten'. In order to understand its substance, therefore, it is necessary to examine the many and various legal and non-legal rules and principles which together comprise the Constitution.

Understanding Public Law is divided into 15 chapters. The early chapters deal with the sources of the Constitution and the principles that form the foundation of the contemporary Constitution: the rule of law, separation of powers and supremacy of the United Kingdom Parliament. Of increasing importance is the UK's membership of the European Union (EU) and the manner in which EU law impacts on domestic law, which is discussed in Chapter 6. The structure and working of central, regional and local government is considered in Chapter 7, while Chapters 8 and 9 deal with electoral law and the role of the United Kingdom Parliament in law-making and scrutinising government policy and administration. Chapters 10 to 12 deal with civil liberties (freedom of expression and privacy; freedom of assembly), public order law and the protection of human rights. Chapters 13 and 14 discuss judicial review of administrative action and Commissioners for Administration (Ombudsmen). The final chapter offers a very brief history of the evolution of the British Constitution, which it is hoped will be helpful in understanding its gradual development over past centuries.

Hilaire Barnett
May 2009

Table of Cases

Table of Statutes

Secondary legislation

European legislation

Chapter 1

Introduction to public law

CONTENTS

Studying public law

Public law is the label given to the laws regulating the state. It may be contrasted with private law, which regulates relationships between individuals such as contracts and marriages.

For the purposes of study, public law comprises constitutional law and aspects of administrative law. Constitutional law is concerned with the role and powers of the institutions within the state and the relationship between the citizen and the state.

Studying public law successfully involves acquiring an understanding of a variety of historical, legal and political factors that have shaped the organisation of the state. This is because, in the United Kingdom (UK), unlike the majority of states around the world, there is no comprehensive, single document known as 'the Constitution'. Aside from conflict in the seventeenth century (see Chapter 15), the constitution has evolved gradually and peacefully over the centuries, and there has never been the need to set all the rules down in a written constitution. As a result, the constitution is contained in numerous legal and non-legal sources – Acts of Parliament, decisions of the judges, the legal powers of the Crown and obligatory but non-legal rules.

The constitution is dynamic, and particularly since 1997, when the Labour government came into power, there has been considerable constitutional reform. In addition to studying from textbooks and the law reports it is also necessary to keep up to date with current affairs and be aware of changes actual and proposed, which may affect the working of the state.

The United Kingdom

The UK comprises England and Wales, Scotland and Northern Ireland. Northern Ireland, Scotland and Wales each has its own legislative body (the Parliament in Scotland, Assemblies in Northern Ireland and Wales) with differing levels of law-making power. The ultimate power to make law for each of the nations lies with the UK Parliament in London.

The Head of State is the Queen and all acts of government are undertaken in her name. Equally, the Queen is the 'fountain of justice' and all the actions of the judges are undertaken in her name: the courts are the Queen's courts. While the Crown has wide-ranging legal powers (for the royal prerogative, see Chapter 2), the government mostly exercises these today on her behalf.

Although a 'united kingdom' with one Crown and one supreme legislature, the UK has more than one legal system. Scotland has always had its own distinctive legal system, one protected under the Acts of Union 1706/1707. Northern Ireland also has its own system. Only England and Wales share a legal system. Devolution of power to national assemblies also reflects diversity within the UK. While Northern Ireland experienced a high degree of legislative autonomy between 1922 and 1974, the civil unrest in the Province resulted in law-making power being recalled to the UK Parliament at Westminster. In 1997 the Labour government was intent on devolving power not only back to Northern Ireland but also to Scotland and Wales. The Northern Ireland Act, Scotland Act and Government of Wales Act 1998 gave effect to devolution (see Chapter 7).

What is a constitution?

Every organisation – whether a state or a university or a trade union or a club – will have a constitution – a set of rules defining the structure and working of the organisation. The constitution of a state will define the principal institutions – the executive, legislature and judiciary – and the nature and scope of their powers. In addition, a constitution will usually define the rights and freedom of citizens, rights with which the government cannot lawfully interfere. Very broadly, a constitution of a state may be defined as being:

> . . . the whole system of government of a country, the collection of rules which establish and regulate or govern the government.[1]

1 Wheare, KC, *Modern Constitutions*, 1966, Oxford University Press.

Classifying constitutions

Constitutions may be:

- written or unwritten;
- republican or monarchical;
- flexible or rigid;
- unitary or federal;
- supreme or subordinate;
- have clearly separated powers or fused powers.

A written constitution is one contained within a single document or a series of documents defining the basic rules of the state. The origins of written constitutions lie in the American War of Independence (1775–1783) and the French Revolution of 1789. More recently, written constitutions have been drafted in the process of dismantling a colonial relationship and restoring independence to a country.

The feature that is common to all countries with a written constitution is that at some point in time there has been a clear break from former constitutional arrangements, providing the opportunity for a fresh start.

A republican state is one having as its figurehead a (usually) democratically elected president. By contrast, a monarchical state is one having as its head of state a king or queen. In Britain the Crown is hereditary, with the line of succession being defined under the Act of Settlement 1700. This restricts the succession to members of the Protestant faith and specifically excludes Roman Catholic. Male heirs take precedence over female heirs.

A flexible constitution is one that may be amended with ease. A rigid constitution, by contrast, is one where there are stringent procedures to be followed before reform can take place. The constitution is usually written, and the rules for reform 'entrenched' – that is, incapable of or exceedingly difficult to reform. Common conditions for amendment would include the need for strict majorities in both Houses of the legislature to agree to reform, and for the proposal to be approved by the people in a referendum.

A unitary state is one with a highly centralised government and legislature, which enacts laws governing the whole state. A federal state is one where the power is divided between central government and more localised state governments. The constitution will define the allocation of power between central and state government.

A supreme constitution is one that is not controlled by any higher source of power. On the other hand, a subordinate constitution is one that has (usually) been conferred by a higher power, with that higher power being able to extend or restrict the degree of autonomy enjoyed by the subordinate state. Subordinate constitutions are usually the product of colonialism, largely but not completely abandoned in the twentieth century.

Constitutions may also be classified according to whether they have separated powers or not. Separation of powers (see Chapter 3) is an ancient concept requiring that the personnel, functions and powers of the principal institutions of the state – the executive, legislature and judiciary – are separate. The purpose of the separation of powers is to avoid the concentration of power in one 'pair of hands', which could lead to the abuse of power. A state with a poor, or nonexistent, separation of powers is likely to be a dictatorship, with no system of checks and balances to avoid the abuse of power.

Characteristics of the United Kingdom constitution

The British constitution today is largely written but uncodified (not brought together in a single document), has a constitutional monarchy, is unitary but with powers diffused among different levels of government (central, regional and local), and highly flexible. Unlike states whose constitutions set out complex procedures for constitutional reform, in the UK an ordinary Act of Parliament can achieve fundamental reforms.

The UK's constitution is not controlled by any higher power, and accordingly may be described as supreme rather than subordinate. This last point needs qualifying in the sense that since 1973, Britain has been a member of the European Community, and now the wider European Union (EU). As such, domestic law must be in line with EU law (see Chapter 6 on this). However, membership is voluntary, and any restriction on Britain's law-making power is accepted as one of the terms of membership.

Only three countries have an unwritten, or uncodified, constitution: Britain, Israel and New Zealand. In the absence of a written constitution – which is the ultimate authority with a state – the void is filled by the concept of the sovereignty of Parliament. Parliament may – subject to non-legal restraints such as politics and economics – legislate on any subject whatsoever (see Chapter 5). Also central to the UK's constitution is the relationship between the three major institutions of the state – the executive, the legislature and the judiciary. While most states have a clear separation of powers and personnel between these institutions, the UK arrangement is more one of checks and balances, so that where overlaps occur, any potential abuse of power is avoided by legal rules or by the non-legal but binding rules of the constitution – constitutional conventions (see Chapter 2).

To conclude, the British constitution:

- is largely unwritten in character;
- flexible;
- supreme;
- formally unitary, but with powers devolved to Northern Ireland, Scotland and Wales;
- has mainly but not completely separated powers;
- is monarchical.

? *SELF-ASSESSMENT QUESTIONS*

1. Write a brief definition of a Constitution.
2. List at least four characteristics that constitutions may have (for example a constitution may be *federal* or *unitary*).
3. List at least four characteristics of the British constitution.
4. What are the primary characteristics of the British Constitution (you should be able to list at least three).

Chapter 2

Sources of the Constitution

CONTENTS

KEY WORDS AND PHRASES

Common law	The law developed through the decisions of judges
Constitutional conventions	Non-legal but obligatory rules
Judicial review	The procedure by which the courts rule on the legality of administrative and executive decisions
Justiciability	The concept that defines those issues upon which the courts will adjudicate

Royal prerogative	The legal powers of the Crown
Statute	An Act of Parliament, the highest form of law

Introduction

In a state with a written constitution, the principal source of the rules regulating the state will be the Constitution itself, supplemented by the judicial decisions that have interpreted the meaning of aspects of the Constitution. In a state such as Britain, which has no written constitution, the situation is very different and it is necessary to look at a number of sources, both legal and non-legal. Among these are Acts of Parliament, judicial decisions,

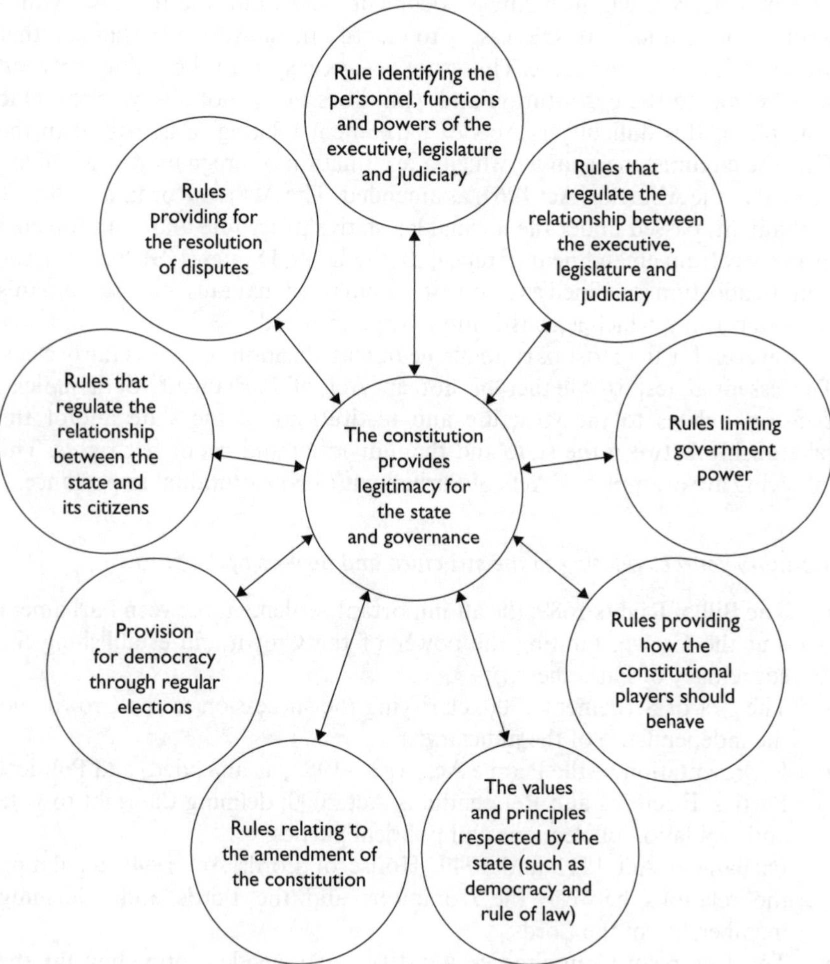

Figure 2.1 A 'Constitution'

the powers of the Crown (the Royal prerogative) and the non-legal but obligatory constitutional conventions. In addition to these sources, there are also principles that underpin the British Constitution. These include the concepts of the rule of law and separation of powers, discussed in Chapters 3 and 4, and parliamentary sovereignty considered in Chapter 5.

Legal sources

Statutes (Acts of Parliament)

Under the United Kingdom (UK) Constitution, Acts of Parliament are the highest form of domestic law. As the rules of the Constitution are not conveniently defined within a single document – as would be the case with a written constitution – it is necessary to identify those Acts of Parliament that are 'constitutional' in nature. This is not always easy as the boundary between what relates to the constitution and what does not is not always clear. One example of this difficulty is Acts of Parliament relating to abortion. In the UK, the circumstances under which a termination of pregnancy is lawful are defined in the Abortion Act 1967, as amended. The Act is an 'ordinary' Act of Parliament, passed under the normal legislative procedure and not protected in any way from amendment or repeal. In the United States (US), however, the right to abortion is defined as a constitutional issue that falls under a woman's right to privacy, which is constitutionally guaranteed.

However, for the most part, the issue of classification of laws is fairly clear. The essential test is whether or not an Act of Parliament, or a judicial decision, relates to the structure and institutions of the state and/or the relationship between the state and the individual and his or her rights. The following are examples of Acts of Parliament of constitutional importance.

Statutory sources relating to the structure and powers of the state

- The Bill of Rights 1689: the all-important settlement between Parliament and the Crown, limiting the power of the Crown and establishing the supremacy of Parliament;
- The Act of Settlement 1700: clarifying the succession to the Crown and the independence of the judiciary;
- Representation of the People Acts 1837–1983, as amended, and Political Parties, Elections and Referendums Act 2000: defining the right to vote and regulation of elections and political parties;
- Parliament Act 1911 and 1949, House of Lords Act 1999: regulating the relations between the Commons and the Lords and reforming membership of the Lords;
- The European Communities Act 1972, as amended: providing for the reception of Community law into domestic law;

- The Scotland Act 1998, Government of Wales Act 1998 and 2006, Northern Ireland Act 1998: providing for the devolution of power from Westminster to national assemblies;
- Local Government Acts: regulating the role and powers of local government.

Statutory sources relating to individual rights and freedoms

- The Race Relations Acts 1965 and 1976: prohibiting discrimination on grounds of race; the Equal Pay Act 1970, Sex Discrimination Act 1975: prohibiting discrimination on grounds of sex; the Disability Discrimination Act 1995: prohibiting discrimination on grounds of disability. The Single Equality Act 2006;
- The Human Rights Act 1998: incorporating rights enshrined in the European Convention on Human Rights into domestic law.

Common law sources (judicial decisions)

The decisions of judges form the common law. Historically, it was the courts that made most of the law, using the doctrine of precedent to ensure that there was consistency in decision-making. Parliament became the principal lawmaker towards the end of the nineteenth century, when – as a result of the Industrial Revolution and social change – the wide-scale and uniform regulation of society became necessary. While Acts of Parliament are the highest form of law and can overrule judicial decisions, judicial decisions that are not replaced by an Act of Parliament remain an important source of law. Accordingly, much of the law remains common law. The judiciary also develop the law through the interpretation of statutes, employing a set of 'rules', which are designed to ensure that judges correctly interpret Parliament's will as expressed in the Act of Parliament.

As with Acts of Parliament, however, not all decisions of the courts will be regarded as 'constitutional' in nature. Those that are so regarded will be decisions that relate – as with Acts of Parliament – to the structure and powers of the state and/or the rights and freedoms of the individual. Accordingly, whenever a case relates to the powers and/or duties of the state and its institutions, or the relationship between those institutions, the case is constitutional in nature. Equally, it can be said that any case that defines and/or protects the rights of individuals against the state and its agents, is constitutional in nature. The following represent just a few of the many important constitutional cases.

Entick v Carrington (1765): in which the court declared that the action of the executive in trespassing on a citizen's property and seizing property without a specific warrant was unlawful.

R v SS for Home Dept ex p Fire Brigades' Union (1995): in which the court declared the proposed use of the Royal prerogative by the Home Secretary rather than a statutory power to amend the Criminal Injuries Compensation Scheme was unlawful. The scheme had been established under the Royal prerogative, but an Act of Parliament made provision for amendments to the scheme. The House of Lords ruled that the Secretary of State was obliged to use the statutory provisions.

M v Home Office (1992).[1] In this case, an application for asylum had been refused and arrangements made for M to be deported. On the day of his departure, a High Court judge ordered that M be returned to the UK. The Home Secretary refused to comply with the order. M's lawyer sought to have the Home Secretary committed for contempt of court. The issue went to the House of Lords, which dismissed the Home Secretary's appeal against a finding of contempt. The Court ruled that while a finding of contempt could not be made directly against the Crown, it could be made against a minister in his personal or official capacity.

Pickin v British Railways Board,[2] in which the House of Lords ruled that once an Act of Parliament had been passed and received the Royal Assent, the court should not look into the procedure under which it was passed – even where there were allegations of wrongdoing.

Inland Revenue Commissioners v Rossminster Ltd (1980).[3] In this case, Inland Revenue inspectors obtained warrants to enter and search premises for evidence relating to fraud. The warrant did not specify the offences that were under investigation. The House of Lords ruled that since the warrant reflected the wording of the statute, the exercise of power was lawful. In a very different way from *Pickin*, the *Rossminster case* emphasises the power of Parliament and the inability of the judges to protect individual rights in the face of powers granted by Parliament.

1 [1992] 4 All ER 97.
2 [1974] AC 765.
3 [1980] AC 952.

A v Secretary of State for the Home Department (2004).[4] Here the House of Lords ruled that section 23 of the Anti-terrorism Crime and Security Act 2001 was incompatible with the right to liberty guaranteed under Article 5 of the Convention on Human Rights. Section 23 permitted the indefinite detention of non-British terrorist suspects. The reason for this power lies in the prohibition against admitting evidence obtained by the security services in court, and the inability of the government to deport the suspects, due to the obligation not to deport a person to his or her country of origin, if that would have the result of that person suffering inhuman or degrading treatment or punishment in that country. As a result, the government was obliged to release the suspects and to reform the law.

The Royal prerogative

The Royal prerogative comprises the powers of the Crown. Historically, as discussed in Chapter 15, the Crown had wide-ranging powers. The monarchy was regarded as handed down by God: an idea expressed in the now-discarded phrase 'the Divine Right of Kings'. The Crown owned all the land. The Crown conferred honours on its supporters and demanded men to form armies. The Crown controlled trade and commerce, including the power to close the ports and to raise taxes on trade. The Crown appointed magistrates and judges, for the courts were the Crown's courts.

But, notwithstanding all this power, the King was nevertheless dependent upon the allegiance of his supporters. As the signing of *Magna Carta* in 1215 shows, the King could ill-afford to ignore the grievances of the Barons.[5] However, until the late seventeenth century, the Crown had real power. It was the abuse of that power, which led to Civil War in the 1640s, the execution of Charles I and an 11-year period of republican rule. The restoration of the monarchy in 1660 restored stability, but the question of religion continued to fester, until King James II abdicated under the threat of invasion from Holland. William and Mary were to assume the throne on conditions laid down by the Bill of Rights 1689, which established the supremacy of Parliament as the principal lawmaker and finally curtailed royal power.

The powers of the Crown, however, remain many and varied and the Royal prerogative is an important source of power spanning the contemporary constitution. Under the doctrine of parliamentary supremacy, Parliament could abolish these powers or place them on a statutory basis. However, the powers have never been exhaustively defined, let alone codified.

4 [2004] UKHL 56; [2005] AC 68.
5 Those on whom he had conferred land and titles.

Defining the Royal prerogative

Sir William Blackstone, the eighteenth-century constitutional authority, defined the prerogative as being:

> . . . that special pre-eminence which the King hath over and above all other persons, and out of the ordinary course of the common law, in right of his regal dignity. It signifies, in its etymology (from prae and rogo) something that is required or demanded before, or in preference to, all others.[6]

Dicey, on the other hand, defines the prerogative as being:

> . . . the residue of discretionary or arbitrary authority, which at any time is legally left in the hands of the Crown. . . . Every act which the executive government can lawfully do without the authority of an Act of Parliament is done in virtue of this prerogative.

What can be deduced from these two differing definitions is the following:

- that the powers are inherent in, and peculiar to, the Crown;
- that the powers derive from common law;
- that the powers are residual;
- that the majority of powers are exercised by the government in the name of the Crown;
- that no Act of Parliament is necessary to confer authority on the exercise of a prerogative power.

Prerogative powers can be classified as relating to either domestic or foreign affairs,[7] and as can be seen from the lists below, cover a wide and diverse range of important issues:

The prerogatives relating to domestic affairs include:

- the summoning and dissolution of Parliament;
- the appointment of ministers;
- the granting of honours;
- the Royal Assent to Bills;
- defence of the realm;
- the issuing of passports;
- keeping the peace;
- the *parens patriae*[8] jurisdiction of the courts;

6 *Commentaries on the Laws of England*, 1765–69.
7 Following the classification used by Blackstone.
8 The protective jurisdiction which the courts exercise over children.

- the power to stop criminal proceedings;
- the reduction of sentences;
- pardoning of offenders;
- regulation of the terms and conditions on Civil Servants; and
- the right to royal fish and swans.

The prerogatives relating to foreign affairs include:

- the power to make declarations of war and peace;
- the power to enter into treaties;
- the recognition of foreign states;
- diplomatic relations; and
- the disposition of the armed forces overseas.

It may seem remarkable that in a twenty-first century democratic state, such a large area of power lies in the hands of the unelected, hereditary Head of State. What requires analysis is the extent to which the exercise of these powers is controlled – either by Parliament or by the courts, and whether – in light of that analysis – reform is needed.

Judicial control of the exercise of the Royal prerogative

The traditional approach of the judges to the prerogative is one of caution, owing to the need to protect the separation of powers and avoid intruding on areas better left to the executive to decide. Accordingly, the court would decide whether a Royal prerogative power existed or not, but would not inquire into the exercise of that power.

However, where an Act of Parliament covered the same ground as a prerogative power, the courts were prepared to uphold Parliament's supremacy and declare that the Act of Parliament applied over the prerogative. Two cases are sufficient to illustrate this principle.

> *Attorney General v de Keyser's Royal Hotel Ltd* (1920).[9] In this case the owner of a hotel which had been requisitioned by the government for the use of troops in wartime, sought compensation. The government argued that any compensation payable was under the royal prerogative. However, the Defence of the Realm Acts 1914–1920, made provision for compensation. The House of Lords ruled that the Act must be applied and that where a prerogative and a statute coexisted, the prerogative is placed in 'abeyance' for as long as the statute remains in force.

9 [1920] AC 508.

R v Secretary of State for the Home Department ex parte Fire Brigades Union (1995). In this case, the House of Lords ruled that the Home Secretary was obliged to make use of statutory provisions, rather than the royal prerogative, to make amendments to a scheme for compensating victims of crime, even though the original scheme was established under the prerogative.

However, while the principle is clearly stated in the above two cases, there is one case which causes concern:

R v Secretary of State for the Home Department ex parte Northumbria Police Authority (1988).[10] In this case the Police Act 1964 provided (in part) that a Police Authority could request the issue of riot-control equipment from the Home Secretary. The Home Secretary issued a Circular stating that the equipment would be despatched to police forces, without a request from the Police Authority. The Court of Appeal had to decide whether the Home Secretary's Circular was lawful. This turned on the interpretation of the Police Act 1964. However, the Home Secretary also claimed that irrespective of the interpretation of the statute, he had the power to issue the equipment under the royal prerogative to keep the peace.

The Court of Appeal ruled that as a matter of statutory interpretation, the Home Secretary had the power he claimed. However, it went on to consider the prerogative and – notwithstanding that there was no precedent case establishing that there was a prerogative power to keep the peace – decided that the Home Secretary did indeed have such a power. There was no appeal to the House of Lords.

In situations where there was no corresponding statutory provision, the courts exercised restraint. However, in *Council for Civil Service Unions v Minister for Civil Service* (1985), the House of Lords made it clear that if the subject-matter of a case was reviewable by the court, the source of the power in question – whether statute or prerogative – was irrelevant to the court's power to review. Having made that important point of principle, however, the House of Lords stepped back and examined the areas of power that were not reviewable by the court. Using the concept of *justiciability* the court ruled

10 [1988] 1 All ER 556.

that there were many areas of prerogative power that are not suitable for review by the court.

The *GCHQ* case concerned the lawfulness of the Minister's order that membership of a trade union by workers at the Government Communications Headquarters was to be prohibited in the future. The trade union sought judicial review of that decision, and at first instance (in the High Court) won its case on the basis that the government should have continued to negotiate with the union. However, in the Court of Appeal and the House of Lords, the government pleaded national security as the justification for its action. The courts ruled that national security was not an issue that was justiciable before the courts: it was an issue that should be left to the executive – which was accountable to Parliament and the electorate – to decide.

Lord Roskill examined the areas that would be regarded as non-justiciable. These included all aspects of the prerogative in relation to foreign affairs,[11] plus the summoning and dissolution of Parliament, granting of honours, the prerogative of mercy,[12] appointment of ministers, and defence of the realm, or national security.

Political control of the exercise of the Royal prerogative

The limits of judicial control leave a large area of unregulated power to the executive. What now needs to be considered is whether Parliament's control is adequate to prevent the actual or potential abuse of power.

It is of course possible for Parliament to place the Royal prerogative under an Act of Parliament, and thereby set out in detail the circumstances in which a power may be used and mechanisms to ensure accountability. An example of this is seen in the Treasure Act 1986, which placed the right to treasure trove – formerly a matter of prerogative – under an Act of Parliament. However, that was a relatively minor and uncomplicated prerogative compared with – say – the right to declare war and peace, the power to enter into treaties, and the need to defend the security of the state. In relation to these, and most other prerogative powers, there are real difficulties of definition and scope, and difficulties involving the potential damage that could be caused by open parliamentary debate on sensitive issues. Accordingly it may not be possible to place all prerogatives on a statutory footing. Instead, it may be preferable to proceed on an individual basis – some prerogatives being deemed suitable for 'codification', others not.

11 In *R v Secretary of State for Foreign and Commonwealth Affairs ex parte Everett* [1989] 2 WLR 224, the Court of Appeal ruled that the granting or refusal of a passport, being an administrative matter rather than an issue of foreign policy, was reviewable.

12 But see now *R v Secretary of State for the Home Department ex parte Bentley* [1994] 2 WLR 101 in which the High Court ruled that some aspects of the prerogative of mercy were reviewable and that the Home Secretary had misunderstood his powers under the prerogative.

The second way in which Parliament can control the exercise of the prerogative is through its usual mechanisms for scrutiny of the executive, discussed in more detail in Chapter 9. Question time, debates – particularly those determined by the Opposition parties – and select committee enquiries are all valuable tools that underpin ministerial responsibility. However, of necessity, the use of these mechanisms in relation to the most sensitive issues is generally going to take place after the power has been exercised and while this may lead to an evaluation of whether the executive has acted lawfully or not, it may not prevent the unlawful action.

Reform of the Royal prerogative?

In 2007, the incoming Prime Minister Gordon Brown announced that a package of constitutional reforms was under consideration – not least of which was the issue of the prerogative. In the government's Green Paper *The Governance of Britain*[13] the following prerogative powers are considered for reform:

- treaty-making powers: the government proposes placing the Ponsonby Rule (page 19 below) on a statutory basis.
- regulation of the Civil Service: there have long been calls for a Civil Service Act, and this the government intends to enact.
- the Dissolution of Parliament: the government proposes requiring the consent of the House of Commons before seeking the formal dissolution from the Crown.

Non-legal sources

Constitutional conventions

As noted in the introduction above, not all constitutional sources have legal status. As the British Constitution has evolved gradually over the centuries, practices have developed which – while not formalised in legal rules – have become regarded as binding or obligatory on those to whom they relate. When these practices harden into rules and impose an obligation they become known as *constitutional conventions*. When a constitutional convention is recognised as such, it defines the constitutionally correct situation or practice, and any deviation from that will give rise to criticism and require justification.

AV Dicey, the nineteenth-century constitutional authority, described conventions as being similar to 'habits', 'understandings' and 'practices'. This approach, however, fails to emphasise the fact that conventions do impose obligations (or duties) and are far more regulatory than habits, understandings

13 Cm 7170, July 2007.

or practices. However, because conventions are not legal rules, the breach of a convention will not have legal consequences: no court of law can enforce a convention, because it is not law.

	Habits	Understandings	Practices	Conventions	Laws
Regularity of conduct	yes	not necessarily	yes	yes	yes
Reflectiveness	no	yes	yes	yes	yes
Degree of obligation imposed	none	weak	srong	absolute	absolute
Sanction attending breach	none	justification required	justification required	change of unconstitutional conduct	unlawful conduct

Figure 2.2

The following examples illustrate the wide-ranging nature and application of conventions.

Conventions relating to the Crown

- Once a Bill has passed through Parliament, the Royal Assent will not be refused. The Crown has the legal right/power to refuse the Royal Assent, but this has not been refused since the early eighteenth century. The legal power is controlled by the non-legal constitutional convention.
- The Crown must remain above party politics. This convention protects the Crown from criticism. The monarch is Head of State but the real political power lies with the Prime Minister. If the political views of the Crown were known, it would be difficult for the Queen to work with a Prime Minister who represented very different political views.
- The Crown will appoint as Prime Minister the leader of the political party that secures a majority at a general election and can command the confidence of the House of Commons. Provided there is such a person, the Crown does not have discretion.
- The Crown will dissolve Parliament at the request of the Prime Minister in order for a general election to be held. The legal power to refuse a request for a dissolution undoubtedly exists. However, that power is controlled by the constitutional convention. Only if a situation where a Prime Minister sought a dissolution for improper purposes (such as increasing his or her party's majority in Parliament following inducements to the electoral) would the Crown be justified in refusing a dissolution.

Conventions relating to the executive

- The government must retain the confidence of the House of Commons and will resign on losing a vote of confidence. A vote of confidence may be proposed by the government or the opposition in order to test the support of the House of Commons in relation to a matter that is central to the government's agenda. If the vote goes against the government, the Prime Minister must tender the government's resignation to the Crown.
- The Prime Minister must appoint a Cabinet and ensure that it meets regularly. Neither the office of Prime Minister nor the institution of Cabinet was created by Act of Parliament. Each came into being as a result of practice. There came a time in the mid-eighteenth century when it was useful for there to be a single minister who could advise the Crown; similarly, with Cabinet. The process of governing would be unwieldy if all ministers were involved in every aspect of decision-making. Accordingly, the practice developed of there being an inner core of ministers, in Cabinet, who reached the most significant decisions (decisions which bind all ministers and prevent them from dissenting from agreed government policy: see below).
- The convention of collective Cabinet responsibility. Once discussion in Cabinet has finished and a decision on policy reached, neither a member of Cabinet nor any non-Cabinet minister may publicly dissent from that decision. To protect decisions from divisive political debate outside Cabinet, collective responsibility also requires that Cabinet discussions remain confidential.
- The convention of individual ministerial responsibility. A minister is responsible for his or her own personal conduct and also for the working of his or her department. In theory, every decision taken by a government department falls within a minister's responsibility. That responsibility entails accounting to Parliament for the successes or failings of the department, and – if personal blame attaches to some damaging circumstance – resigning from office.

  While the convention relating to personal conduct – sexual and financial – is relatively clear-cut (if your conduct is going to embarrass the government, resign), responsibility relating to the department is not. In the *Crichel Down affair* in 1954, a minister (Thomas Dugdale) resigned office, taking responsibility for his department's failings even though he had no personal knowledge or involvement in the matter. Since that time, however, it has become clear that ministers distinguish between failures of administration and failure of policy. For example:

  > In the 1980s the then Secretary of State for Northern Ireland, James Prior, refused to resign over escapes from a high-security prison. He blamed the prison governor and remained in office.
  >
  > That precedent was followed in the 1990s by the then Home

Secretary who refused to resign over failings in the prison service, instead sacking the prison governor.[14]

Conventions relating to Parliament

- Members of Parliament will not criticise the judiciary. This convention is designed to protect the independence of the judges and the integrity of the legal system (note that to protect judicial independence senior judges can only be dismissed following a successful address to both Houses of Parliament).
- The House of Lords will not oppose government Bills that contain proposals put to the electorate before a general election. Proposals that have been put to the voters are deemed to be 'mandated' by the people and accordingly, protected from attack by the unelected House of Lords.

  In the first decade of the twentieth century, the House of Lords refused to pass the government's financial proposals (the Budget), in breach of the convention that matters of finance were for the elected lower House. The outcome of this breach of convention was the Parliament Act 1911, which placed the convention on a statutory basis.
- Ministers are accountable to Parliament for the conduct of their department and for personal conduct (see the discussion above).
- Known as the Ponsonby Rule, treaties that are to come into force at a date later than their signature must be laid before Parliament for at least 21 days.

Conventions relating to the judiciary

- Judges will not engage in party-political debate. This is an extremely important aspect of judicial independence. If the political views of the judges were public knowledge, it would be difficult, if not impossible, for judges to be regarded as impartial, unbiased, decision-makers.
- Judges will withdraw from cases where there might be a suspicion of personal bias. This protects the integrity of the legal process and ensures that judges cannot be wrongly accused of personal bias. The rule is very strict: if the reasonable person would think that a judge is biased then that is sufficient to ensure that they should not sit – even if in fact there is no actual bias. The governing principle is that justice should not only be done, but it should also be seen to be done.

14 Who subsequently sued the government and was awarded significant damages.

Do constitutional conventions need reform?

It has been seen that constitutional conventions play a very important role in the Constitution, often controlling the manner in which legal powers are exercised. Despite this, many conventions remain uncertain in their scope and application. It is for this reason that there are calls for reform.

One means of clarifying conventions could be to codify them: bring them together in a formal document, which defines their scope and the circumstances under which they apply. Two forms of codification are possible: a legal code, and an authoritative, but non-legal code. However, while superficially attractive, codification has difficulties. The first is that of identification and definition: how can all the possible scenarios that might occur be envisaged in advance? The second difficulty lies in the relationship between the code and actual practice – if there is a conflict, how is this to be resolved?

If conventions were to be placed in a legal code, the question of the courts' jurisdiction arises. The courts currently will recognise, but have no power to enforce, conventions.[15] Would this change? If conventions became legal rules, it is inevitable that the courts would become involved. However, it is unlikely that the judges would be prepared to change their approach to sensitive political issues – namely to regard them as non-justiciable and hence unenforceable by the courts. If the code were to be non-legal, then this difficulty falls away. However, the question then becomes, of what use is the code?

The other matter that would have to be resolved is the loss of flexibility, which would be entailed in codification. The essence of constitutional conventions is that they are flexible and can adapt to differing circumstances as required. Would the certainty gained through codification outweigh any loss of flexibility? Or would the constitution be damaged by its inability to evolve? It may be argued that the code could retain flexibility. However, if the code is to reflect flexibility, then it becomes more difficult to regard it as a binding code with sanctions for its breach.

Summary

In the absence of a written constitution, it is necessary to study the different constitutional sources that make up the partly written, but uncodified, UK Constitution. This involves understanding which Acts of Parliament have constitutional relevance, and also a study of the common law to gain an insight into those constitutionally important judicial decisions. In addition, the Royal prerogative – the powers and immunities of the Crown – remains an important, residual source of power.

15 *Attorney General v Jonathan Cape Ltd* [1976] 1 QB 752.

Supplementing the legal sources of the Constitution are the all-important, but rather ill-defined, constitutional conventions. These are non-legal, but binding, rules, the breach of which will give rise to the allegation of 'unconstitutional conduct'.

Further reading

Blackburn, R, 'Monarchy and the Personal Prerogatives' [2004] PL 546.

Brazier, R, 'The Non-Legal Constitution: Thoughts on Convention, Practice and Principle' (1992), 43 NILQ 262.

Chitty, J, *Prerogatives of the Crown*, 1820, Butterworths.

Craig, P and Tomkins, A (eds), *The Executive and Public Law*, 2006, Oxford: OUP.

Hood-Phillips, O, 'Constitutional Conventions: Dicey's Predecessors' (1966), 29 MLR 137.

Jaconelli, J, 'The Nature of Constitutional Conventions' (1999), Legal Studies, 19: 24.

Jaconelli, J, 'Do Constitutional Conventions Bind?', [2005] 64 CLJ 149.

Munro, CR, *Studies in Constitutional Law* (2nd edn, 1999), London: Butterworths, Chapters 3 and 8.

Sampford, CJG, 'Recognise and Declare: An Australian Experiment in Codifying Constitutional Conventions' (1987), 7 OJLS 369.

Sunkin, M and Payne, S (eds), *The Nature of the Crown: a Legal and Political Analysis*, 1999, Oxford: Clarendon Press.

Wilson, R, 'The Robustness of Conventions in a Time of Modernisation and Change' [2004], PL 407.

? *SELF-ASSESSMENT QUESTIONS*

1. Write a brief definition of the Royal prerogative (you may draft your own definition or recite either Blackstone or Dicey).
2. Name at least one difference between Blackstone's and Dicey's definition.
3. List at least three prerogative powers relating to the Crown.
4. Write a brief definition of a constitutional convention.
5. Name three differences between a legal rule and a constitutional convention.
6. Name three conventions relating to the Crown.
7. Name three conventions relating to the government.
8. Name two conventions relating to the judiciary.

SAMPLE EXAMINATION QUESTIONS

1. To what extent is it accurate to describe the British Constitution as 'unwritten'?
2. To what extent is the exercise of the Royal prerogative compatible with the rule of law?
3. 'The acts of the prerogative are as reviewable as any other executive act.'

   Discuss.
4. 'It is high time that the Royal prerogative be placed under statutory authority.'

   Do you agree? What are the constitutional implications entailed in this proposal?

Chapter 3

Separation of powers

CONTENTS

KEY WORDS AND PHRASES

Constitutional convention	The unwritten, non-legal but binding rules of the Constitution
Crown	The monarch, Queen Elizabeth II, in whose name all acts of government are undertaken
Executive	Principally the Crown, government and civil service, but also technically the armed forces and police
Judiciary	The judges
Legislature	The law-making body: Parliament

Introduction

Under any constitution there will be three major institutions: the executive, the legislature and the judiciary. In order to prevent a concentration of power in one institution – which could give rise to an abuse of power – under most Western liberal constitutions there will be a defined 'separation of power' between the three institutions. The idea of separation of powers goes back to ancient Greece, but the idea was later given prominence by the French political philosopher Montesquieu (1689–1755) in his comparative analysis of forms of government *L'Esprit des lois* (1748).

The ideal form of separation is seen in the written constitution of the United States of America, which the following diagram illustrates.

EXECUTIVE: PRESIDENT
Separately elected. Fixed term. May veto Bills from Congress but Congress may override (2/3 majority in each House). Appoints judges, with Senate advice and consent. Commander-in-Chief, armed forces.

LEGISLATURE: CONGRESS
Bicameral (Senate and House of Representatives). Sole Legislature. House of Representatives may impeach judges. Financial powers limiting what the President may do.

JUDICIARY: SUPREME COURT
Polices the constitution and limits government by judicial review for unconstitutionality.

Figure 3.1

Before examining the arrangement under the United Kingdom's Constitution, the institutions require more detailed consideration.

The executive

The executive includes the Crown, Prime Minister, cabinet and other and government ministers, civil servants, the armed forces (air force, army and navy) and the police.

All acts of government are undertaken in the name of the Crown. The core of government – the Prime Minister and cabinet ministers – formulates policy that will be presented to Parliament for enactment into law. The civil service administers government policy into effect. The armed forces and police protect the government from internal or external threat.

The Crown is a hereditary position, with succession determined by the Act of Settlement 1700.

The Prime Minister is the head of the government. The position is awarded to the leader of the political party that wins a majority of seats in Parliament at a general election. The position of Prime Minister evolved over time and is the creation of constitutional convention. It is not governed by statute. The powers of the Prime Minister are set out in Chapter 3.

The Cabinet is the innermost circle of government and is made up of those ministers representing the most important departments of state. As with the office of Prime Minister, the cabinet has arisen through practice and remains regulated by convention rather than statute. By convention, approximately 20–24 ministers will sit in cabinet. The Prime Minister controls the membership of cabinet and its working.

Ministers are those Members of Parliament or Peers (members of the House of Lords) who are appointed to a ministerial position in a government department by the Prime Minister. The most senior ministers, representing the most important departments of state, sit in cabinet (see above). There will be approximately 120 ministers, including cabinet ministers.

Civil Service. Civil servants are employees of the Crown. The Civil Service includes those working in central government departments as well as those working in regional and local offices.

The armed forces and police. The control of the armed forces is largely under the Royal prerogative (see Chapter 2) rather than statute. Members of the armed forces are subject to a separate legal system – military law. There is no national police force in the UK. There are 44 local police forces in England and Wales, six in Scotland and one in Northern Ireland. The powers of the police are defined in statute. Collectively the armed forces and police have the responsibility of protecting the state from internal or external attack.

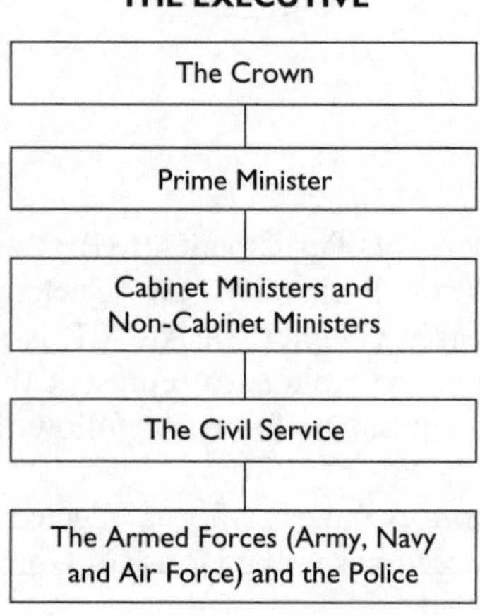

Figure 3.2

The legislature

The United Kingdom Parliament is made up of the Crown, the House of Commons and the House of Lords. Parliament alone enacts law. It can repeal any previous law and overturn judicial decisions. Note that Northern Ireland has its own legislature – the Northern Ireland Assembly and that Scotland has its own Parliament. Both have limited law-making power that is defined in an Act of Parliament enacted by the UK Parliament. Wales also has an Assembly with more restrictive powers than Northern Ireland or Scotland.

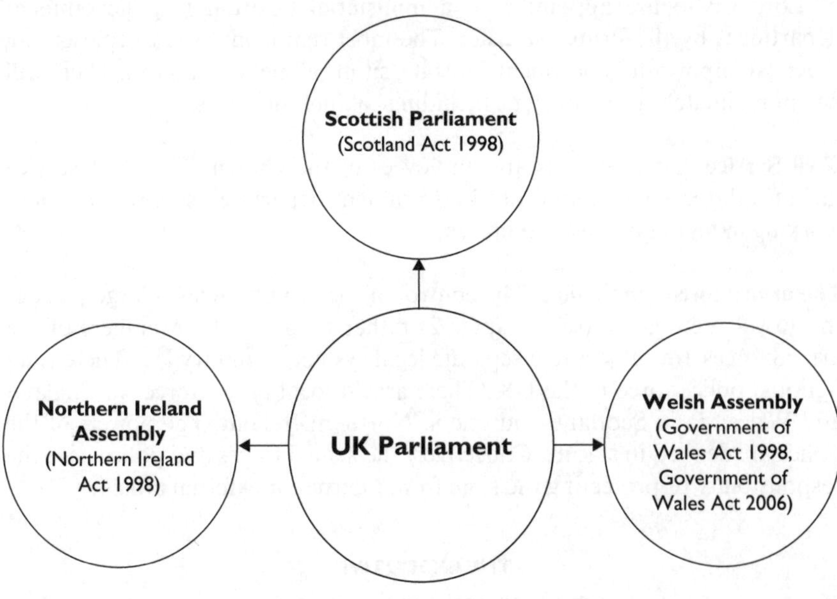

Figure 3.3

The House of Commons

There are 646 Members of Parliament (MPs), each representing one constituency. Members of Parliament are elected through the simple majority voting system (see Chapter 8). An MP is not a 'delegate' of his or her constituents. His or her role is to represent the interests of the constituency, but he or she cannot be forced to follow the views of his or her constituents.

The politically neutral Speaker, who is elected by all Members of Parliament, controls proceedings in the House of Commons.

The House of Lords

Historically, all members of the House of Lords (Peers) became members on the basis of inheritance rather than election: they were unelected 'hereditary peers'. The majority of these were expelled from the Lords under the House of Lords Act 1999.

Life peers (who hold the title for their lives only) were introduced under the Life Peerage Act 1958. In addition, there are Lords Spiritual – the Archbishops of Canterbury and York and 24 other senior Church of England bishops. Finally, there are the judicial peers (judges) appointed under the Appellate Jurisdiction Act 1886. Under the Constitutional Reform Act 2005, those who are still working as judges are not allowed to participate in the legislative work of the House of Lords; only retired judges may do so.

The Constitutional Reform Act 2005 makes provision for the establishment of a Supreme Court separated from Parliament (see pages 30–31 below).

Despite several attempts to reform the House of Lords, the Upper House remains unelected and unaccountable to the electorate. The issue of reform will be discussed in Chapter 9.

The judiciary

The judiciary comprises all the judges, from the lowest court to the Supreme Court. The judges have developed the law through judicial decisions (common law) and through the interpretation of Acts of Parliament. As noted above, if Parliament disapproves of a decision it may overturn it by passing an Act.

Appointment and tenure

The Crown appoints the judges. Prior to the Constitutional Reform Act 2005, the Lord Chancellor was the formal head of the judiciary with powers of appointment. The Lord Chancellor was also a member of the cabinet and the Speaker of the House of Lords. The 2005 Act reformed the office of Lord Chancellor, establishing a clearer separation of powers between his various previous roles. The Lord Chancellor is no longer head of the judiciary: that task is now conferred on the Lord Chief Justice. The Lord Chancellor also no longer acts as Speaker of the House of Lords, the 2005 Act providing that the House of Lords shall elect its Speaker. Indeed, it is no longer necessary that the Lord Chancellor is a member of the House of Lords.[1]

1 The first holder of the reformed office was Jack Straw, who acts as both Lord Chancellor and Secretary of State for Justice and sits in the House of Commons.

In relation to judicial appointments, under the 2005 Act, there is established a Judicial Appointments Commission with the task of selecting candidates for appointment. The Judicial Appointments Commission's recommendations go to the Lord Chancellor, who advises the Crown on appointments.

To preserve judicial independence, by convention there is no parliamentary discussion of judicial salaries, which are paid out of the Consolidated Fund (a fund set aside for several purposes without open debate in Parliament). While junior judges can be dismissed for incompetence or wrongdoing, the Supreme Court Act 1981, section 11(3), provides that judges of the Crown Court, High Court and Court of Appeal hold office 'during good behaviour', but may be removed by the Crown following an 'address' to both Houses of Parliament. The judicial retirement age is 70, which may be extended to 75.[2]

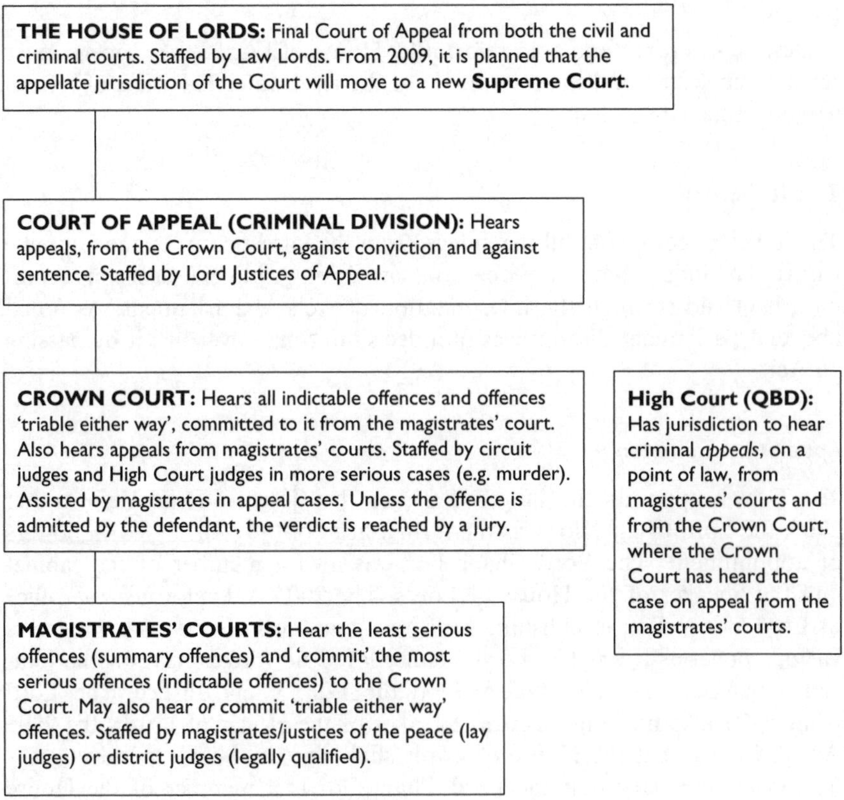

THE HOUSE OF LORDS: Final Court of Appeal from both the civil and criminal courts. Staffed by Law Lords. From 2009, it is planned that the appellate jurisdiction of the Court will move to a new **Supreme Court**.

COURT OF APPEAL (CRIMINAL DIVISION): Hears appeals, from the Crown Court, against conviction and against sentence. Staffed by Lord Justices of Appeal.

CROWN COURT: Hears all indictable offences and offences 'triable either way', committed to it from the magistrates' court. Also hears appeals from magistrates' courts. Staffed by circuit judges and High Court judges in more serious cases (e.g. murder). Assisted by magistrates in appeal cases. Unless the offence is admitted by the defendant, the verdict is reached by a jury.

High Court (QBD): Has jurisdiction to hear criminal *appeals*, on a point of law, from magistrates' courts and from the Crown Court, where the Crown Court has heard the case on appeal from the magistrates' courts.

MAGISTRATES' COURTS: Hear the least serious offences (summary offences) and 'commit' the most serious offences (indictable offences) to the Crown Court. May also hear *or* commit 'triable either way' offences. Staffed by magistrates/justices of the peace (lay judges) or district judges (legally qualified).

Figure 3.4a Outline of the criminal courts

2 Judicial Pensions and Retirement Act 1993.

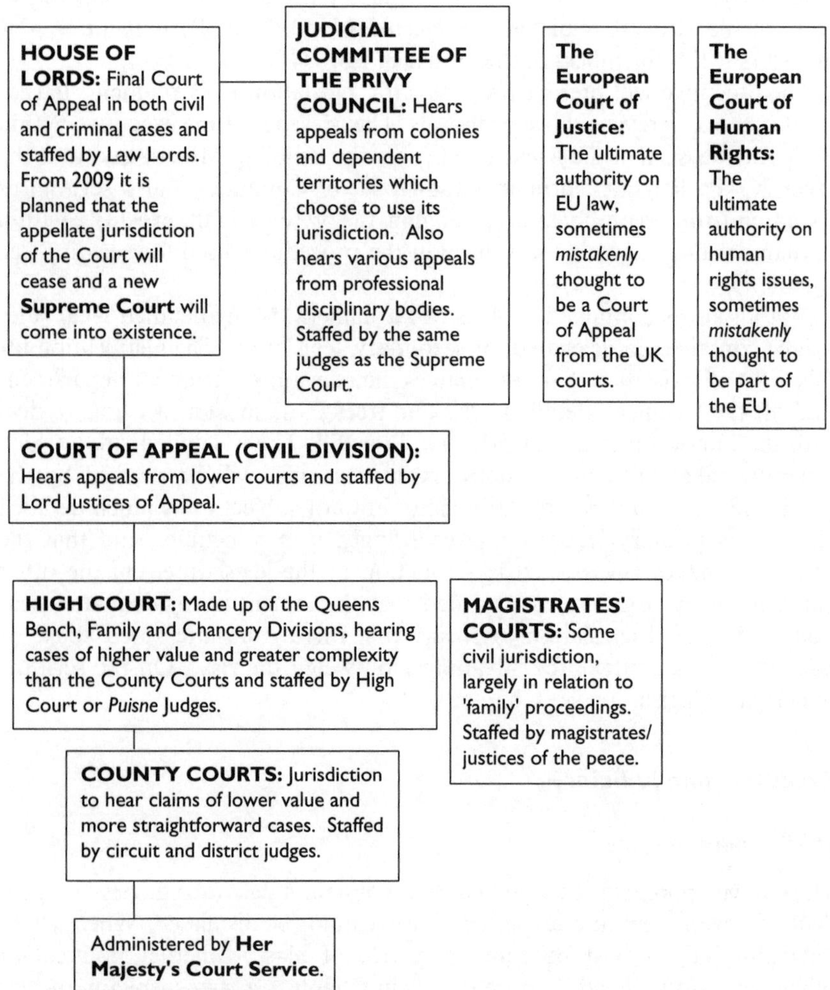

Figure 3.4b Outline of the civil courts

The relationship between the institutions

Executive and legislature

Under a written constitution such as that of the US, it is usual for there to be a complete separation of the executive and legislature. In the UK, however, the executive – in terms of the Prime Minister, cabinet and non-cabinet ministers – is drawn from the personnel of Parliament (Members of Parliament and Peers). Furthermore, the executive sits in Parliament: the Prime Minister and the majority of ministers are elected Members of Parliament. A few ministers will be members of the House of Lords (Peers).

The executive will present proposals for legislation to Parliament. Parliament accepts or rejects those proposals. The presence of the executive within Parliament assists in the legislative process by enabling MPs to question the executive. Parliament – primarily the House of Commons – also scrutinises the administration of the state. Here again, the presence of the executive within Parliament facilitates this scrutiny. On the procedures used for scrutiny, see Chapter 9.

Not all law is contained in Acts of Parliament. Many detailed legal rules will be contained in delegated, or secondary, legislation. The justification for this form of legislation is that it enables the relevant government department to draft the technical, detailed rules and frees Parliament as a whole to deal with the important issues of principle in a Bill. These detailed rules, which generally take the form of statutory instruments, will be drafted by the government and laid before Parliament, but not subject to as much detailed scrutiny as primary legislation. Accordingly, it is sometimes said that the executive 'makes law', which is a function of the legislature. On the other hand, it can be argued that provided that Parliament pays adequate attention to delegated legislation to ensure that there is no attempted abuse of power by the executive, the advantages outweigh the risks. On the scrutiny of delegated legislation see Chapter 9.

Executive and judiciary

Judicial independence

The Crown appoints the judges. Once appointed, judges are entirely independent of government and, as noted above, cannot be dismissed. When acting judicially, judges must be completely free of bias – whether political or otherwise. As discussed in more details in Chapter 14, any suspicion of bias may lead to an appeal.

By convention, there should be no parliamentary criticism of judicial decisions.

The Supreme Court

The most senior judges – the Law Lords[3] – until 2009, sat as the Appellate Committee of the House of Lords located in Parliament. The Law Lords also participated in the law-making work of the House of Lords, sitting

3 Officially the Lords of Appeal in Ordinary.

as non-political crossbenchers. The Constitutional Reform Act 2005, in addition to reforming the office of Lord Chancellor, provides for the establishment of a Supreme Court, physically separate from Parliament. This clarifies the separation of powers by removing the Law Lords from Parliament. In future, only retired Law Lords will be allowed to sit in the House of Lords.

The Supreme Court will exercise the same powers as those currently exercised by the Appellate Committee of the House of Lords and the Judicial Committee of the Privy Council. The Judicial Committee of the Privy Council hears appeals from those Commonwealth countries that choose to retain the right of appeal, plus appeals from various professional bodies.

Public inquiries

Judges are occasionally appointed to chair inquiries, the outcome of which can give rise to criticism on the basis that the judge's political impartiality is brought into question. An example of such inquiries include the government's claim that Iraq had weapons of mass destruction capable of being activated within 45 minutes, a claim which was central to the decision to support America's invasion of Iraq in 2003.

Judicial review

From a separation of powers perspective, one of the most constitutionally controversial aspects of judicial work is that of judicial review (discussed in detail in Chapter 13). Judicial review is a procedure by which an individual or representative group who has a particular interest in an administrative decision made by a public body may challenge the legality of that decision. The court – the Administrative Court, which has High Court status – is not concerned with the rights and wrongs of the actual decision but with whether the decision-maker reached the decision lawfully. It is therefore procedural in nature. The court will not substitute its own decision for that of the administrator, but will rule on whether the administrator decided the issue in a lawful manner. If it did not, the court may quash (set aside) the decision and require the administrator to remake the decision in the correct, lawful, manner.

Judicial review is controversial insofar as it raises the question 'is the judiciary interfering with the work of the executive?' In other words, are the judges violating the separation of powers by ruling on the legality of acts of the executive? The answer to these questions lies in the central purpose of judicial review, namely to keep those public bodies on whom power has been conferred by Parliament within the scope of the power conferred. In other words, the judges are upholding the will of Parliament by ensuring that the executive acts within the law. This function can only be fulfilled successfully by a judiciary that is independent of the executive and free from executive influence.

Judiciary and legislature

Parliament is the sovereign law-making body and accordingly the judges are constitutionally subordinate to Parliament. However, it has always been the case that judges contribute to the law-making process, both through the development of the common law and through statutory interpretation. From the perspective of the separation of powers, it is important to understand the apparent paradox of judges, the judiciary, 'making law' – a function of the legislature.

Common law

The common law comprises those legal rules and procedures that are 'common' to the whole country. In the earliest times, Parliament was remote from the people, whereas the courts were local and accessible. Accordingly, it was the judges who developed the law through their decisions. In order to achieve some consistency, the doctrine of precedent applied. The main principle of precedent is that of *stare decisis: let like cases be decided alike*.

Statutory interpretation

In addition to developing the common law, the judges are required to interpret Acts of Parliament and give them effect. As with precedent, consistency is important and the judges developed the 'rules' of statutory interpretation to achieve this. For much of history, the dominant rule was the 'literal rule', which provided that if the words of the statute (Act of Parliament) were clear, they were to be given their plain, ordinary meaning and applied. Only where there was ambiguity in the meaning of the words should this rule be set aside in favour of a rule that gave proper meaning to the Act.

In addition to achieving consistency, the rules of statutory interpretation were designed to restrict the scope of the judges and keep them within the meaning intended by Parliament rather than leading to some decision favoured by the judges but not intended by Parliament.

Assessing the separation of powers in the UK

It has been seen above that there are many overlaps in both personnel and functions under the UK Constitution. However, while these may be criticised as being contrary to an ideal separation of powers, what must be noted is that there are many 'checks and balances' within the system, which are designed to prevent an abuse of power.

Returning to the diagram representing the US's Constitution, it might be concluded that the British Constitution is arranged in the following manner:

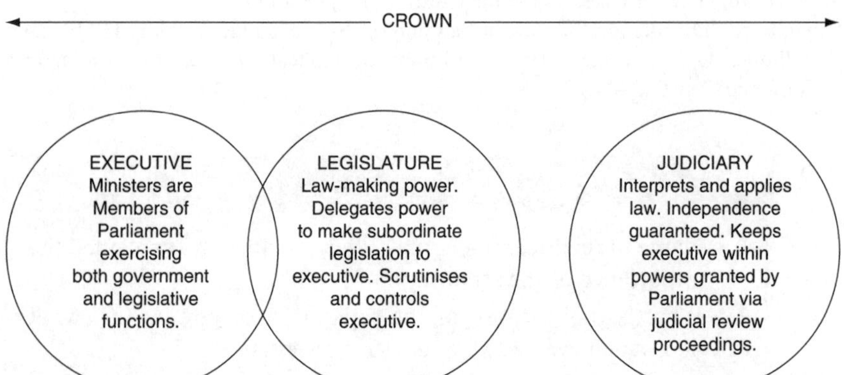

Figure 3.5

Summary

The separation of powers is a key constitutional concept. The separation of powers explains the personnel, functions and powers of the three major institutions of the state: the executive, the legislature and the judiciary. The principal purpose it serves is to prevent the concentration of powers in one institution. Under a written constitution the separation of powers will be clearly defined. Under the UK Constitution, however, this is not the case and it is necessary to examine the relationship between the executive and legislature, legislature and judiciary, and judiciary and executive in order to ascertain the extent to which the concept applies. Undertaking this exercise reveals that while the separation of powers is not as clear and certain as it would be under a written constitution, there are nevertheless sufficient checks and balances that prevent the abuse of power. Accordingly, it is not inaccurate to state that the separation of powers is a concept respected under the constitution.

Further reading

Barendt, E, 'Separation of Powers and Constitutional Government' [1995] PL 599.

Bingham, Lord, 'The Old Order Changeth' (2006), 122 LQR 211.

Cooke, Lord, 'The Law Lords: An Endangered Heritage' (2003), 119 LQR 49.

Legal Studies, Special Issue, Constitutional Innovation: the Creation of a Supreme Court for the United Kingdom; Domestic, Comparative and International Reflections, (2004) 2, 3, 5, 7, 8, 9, 10.

Munro, CR, *Studies in Constitutional Law* (2nd edn, 1999), London: Butterworth, Chapter 9.

Steyn, Lord, 'The Weakest and Least Dangerous Department of Government' [1997] PL 84.

Steyn, Lord, 'The Case for a Supreme Court' (2002), 118 LQR 382.

Steyn, Lord, 'Democracy, the Rule of Law and the Role of Judges' [2006] EHRLR 243.

Woodhouse, D, 'The Constitutional and political implications of a United Kingdom Supreme Court' (2004), 24 LS 134.

SELF-ASSESSMENT QUESTIONS

1. Name the eighteenth-century French writer who explained the importance of the separation of powers.
2. What is the purpose of the separation of powers (i.e. what does it achieve and what does it prevent?)?
3. Name the three principal institutions of the state and write a brief definition of their role and functions.

SAMPLE EXAMINATION QUESTIONS

1. To what extent is the doctrine of separation of powers respected under the constitution of the UK?
2. Critically assess the view that the 'British constitution is firmly based on the doctrine of the separation of powers'.
3. To what extent was Walter Bagehot correct in his assertion that the close fusion of the executive and legislature represents the 'efficient secret' of the constitution? (Walter Bagehot, *The English Constitution* (1867)).

Chapter 4

The rule of law

CONTENTS

KEY WORDS AND PHRASES

Social contract — A fictional agreement between government and citizen under which citizens confer power on government, which is held on trust and

subject to the condition that government
protect the citizens' rights

Introduction

The rule of law is a concept regularly invoked by lawyers and politicians without offering any explanation as to the meaning to be given to it. This is problematic in that it is a concept that is capable of several very different meanings. In this chapter we shall explore some of these meanings and assess the significance of the rule of law to the UK Constitution.

The rule of law may be viewed in different ways. First, it has been a key concept in legal and political philosophy. Secondly, the rule of law has a practical application in that it can offer guidance on the requirements that a good legal system must adhere to.

Western liberalism

In Western liberal democratic societies, it is generally assumed that the rule of law is a force for good. It is law that controls the power of the state and law that protects the rights and freedoms of citizens. However, the 'rule of law' is a concept far wider than 'the law'. In a democratic society, where government is dependent ultimately on the will of the people to retain its power, the law will in general be 'benevolent'. In non-democratic societies, or societies that are ruled by a harsh regime the law may be far from benevolent – as Nazi Germany so starkly showed in the twentieth century and until more recently the South African regime with its discriminatory system of apartheid. So law, of itself, is not necessarily consistent with the 'rule of law'.

The 'rule of law' implies certain values that the law should respect. Consistent with liberalism the law should control the exercise of government power: government under the law rather than above the law is a key requirement. So too is the idea that law protects people's freedoms and rights against the power of the state. Both of these aspects of the rule of law are consistent with the concept of 'constitutionalism'.

Under a written constitution such as the United States of America's, the protection of rights is easier to evaluate because of its Bill of Rights. In the UK, with its uncodified constitution and the concept of parliamentary supremacy, the position is less straightforward, although the European Convention on Human Rights and now the Human Rights Act 1998, together go a long way towards providing a charter of rights.

Marxism and the rule of law

One of the intellectual giants of the twentieth century, Karl Marx (1818–81) viewed law – and the rule of law – with suspicion. Put simply, it was Marx's thesis that one's position in society is determined not by law but by one's place in the economy. In a capitalist society, the role of law was designed to uphold the economic system, which, owned by the few, extracts from the working class their labour at less than its full value. The laws that regulate factories and terms and conditions of employment are all underpinned by an implied acceptance of the capitalist system, which is exploitative of the ordinary man. Furthermore (some Marxist followers argue), those laws that are supposedly designed to protect the weak in society – housing and social welfare provisions – far from being beneficial, in fact simply mask the reality and keep men and women in their position of subservience within the capitalist system. The law, and the rule of law, it follows, are sham concepts. Only when the capitalist system is overthrown will the law that upheld it die away, leaving men and women truly free and equal in a communist society.

Traditional oriental thought

A quite different approach to the rule of law is seen within traditional oriental thought. As authors David and Brierley demonstrate in *Major Legal Systems*,[1] in many societies personal and business relationships are regulated not by law but by the principle of equal respect and a process of mediation resulting in a solution to whatever problem has arisen. This informal but binding system works well. However, once the concept of law and enforceable legal rights are introduced, people may resort to the courts. This undermines the mediation system and weakens society. From this perspective, law is unwelcome and socially damaging.

Western social contract theory

The essence of social contract theory is that individuals in society come together and enter into a fictional contract, which establishes the legitimate authority in the state. In turn that authority protects the citizens and their rights. It is a reciprocal arrangement. However, philosophers differ over the details of the contract.

Social contract theory can be traced back to Thomas Hobbes[2] in the seventeenth century. Hobbes was writing against the background of the English Civil War 1641–1648, an upheaval that led to the execution of the King and to the only republican government (albeit brief) that Britain has known. It was Hobbes' central thesis that citizens contract with one another to create a sovereign power within the state. This sovereign power, 'the Mortal God', had the duty to protect citizens from harm. However, Hobbes did not believe in human rights in the contemporary sense and this was reflected in *The*

1 Third edition, 1985, London: Sweet & Maxwell.
2 1588–1679.

Leviathan.[3] The only right that a citizen retained was the right to defend him or herself against any unlawful violence on the part of the state.

Before the end of the seventeenth century came the seminal work of John Locke[4] – *Two Treatises on Government.*[5] John Locke was forced into exile as a result of his views. In 1689 – the year of the Bill of Rights – Locke returned to England and *Two Treatises* was published, initially anonymously. The central thesis was a critique of royal power (the royal prerogative) and the assertion of individual rights and freedoms that were inalienable. The contract between citizen and state conferred to the government the legitimate power to rule. That power, however, was conditional upon the government acting for the good of the people and not taking away their rights. The power was held on trust, for the people. If that trust was broken, the people had the right to overthrow the government and replace it with one that would respect their rights.

A full-blown theory of the natural rights and freedoms of the people was provided by Thomas Paine who was influential in both the American and French revolutions.[6] In *Rights of Man*[7] Paine argued that individuals have both natural rights and civil rights. Natural rights are inherent: they exist because we are human. Civil rights arise out of our involvement in society. These rights cannot be taken away: they must be respected by government.

Twentieth-century thought

Lon Fuller

Professor Lon Fuller, of Harvard University, provided a different perspective on the rule of law.[8] Fuller was greatly concerned with the role of law and its relationship with citizens. The role law should play is to set a framework within which people can pursue their legitimate goals in life. Law should be facilitative and serve the people. There is, for Fuller, an essentially moral quality in law, which presents itself in two forms. First, there is the 'morality of duty', which leads Fuller to identify the necessary qualities that a good legal system will have if it is to serve the people. These qualities are analogous to the foundations of a house. For a house to be safe and to endure, it must be built on sound foundations; so too the legal system. The basic requirements of the legal system are that:

3 1651. 1973, London: Dent.
4 1632–1704.
5 1690. 1977, London: Dent.
6 1737–1809.
7 1792. 1984, rep. 1998, Collins, H (Ed), New York: Penguin.
8 *The Morality of Law*, Yale University Press, 1969.

- it operates prospectively, not retrospectively.
- the law is clear and relatively certain.
- the law is publicised, not secret.
- laws must be non-contradictory.
- there must be an accessible court system.
- it is staffed by independent judges.

Over and above these basic requirements there is a 'morality of aspiration', an intangible concept, which nevertheless directs the law to serve the people by allowing them the means to pursue their own legitimate goals. A legal system that failed to serve the people is, for Fuller, no legal system at all: it lacks an essential defining quality – that of morality.

Fuller's morality of law gives rise to difficult issues, issues explored in the dialogue between Fuller and Professor HLA Hart of the University of Oxford, published in the *Harvard Law Review*.[9] From the rule of law perspective, we could borrow just one example from their debate on law and morality. Under German law, during the Nazi regime, it was a criminal offence to criticise Hitler. As Hart explains, in 1944 a woman reported her husband to the authorities for insulting remarks he made about Hitler. The wife was under no legal duty to report his acts. The husband was arrested and sentenced to death, although he was not executed but sent to the front. In 1949, the wife was prosecuted for unlawfully depriving a person of his freedom, under a law that had remained in force throughout the period. She pleaded in her defence that her husband's imprisonment was pursuant to Nazi statutes and that she had committed no crime. She was convicted, the Nazi statute being declared by the court to be 'contrary to the sound conscience and sense of justice of all human beings'.

Hart objects to this approach on the basis that it involved a court declaring a statute to be invalid. The alternatives were either to let the woman go free or to punish her but recognise that in doing so, retrospective law was being applied. Hart prefers the retrospectivity approach, arguing that:

> It would have made plain that in punishing the woman a choice had to be made between two evils, that of leaving her unpunished and that of sacrificing a very precious principle of morality endorsed by most legal systems.

The central difficulty that arises from the differing approaches to immoral laws is that it becomes impossible to decide what law *is*. To claim that a law that has been enacted, according to the rules of the constitution, is invalid because it is immoral involves the imposition of personal subjective values on

9 HLA Hart, *Positivism and the Separation of Law and Morals*, (1958) 71 Harvard Law Review, 593.

to law. On the most difficult moral dilemmas facing society, there may well be little or no agreement on what constitutes the 'correct' interpretation of morality, and confusion will arise as to whether or not law is valid.

From Hart's perspective, it is preferable to accept that a law – however immoral – is valid, and then to decide what to do about it. To say that it is invalid is to invite argument and doubt, which itself is contrary to the clarity and certainty demanded by the rule of law.

Joseph Raz

The requirements of Fuller's morality of duty are reflected in the writings of Professor Joseph Raz of the University of Oxford in *The Rule of Law and its Virtue*. To Fuller's requirements Raz (recognising that even now this is an incomplete list) adds the principles that:

- the independence of the judiciary must be guaranteed.
- the principles of natural justice must be observed.
- the discretion of the crime preventing agencies should not be allowed to pervert the law.

However, Professor Raz rejects Fuller's view on the moral nature of law and the link between law and morals and argues that the rule of law is a morally neutral concept. Indeed, he goes further and argues that even a morally repugnant regime could be perfectly in compliance with the rule of law. Hart objects to this, arguing that an evil regime would be forced, one way or another, to violate the basic principles of the rule of law in order to hide what they were attempting to achieve. Retrospective law, or secret laws, or contradictory, confusing laws would inevitably be enacted.

It may be that the example of evil regimes raises morally intractable questions, which require exceptional solutions. Fuller's solution of designating an evil regime as 'invalid' – while morally appealing – is unhelpful in that it cannot solve the problem of how to deal with those who acted under the unjust or immoral law. Hart's solution of treating such law as valid at the time of the actions in question, but imposing a retrospective liability on those complying with it, is, in Hart's own admission, the 'least worst alternative' rather than a satisfactory solution. Retrospectivity itself infringes the rule of law, going against the whole idea of the law guiding conduct, which is lawful if in accordance with law.

The question of 'what to do about' evil regimes, however, remains one of the most difficult contemporary questions for the international community. The role of the International Criminal Court in bringing those guilty of war crimes to justice is one response. The recourse to war in Iraq in 2003 is another. Neither is free of controversy.

The obligation to obey law

The debate about law and morality gives rise to an important question – namely, what is the nature of an individual's obligation to obey the law? An authoritarian interpretation of the rule of law is to argue that where law exists, so too does the duty of absolute obedience. This, however, is unsatisfactory, as the example of the woman who denounced her husband shows.

The debate over whether there is a duty to obey law, and the nature and extent of that duty, goes back to ancient Greece,[10] and it remains one of the most difficult questions relating to law.

Leaving aside the particular tragedy of the Nazi regime and that of the system of apartheid practised in South Africa before reform, it needs to be recognised that laws and legal systems can and do 'go wrong', albeit generally in less spectacular fashion than those of Germany and South Africa. A key example from the US in the twentieth-century illustrates the difficulty. The law provided for the segregation of blacks and whites, and ensured that white people were advantaged over black people. The question that arises is, did black Americans have a duty to obey the law, which treated them as second-class citizens?

Martin Luther King led the campaign of civil disobedience against discrimination.[11] In doing so he broke the law and was frequently imprisoned. King was campaigning for the removal of legal disabilities, which were imposed on the grounds of race. In doing so he sought a society free of prejudice, based on the equality of the individual. By serving his punishment, King showed his acceptance of and loyalty to the legal system as a whole, while rejecting the immoral laws.

Unjust laws cannot give rise to a duty of obedience. The obligation to obey law, therefore, is not absolute. The duty to obey arises out of membership of society. It can be viewed as one aspect of the social contract: accepting not only the benefits that membership brings but also the obligations it imposes. WD Ross argued that:

> . . . the duty of obeying the laws of one's country arises partly . . . from the duty of gratitude for the benefits one has received from it; partly from the implicit promise to obey which seems to be involved in permanent residence in a country whose laws we know and we are expected to obey, and still more clearly involved when we ourselves invoke the protection of its laws . . . and partly (if we are fortunate in our country) from the fact that its laws are potent instruments for the general good.[12]

10 See, e.g., Plato in the *Crito*.

11 See ML King, *Why We Can't Wait*, 1963, New York: Signet.

12 (1955) 64 Philosophical Review, 175, 185.

Where unjust law exists, action to reform that law is aimed at restoring the terms of the social contract. A supporter of a limited right to civil disobedience – where the democratic process has been unresponsive – is Professor John Rawls of the University of Harvard. In *A Theory of Justice*, 1973,[13] Rawls argued that an entirely peaceful campaign of civil disobedience is a legitimate mechanism to raise the awareness and 'sense of justice' in the community and bring about change. The protest must be non-violent, for violence is destructive. Further, when in the course of the protest the law is broken, the individual must accept the punishment handed down by law. Finally, should the campaign fail to attract the support of the community, it must be brought to an end.

AV Dicey and the rule of law

Writing in the nineteenth century, and in one important respect inaccurate today, AV Dicey's writing on the rule of law has nevertheless been influential and still provides guidelines for a good legal system.[14] In Dicey's view there are three main aspects of the rule of law, each of which can be broken down into further detail.

- First, no one should be punished other than for a distinct breach of law: 'No man is punishable or can be lawfully be made to suffer in body or goods except for a distinct breach of law established in the ordinary legal manner before the ordinary courts.'
- Second, irrespective of status, all are equal under the law.
- Third, individual rights and freedoms are best protected by the ordinary law rather than by a Bill of Rights.

It is this third proposition that can no longer be supported, as discussed further below.

The first two Diceyan principles do, however, offer scope for development.

No punishment without a crime

This apparently straightforward requirement masks a number of other factors. Dicey was very much a champion of the unwritten constitution and the common law. He disapproved of vaguely worded laws that encouraged uncertainty and might result in too much discretion being given to officials who interpret the laws. Accordingly, law must be clear and certain in order to offer real guidance as to the behaviour required or prohibited by the law.

13 Revised edition, 1999, Oxford University Press.

14 *Introduction to the Study of the Constitution*, London: Macmillan, 10th edn, 1959.

Discretion

Dicey's objection to discretionary powers is that broad discretion is capable of leading to arbitrariness, which is contrary to the rule of law. To take a simple example, if the law provides that a police officer may arrest anyone who s/he thinks *might* have committed a crime, this will lead to arbitrary arrests with the police having the power to arrest anyone on any basis whatsoever according to his or her personal whim. Accordingly, the usual formula relating to the power of arrest is one that is capable of being assessed objectively by the courts to ensure that the police act lawfully. Section 24(1)(d) of the Police and Criminal Evidence Act 1984, for example, provides that a constable may arrest without a warrant anyone whom he has *reasonable grounds for suspecting to be committing an offence*. The concept of 'reasonableness' is capable of objective analysis and judgement.

However, not all actions or decisions can be controlled by detailed rules that exclude the exercise of any judgement by decision-makers. Some discretion is inevitable and necessary. It is when the exercise of discretion is tainted by arbitrariness that it becomes contrary to the rule of law. There are many examples of this aspect of the rule of law in case law relating to judicial review.[15] To take just one example, in the case of *Sagnata Investments v Norwich Corporation*,[16] the local authority had the power to grant licences for amusement arcades. However, it adopted a policy that it would never grant any licences – irrespective of the merits of the application. The court ruled this to be unlawful: the authority had fettered its discretion by adopting a rigid policy.

Prospective, not retrospective, law

Law should be prospective, not retrospective. As noted above, it is morally wrong for the state to punish someone for conduct that when undertaken was lawful, but has now become unlawful. Retrospective law is capable of being beneficial: for example to confer retrospectively on individuals a right to compensation for loss suffered for which no provision had previously been made, cannot be criticised as wrong. However, to punish someone for conduct which was lawful at the time is clearly wrong.

One case that raises difficult questions is that of *R v R*.[17] In this case, a husband was prosecuted for raping his wife. At the time there existed a legal immunity from liability for rape for husbands in relation to their wives (with limited exceptions). The reason for this lay in the centuries-old fiction that on marriage husband and wife were united – they became one. This is the doctrine of 'one flesh'. An alternative fiction is that on marriage the wife

15 See Chapter 13.
16 [1971] 2 QB 614.
17 [1992] 3 WLR 767.

consents to sexual intercourse throughout the marriage and that her consent to the specific act is not required. However, in *R v R*, the House of Lords abolished the immunity and found the husband guilty of rape. The husband took the case to the European Court of Human Rights, arguing that the English court had violated the principle of non-retrospectivity, enshrined in Article 7 of the European Convention on Human Rights. The Court of Human Rights upheld the House of Lords' decision: the doctrine of one flesh was contrary to the principle of equality between the sexes, which the law should protect. Accordingly, the husband was punished for conduct that was thought to be lawful at the time, but which became unlawful subsequently, in order to give effect to the principle of sexual equality.

Law must be clear

In addition to non-retrospectivity, if law is to guide conduct it must be clear and relatively certain and it must be accessible (i.e. published rather than secret). These requirements are implicit in Dicey's first requirement and find echoes in the writing of Fuller and Raz. Laws that are unclear or contradictory, or that are changed frequently, offend against the rule of law in failing to provide guidance and placing the individual at risk of punishment for conduct that s/he did not know was unlawful.

Equality before the law

This aspect of Dicey's analysis of the rule of law causes problems and is often misinterpreted. The principle of equality before the law does not mean that each and every individual in society should have equal powers, rights, freedoms or obligations. It is an important principle of justice that like situations be treated alike and that different situations are treated differently. To treat all in exactly the same way, irrespective of differing capacities, characteristics, needs, etc. would be arbitrary and itself contrary to the rule of law. Accordingly, it is necessary to make adjustments to ensure that differing factors are dealt with differently. It would be wrong, for example, for the law to treat a child of seven in exactly the same way as an adult, in relation to criminal liability. Equally, it would be wrong to treat a mentally ill person as having the same legal capacity as a person without a mental illness. The law must also make provision for different treatment towards those who are physically disabled. To act justly is to treat like cases alike and to treat different cases differently, taking relevant differences into account and make adjustments for them.

Powers and immunities

Dicey never intended that equality be an absolute concept. The law confers on the police powers over and above those of ordinary citizens. The law also provides immunities from the legal process in relation to certain categories of person. For example, Members of Parliament are protected against the law of defamation for words spoken in the course of parliamentary proceedings.[18] The justification for this immunity is that it is necessary to provide protection in order that there can be full and frank debate on matters of public importance. This could not occur if there was a risk of legal action: the democratic process provides the justification. A further immunity is given to judges who are protected against legal action related to the exercise of their judicial function. Diplomats are also given immunity from the criminal law on the basis that another country's embassy is fictionally a part of that country's territory and jurisdiction, and each country respects this principle of international law.

What Dicey did demand, however, is that irrespective of rank and status in society, all should be equally accountable to the law for the exercise of their powers. In relation to MPs, their immunity is strictly limited to parliamentary proceedings. If in the course of debate they slander an individual, that slander is not actionable. However, should the slander be repeated outside Parliament, it then becomes actionable. In relation to judges and the protection of their judicial functions, should a judge misinterpret his or her powers and act wrongly, that wrong can be corrected on appeal.

Accountability

The most important accountability is that of state officials on whom powers are conferred. In relation to government officials and public bodies, where powers are conferred by Act of Parliament the courts will – through judicial review – ensure that officials and bodies are kept within the law: *intra vires*. If a public body acts outside its powers, the courts will correct that error by requiring the decision-maker to decide according to law. The courts will also hold a minister of the Crown accountable to law. For example, in *M v Home Office* (1993)[19] the Home Secretary, ignored an order of the court and was held to be liable in his personal or official capacity.

The police have wide-ranging powers. Nowadays these are controlled by detailed Acts of Parliament and Codes of Practice, which, while not law, govern the way that powers are exercised. For example, Code G relates to the Police and Criminal Evidence Act 1984 power of arrest. Paragraph 1.4 provides, in part, that:

> If the provisions of the Act and this Code are not observed, both the arrest and the conduct of any subsequent investigation may be open to question.

18 See Chapter 9.
19 [1993] 3 All ER 537.

Furthermore, to ensure that everyone has access to the Code, it is required to be 'readily available' at all police stations for consultation by 'police officers and police staff, detained persons and members of the public'.

The police are not protected from liability for unlawful conduct in the course of their duties. While miscarriages of justice occur from time to time because of wrongful action of the police, these are fortunately rare. The police only have the power to act according to law – if they step outside their lawful powers they will be liable under the law. For example, the law provides that confessions that have been obtained by force are inadmissible in a court of law. In relation to suspected terrorists, evidence that has been obtained through torture is not admissible.[20]

The legal system and equality

Equality before the law also has implications for the organisation of the legal system. It is essential, if rights and freedoms are to be protected, that everyone has access to the law and to the courts. In turn, this requires that if legal representation is needed, the state will make provision for legal aid and assistance. It requires also that the cost of court proceedings should be within people's reach. The old maxim that the law is like the Ritz Hotel and open to everyone is unfortunately true. The law may be open, but it is also exceedingly expensive and only the very poorest in society are eligible for legal aid.

The case of *Granger v United Kingdom* (1990)[21] illustrates the principle that legal representation is a central feature of the right to fair trial under Article 6 of the European Convention on Human Rights. Granger had been refused extended legal aid in order to pursue an appeal. The Court of Human Rights held that this denial was a violation of the right to fair trial.

The protection of rights and freedoms under common law

This last aspect of Dicey's analysis can be dealt with briefly. While in the nineteenth century (Dicey's work was published in 1865) it may have been tenable to argue that the judges in the ordinary courts of law were the best protectors of rights, it is certainly not so today. The concept of parliamentary sovereignty and its application by the judges means that if Parliament chooses to enact harsh law the judges must apply it. For example, in the case of *Entick v Carrington* (1765),[22] the court held that the Home Secretary had no power to enter and seize a citizen's property without a specific warrant of the court. By contrast, in *R v Inland Revenue Commissioners ex parte*

20 *A v Secretary of State for the Home Department (No 2)* [2006] 2 AC 221.
21 (1990) 12 EHRR 469.
22 (1765) 19 St Tr 1029.

Rossminster (1980)[23] Parliament had given a general power to tax inspectors to enter and search private premises. The court was powerless to protect the citizen against entry into and search of property in light of this wide-ranging power conferred by statute.

However, the Human Rights Act 1998 now provides an additional jurisdiction for the judges to protect rights. Parliament must be informed as to whether or not a Bill complies with Convention rights. In addition, the courts are 'public bodies' within the meaning of section 6 of the Act, a definition that compels the judges to interpret the law in a manner that protects Convention rights. As will be seen in Chapter 10, however, there are limits to this protection. It is not as absolute as the protection provided under a written constitution with a Bill of Rights. Nevertheless, it is correct to argue that the Human Rights Act 1998 undoubtedly reinforces the rule of law and extends the protection of rights and freedoms.

Summary

The rule of law is a controversial concept that lends itself to several interpretations that reflect very different political arrangements – the Western liberal interpretation, the Marxist interpretation and the traditional oriental interpretation being just three. From the Western liberal perspective, law is a positive force in society, providing a framework for government under law and accountable to law, and a framework also for the maximisation of individual freedom and rights within the law and protected by the courts.

The rule of law also has a very practical application. The rule of law can act as a yardstick for measuring the extent to which a legal system complies with the concepts of legality and constitutionalism. The requirement of certainty in law underpins the idea that no one shall be punished except for a breach of law. The idea of equality before the law, so easily misunderstood, acts as a guide to the manner in which a legal system must be arranged to maximise access to law and the protection of the law. It also requires that those who hold special powers are accountable to the law: that no one, irrespective of rank and station, is above the law.

Further reading

Allan, T, *Law, Liberty and Justice: the Legal Foundations of British Constitutionalism*, 1993, Oxford: Clarendon Press.

Allan, T, 'The Rule of Law as the Rule of Reason: Consent and Constitutionalism', (1999) 115 LQR 221.

Allan, T, *Constitutional Justice: a Liberal Theory of the Rule of Law*, 2001, Oxford: OUP, Chapters 1–4.

23 [1980] AC 952.

Barendt, E, 'Dicey and Civil Liberties' [1985] PL 596.
Bingham, Lord, 'Dicey Revisited' [2002] PL 39.
Bingham, Lord, 'The Rule of Law' [2007] CLJ 67.
Ekins, R, 'Judicial Supremacy and the Rule of Law' (2003) 119 LQR 127.
Jowell, J, 'The Rule of Law Today' in J Jowell and D Oliver (eds), *The Changing Constitution*, 6th edn, 2007, Oxford: OUP.
Raz, J, 'The Rule of Law and its Virtue', [1977] LQR 93.
Steyn, Lord, 'Democracy, the Rule of Law and the Role of Judges' [2006] EHRLR 243.
Tomkins, A, 'Readings of *A v Secretary of State for the Home Department*' [2005] PL 259.
Woolf, Lord, 'The Rule of Law and a Change in the Constitution' [2004] CLJ 317.

? *SELF-ASSESSMENT QUESTIONS*

1. List three different approaches to the rule of law offered by political philosophy.
2. Write a brief definition of the rule of law as understood in contemporary Britain.
3. List the three principles identified by AV Dicey as crucial to the rule of law.

SAMPLE EXAMINATION QUESTIONS

1. Given the vagueness of the term 'the rule of law', it can offer little guidance as to the legality, or otherwise, of government action.
2. 'The doctrine of the rule of law is so vague as to be almost meaningless.'

   Discuss.
3. Does any aspect of Dicey's definition of the 'rule of law' have relevance today?

Chapter 5

Parliamentary sovereignty

CONTENTS

KEY WORDS AND PHRASES

Act of Parliament	Statutes: the highest form of domestic law
Colonies	Overseas territories subject to foreign rule

Entrenchment	The process by which legislation is protected against amendment and/or repeal
Express repeal	The intentional repeal of previous law, as stated in a later statute
Implied repeal	Theory ensuring that the most recent legislation is given effect in preference to an earlier piece of legislation by repealing 'by implication' an inconsistent earlier provision
Manner and form	Theory holding that procedural requirements for law-making limit Parliament's sovereignty
Parliament	The Crown, House of Commons and House of Lords
Redefinition theory	Theory that redefining the composition of Parliament limits Parliament's sovereignty
Standing Orders	The formal parliamentary rules regulating procedures
Sovereignty	The ultimate source of power in a state – legal or political

Introduction

Under any constitution there must be an ultimate authority, or power. In a country with a written constitution, the constitution will have its origins in the historical formation of the state and the drafting of a set of rules to govern the state. The original authority of the constitution comes from the people within the state, who are said to be *politically sovereign*. Once drafted the constitution becomes the supreme legal power within the state and any laws that contradict the constitution will be declared to be null and void by the Supreme Court. In other words the constitution is *legally sovereign*.

In the UK, by contrast, the Constitution has evolved over the centuries and never been committed to a single authoritative document. The people hold *political sovereignty* while Parliament, as the highest law-making authority, is the source of *legal sovereignty*.

The rule that Parliament is sovereign – or supreme – derives from common law. Parliament's sovereignty is both recognised and upheld by the judges. Whenever an Act of Parliament is recognised as valid law and is applied by the judges in a court of law, the judges are giving practical effect to Parliament's authority. If a time comes when the judges rule that an Act of Parliament is not valid because it conflicts with some higher source of law, the sovereignty of Parliament will be lost.

However, as will be discussed below, while Parliamentary sovereignty or supremacy may be the orthodox, theoretical foundation of the Constitution and one well-suited to an independent isolated nation state, in today's more complex world the doctrine is subject to many challenges. One key question is whether the traditional theory of sovereignty continues to have any relevance in light of these many challenges.

The orthodox theory of sovereignty

The classic definition and explanation of sovereignty is that of Albert Venn Dicey, the nineteenth-century constitutional authority. In his *Introduction to the Study of the Constitution*, 1885, Dicey laid down three basic principles:

- parliament may enact laws on any subject matter it chooses;
- no Parliament's powers may be restricted by a previous Parliament nor may one Parliament restrict the powers of a future Parliament;
- no one – including a court of law – may challenge the validity of an Act of Parliament.

Parliament may enact laws on any subject matter

Examples of the unlimited power of Parliament include:

- extending its own term of office without any need for elections, as in wartime. See, for example, the Prolongation of Parliament Act 1944;
- changing the succession to the Crown, as in: the Act of Settlement 1700 (succession only through male line and excluding Roman Catholics); His Majesty's Declaration of Abdication Act 1936 (ending the reign of Edward VIII);
- altering its own composition and powers as in: the Parliament Acts 1911 and 1949 (altering the powers of the House of Lords); the House of Lords Act 1999 (altering the composition of the House of Lords);
- granting independence to formerly dependent countries, as in the Zimbabwe Independence Act 1979;
- legislating with retrospective effect, as in the War Damage Act 1965, which nullified the decision of the House of Lords in *Burmah Oil v Lord Advocate* [1965] AC 75, awarding compensation to a company that had suffered damage to its property as a result of war;
- legislating with extraterritorial effect as in the Aviation Security Act 1982, which extends the jurisdiction of the domestic courts to try alleged acts of hijacking, irrespective of the nationality of the accused or place of the hijack.

Unrealistic examples are offered by academics. The most noteworthy are those of Sir Ivor Jennings, who, in *The Law and the Constitution* 1959, argues that Parliament can ban smoking in the streets of Paris and also legally make a man into a woman, and Sir Leslie Stephens, who, in *The Science of Ethics*

1882, states that Parliament can lawfully require that all blue-eyed babies be put to death.

These academic examples highlight the question of what, if any, practical limitations there are on what Parliament may enact. This issue is discussed once the other two aspects of Dicey's definition are considered.

Parliament cannot be restricted by a former Parliament or restrict a future Parliament

The justification for this second rule lies in the fact that if one Parliament could be restricted by another Parliament – whether an earlier or later Parliament – then the restricted Parliament would not be truly 'sovereign'. Sovereignty is, theoretically, an all-or-nothing concept: it is not logical to speak of 'limited sovereignty' for the true meaning of sovereignty is ultimate, unlimited power.

In order to comply with their constitutional duty and ensure that the intention of each Parliament is given effect, the judges employ the doctrine of 'implied repeal'.

Implied repeal

If, usually because of an error, Parliament should enact a part of a statute that conflicts with another, earlier, statute, the judges will give effect to the latest expression of Parliament's will. That is to say, they will hold that the earlier piece of legislation is 'repealed by implication' or 'impliedly' and that the later piece of legislation will be applied.

Two examples of the working of implied repeal are shown in the cases of *Vauxhall Estates Ltd v Liverpool Corporation* [1932] 1 KB 733 and *Ellen Street Estates Ltd v Minister of Health* [1934] 1 KB 590, the facts of which are similar. The Acquisition of Land Act 1919, section 7, seemed to provide that all future land acquisitions would be subject to the provisions of the 1919 Act. This was tested in relation to the Housing Act 1925, which provided a less generous scheme of compensation for land compulsorily acquired. The plaintiffs wanted the 1919 Act, which was more favourable to them, to apply. However, using the doctrine of 'implied repeal', the Court of Appeal ruled that the later Act must apply – thereby impliedly repealing the inconsistent provisions of the earlier Act.

The constitutional function of implied repeal is to ensure that the latest expression of Parliament's will is enforced, thereby ensuring that the latest Parliament in time is fully sovereign, or unrestricted by a former Parliament. Implied repeal also ensures that there can be no 'entrenchment' under the UK Constitution.

However, the judges have recently recognised that there are some statutes – namely the European Communities Act 1972 and the Human Rights Act

1998 – which are immune from implied repeal. The explanation for this exception to the normal rule is that these Acts (and others may be added to the list in future) are regarded by the judges as of such constitutional importance that they should not have their validity affected by some parliamentary oversight or error. Accordingly, only express repeal will be effective in relation to these Acts.

Arguments against Dicey's second principle

This second Diceyan rule has given rise to a great deal of argument. We can examine these under the following headings:

- grants of independence;
- the Acts of Union with Scotland 1706/1707;
- 'manner and form' and 'redefinition' theories.

(a) GRANTS OF INDEPENDENCE

The argument against Dicey here is encapsulated in Lord Denning's remark that freedom once given cannot be taken away (see further below). Essentially the argument is that by granting independence to a former colony Parliament has surrendered its legal power to reclaim that territory as a dependent country. The fact that Parliament *could* pass an Act reclaiming its power over the territory (and the judges would recognise it as a valid Act), is less relevant than the fact that the country in question would ignore such an Act. Furthermore, the international community of nations would support that country against any attempted power to reclaim it, if necessary by imposing sanctions.

(b) THE ACTS OF UNION WITH SCOTLAND 1706/1707

The Acts of Union between England and Scotland created a political union under one sovereign Parliament of Great Britain. In effect, the parliaments of the formerly independent England and Scotland abolished themselves, coming together under the newly established, and sovereign, Parliament.

It is the argument of some eminent academics that these Acts constitute an early form of written constitution, which set out the terms on which the new Parliament of Great Britain would come into being and the terms on which it would operate. If that is correct, it would follow that every future Parliament was bound by (or controlled by) the Acts of Union and was therefore 'not fully sovereign'.

The Acts of Union were phrased in language that made it clear that the union was to be permanent ('for ever lasting'), and included a number of provisions that gave protection to, for example, the Scottish legal system, the Scottish Presbyterian Church and Scottish university system. These provisions, so those in favour of this view argue, represent very real restrictions on what Parliament can lawfully do.

How has this argument stood up to judicial scrutiny?

The key case is *MacCormick v Lord Advocate* 1953 SC 396.

In *MacCormick v Lord Advocate* it was argued that the Royal Titles Act 1953, which provided for the new Queen to assume the title of Queen Elizabeth II, conflicted with the Acts of Union that came into being in 1707 (Queen Elizabeth I being Queen of England, not Queen of Scotland). The Scottish court rejected the argument, holding that the Royal Titles Act 1953 was valid law.

However, Lord President Cooper suggested, *obiter*, it was by no means certain how the court would rule if the UK Parliament passed an Act that affected the key issues in the Acts of Union – namely protection of the Scottish legal system and Church.

This same issue was argued in *Gibson v Lord Advocate* [1975] 1 CMLR 563.

In *Gibson v Lord Advocate* the right of fishermen from other European Community countries to fish in Scottish waters was argued to conflict with Article 18 of the Acts of Union, which provides that no law shall be passed unless it is for the benefit of the Scottish people.

Once again the Court rejected the argument. In this case, however, the Court took the approach that matters relating to Community law were Public Law matters and not related to the private rights of the people. Again, however, there is the judicial suggestion that the argument regarding the validity of law that potentially or actually conflicts with the Acts of Union is not conclusively settled.

(c) 'MANNER AND FORM' AND 'REDEFINITION' THEORIES

This approach focuses on procedural matters: the term 'manner and form' meaning no more than the procedure that must be followed in the law-making process if valid law is to be created. The phrase derives from the 1865 Colonial Laws Validity Act, an Act of the UK Parliament, which laid down procedures to be followed by subordinate, colonial legislative bodies.

Redefinition theory refers to the actual composition of the law-making body. In both cases (and there may well be overlaps between the two) the central argument is that a legislature that intends to make valid law is restricted by procedure or composition. It is therefore not 'sovereign'.

In order to see the manner and form argument clearly we can look at the case of *Attorney General for New South Wales v Threthowan* [1932] AC 526.

The government of New South Wales, Australia, wanted to ensure that an incoming government (of a different political party) did not pass a law abolishing the Legislative Council (the Upper House, the equivalent of the United Kingdom's House of Lords). To protect the Legislative Council an Act was passed in 1929 which provided that if a Bill attempting to abolish it was to pass it had to have the agreement of *both* Houses with a two-thirds majority *and* be approved by a referendum of the people. Furthermore, to prevent the new Parliament repealing the 1929 Act it was provided that the same procedures must be followed if the 1929 Act was to be repealed.

At a general election a new government was elected. It decided to abolish the Legislative Council and produced a Bill which ignored the requirements laid down in the 1929 Act. When the Bill was presented to the Governor General for the Royal Assent, it was argued that the Royal Assent could not be given because the Bill had not been passed following the correct procedure.

The matter went to the Australian High Court and then to the Privy Council in London. Both courts ruled that the Royal Assent could not be granted: the New South Wales Parliament was obliged – ie bound – to follow the 1929 Act and was not free – sovereign – to ignore it. The key factor in this case was the Colonial Laws Validity Act 1865: an Act of the United Kingdom Parliament.

Section 5 of the 1865 Act provided that a colonial legislature could pass laws amending its own composition and procedure *provided that* the legislature followed any procedural requirements which were legally in force at the time. The new Parliament was not able to repeal the 1929 Act which laid down the procedures: the procedures were therefore still in force and had to be followed.

This can be portrayed diagrammatically as follows:

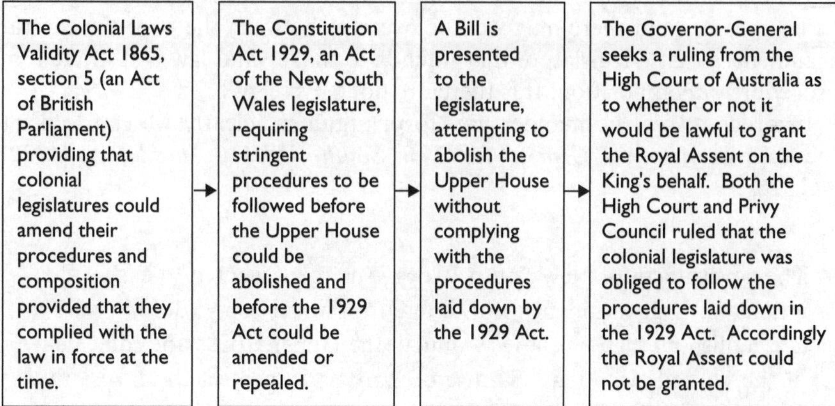

Figure 5.1

The key point to note from this case is that a colonial legislative body is not supreme. By definition, there is a superior law-making body (here the UK Parliament) with power to restrict what the colonial institutions can and cannot do. Only once a colony becomes a free, independent state does it acquire the full power of sovereignty. Accordingly, it is not possible to argue that a case such as *Trethowan* is authority for the fact that the UK Parliament can restrict itself.

Redefinition theory can be dealt with briefly. It is undeniable that if a parliamentary body redefines its membership that the parliament in future is restricted by that membership. For example, the Life Peerage Act 1958 introduced Life Peers to the House of Lords. Thereafter the House of Lords comprised not just hereditary peers and judicial peers and bishops, but also those appointed as members for their life time. However, that redefinition of membership does not in fact or law restrict what a future Parliament can do. As the House of Lords Act 1999 (which abolished the right of most hereditary peers to sit in the House of Lords) illustrates clearly, a sovereign Parliament can amend its own composition and procedure with a minimum of formality. A further example can be seen with the Constitutional Reform Act 2005, which provides that once a new Supreme Court is established, the Law Lords (judicial peers) will no longer be entitled, as now, to sit in the House of Lords when it is acting in its law-making capacity.

No body, including a court of law, may question the validity of an Act of Parliament

It is a fundamental constitutional principle that once a Bill has passed through its various stages of scrutiny in Parliament and has received the Royal Assent, it is a valid Act of Parliament. Regardless of its subject matter, the judges will uphold its validity. One case emphasising this principle is *Pickin v British Railways Board* [1974] AC 765[1] in which the dicta of Lord Reid represents the contemporary view:

> The function of the court is to construe and apply the enactments of Parliament. The court has no concern with the manner in which Parliament or its officers carrying out its Standing Orders [the rules regulating procedure] perform these functions. Any attempt to prove that they were misled by fraud or otherwise would necessarily involve an inquiry into the manner in which they had performed their functions . . . .[2]

Practical limitations on Parliament's powers

The effectiveness of law

The law must be acceptable to the people: if a law is passed which no one obeys or recognises as law, it will be ineffective. Accordingly, although it is technically valid, it is not viable as a mechanism for controlling behaviour. An extreme example of such a law would be if Parliament passed an Act stating that pet dogs could only be taken for a walk lawfully at two o'clock in the morning. A real example lies with the Poll Tax legislation introduced in the 1980s, which proved unacceptable to the people who protested against it and refused to obey it, despite threats of prosecution. The law was changed.

The law must also be workable in practice: banning smoking in the streets of Paris, for example, would be ignored by the French courts and probably unenforceable before the English courts.

Grants of independence and devolution of law-making power

Lord Denning MR once remarked judicially (in *Ndlwana v Hofmeyr* (1937)) that 'freedom once given cannot be taken away'. This principle applies most to formerly dependent territories. The example of the Zimbabwe Independence Act is given above. No Parliament would intentionally revoke the grant of power to a now independent, sovereign, country.

The principle is also relevant to the devolution of power away from the UK Parliament (Westminster) to the parliaments/assemblies of the nations of the UK. The Northern Ireland Acts, the Scotland Act 1998 and the Government

1 See also the earlier case of *Edinburgh & Dalkeith Railway v Wauchsupe* (1842) 8 Cl & F 710.

2 The most recent case in which the validity of an Act was challenged is *Jackson v Attorney General* [2005] UKHL 56; [2005] 2 WLR 1015. *Jackson* concerned the validity of the Hunting Act 2004, which in turn involved consideration of the validity of the Parliament Act 1949. The challenge failed.

of Wales Acts 1998 and 2006 confer law-making powers. While in theory the UK Parliament could take back the powers conferred, it would only do so if the people of the nations – who voted for devolution – were to support such a move.

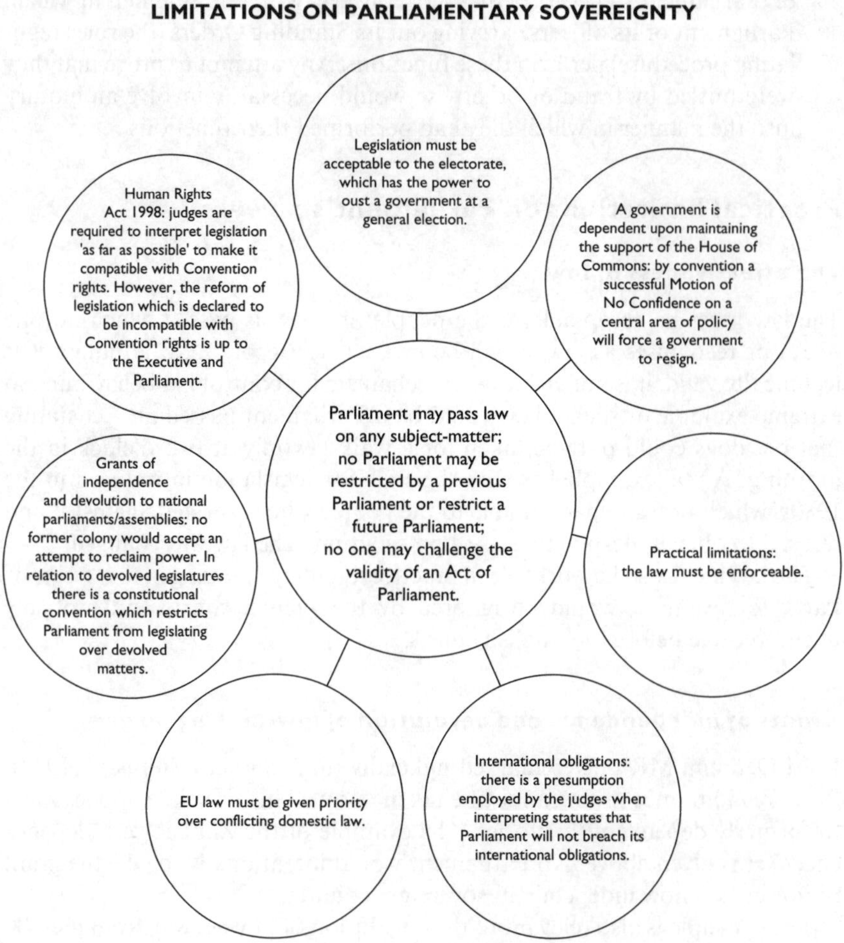

LIMITATIONS ON PARLIAMENTARY SOVEREIGNTY

Figure 5.2

International obligations

Countries enter into international agreements – treaties – which entail obligations, either to do something (for example to improve air quality), or to refrain from doing something (for example using torture techniques in wartime). While these international obligations could be overridden by

Parliament, it would be unusual for Parliament intentionally to damage international relations and the standing of the country internationally.

In order to prevent inadvertent breaches of international law by Acts of Parliament that conflict with international law, there is a judicially created presumption of statutory interpretation that requires the judges – as far as possible – to interpret domestic law in a manner that makes it compatible with international law.

European Union (EU) law

A sub-species of international obligations, by becoming a Member of the European Communities – now European Union – Member States accept the supremacy of the law of the EU and any domestic laws that intentionally or inadvertently contradict EU law must be disapplied (set aside) by the courts. On this, see further, Chapter 6.

European Convention on Human Rights (ECHR)

This treaty represents a charter of enforceable rights and freedoms, which must be respected by the states that sign the Convention. In practice, all member states of the EU are signatories to the European Convention. The Convention rights are now directly enforceable in the domestic courts of the UK under the Human Rights Act 1998. See further, Chapter 10.

The judiciary

The work of the judges – whether through developing the common law or the interpretation of statutes – affects the meaning of the laws passed by Parliament. As seen above with the case of *Burmah Oil v Lord Advocate*, Parliament may choose to nullify a judicial decision; in practice this is rare. It is particularly apparent in relation to EU law (Chapter 6) and to the law relating to the European Convention on Human Rights (Chapter 10) that the judges play a pivotal role in developing the law. As Parliament for the most part will allow a judicial decision to stand, judicial decisions represent a vital source of law – extending, restricting or modifying the law.

The relationship between Parliament and the judges is illustrated in the following three cases:

> *Burmah Oil v Lord Advocate (supra)*: Parliament overturns the decision with the War Damage Act 1965.
>
> *Shaw v Director of Public Prosecutions* [1962] AC 220. The defendant was prosecuted for conspiracy to corrupt public morals, a criminal

offence not previously known to the law. The House of Lords upheld his conviction, ruling that the judges were the guardians of public morals and declaring that such an offence had always existed, albeit not articulated. Parliament allowed the decision to stand.

R v R [1992] 3 WLR 767. A husband was prosecuted for raping his wife. At the time husbands had enjoyed an immunity from the law of rape in relation to their wives. The House of Lords overturned that immunity. Parliament later endorsed the decision by redefining rape in the Criminal Justice and Public Order Act 1994.

Summary

The UK Parliament is theoretically sovereign in that it can make any law that it chooses. Sovereignty is both legal and political. The people hold political sovereignty and confer authority (legal sovereignty) on Parliament to legislate on their behalf.

However, Parliament's legal sovereignty or supremacy is limited by practicalities such as the acceptability of the law to the people. It is also limited by international obligations undertaken under treaties, those having the most impact being the European Union treaties and the Council of Europe's Convention on Human Rights.

Further reading

Allan, TRS, 'Parliamentary Sovereignty: Law, Politics and Revolution' (1997) 113 LQR 443.

Bamforth, N, 'Parliamentary Sovereignty and the Human Rights Act 1998' [1998] PL 572.

Bogdonor, V, 'Our New Constitution' (2004) 120 LQR 242.

Bradley, A, 'The Sovereignty of Parliament – Form or Substance?', in J Jowell and D Oliver (eds) *The Changing Constitution* (6th edn, 2007), OUP.

Coke, Lord, 'A Constitutional Retreat' (2006) 122 LQR 224.

Craig, P, 'Constitutional Foundations, the Rule of Law and Supremacy', [2003] PL 92.

Ekins, R, 'Acts of Parliament and the Parliament Acts' (2007) 123 LQR 91.

Goldsworthy, J, *The Sovereignty of Parliament: History and Philosophy* (1999), Oxford: Clarendon.

Hart, HLA, *The Concept of Law*, 1961, Oxford: Clarendon.

Jowell, J, 'Parliamentary Supremacy under the New Constitutional Hypothesis' [2006] PL 562.

Lester, Lord, 'The Art of the Possible: Interpreting Statutes under the Human Rights Act' [1998] EHRLR 665.

Munro, CR, *Studies in Constitutional Law* (2nd edn, 1999), London: Butterworths, Chapters 5 and 6.
Wade, HWR, 'The Basis of Legal Sovereignty' [1955] CLJ 172.
Wade, HWR, 'Sovereignty – Revolution or Evolution?' (1996) 112 LQR 568.

?

SELF-ASSESSMENT QUESTIONS

1. Write a brief sentence explaining the difference between legal and political sovereignty.
2. List the three main aspects of Dicey's theory of sovereignty.
3. Write a sentence explaining the meaning of 'entrenchment'.
4. Giving reasons, explain whether entrenchment is or is not possible under the UK's constitution.

SAMPLE EXAMINATION QUESTIONS

1. To what extent can AV Dicey's nineteenth-century theory of parliamentary sovereignty be supported today?
2. 'Despite many challenges to its nature and existence, parliamentary sovereignty remains the cornerstone of the constitution.'

   Discuss.

Chapter 6

The European Union

CONTENTS

KEY WORDS AND PHRASES

Acquis communautaire	The whole body of laws and policies of the Community which must be adopted by all Member States
Competence	The right/power to act in relation to a particular matter. Competence may be exclusive or shared
Decisions	A secondary source of EC law, binding on those to whom they are addressed
Directives	A secondary source of EC law, binding as to the objective to be achieved but leaving a measure of discretion to the Member State as to how to achieve that objective
Direct applicability	The concept which means that a provision of EC law automatically becomes part of the law of all Member States
Direct effect	A doctrine developed by the Court of Justice, which provides that European law may confer rights on individual citizens, enforceable in the domestic courts
Indirect effect	The concept developed by the Court of Justice, which provides that European law must be complied with by Member States and their courts in order to comply with the duty imposed by Article 10 of the Treaty (see pages 78–79 below)
Proportionality	A key concept in European law: the action taken must be no greater than necessary to achieve the objective being sought
Regulations	Secondary sources of EC law, binding in their entirety and coming into effect without any further action by the Member States
State liability	Where a Member State breaches EC law and that breach causes loss, the State is liable to compensate for that loss

Subsidiarity	The principle that requires that decisions be taken at the level closest to the people
Treaty	A binding legal agreement between States under international law

Introduction

The Second World War (1939 to 1945), left Europe economically and physically devastated. In order to ensure that no one country had the physical resources to start a future conflict, an agreement was reached between several nations,[1] which resulted, in 1951, in the setting up of the European Coal and Steel Community (ECSC). This Community established an administrative, executive, judicial and parliamentary framework that today represents the key institutions of the EU: the Commission, Council and Court of Justice. The central objective of the ECSC was to place the control over the raw material of war – coal and steel – under the authority of the newly established institutions.

In 1957, the same nations reached agreement to establish a Community designed to control the management and use of atomic energy – the European Atomic Energy Community (Euratom), and intended to last for 50 years. Also in 1957, under the Treaty of Rome, these same nations reached agreement on the establishment of a European Economic Community (EEC), or Common Market. This Common Market was based on four central freedoms: freedom of movement of persons, goods, capital and services. The key objective of the EEC was to create an economic block that was free of internal tariffs and which imposed a common tariff on goods, etc., which entered the EEC from non-EEC countries.

Aims and objectives of the European Union

The aims and objectives of the original three Communities were relatively modest. The ECSC set up a system of supranational control over coal and steel, while Euratom placed atomic energy under supranational control. The EEC, as it was originally called, aimed to create a 'common market' in which people, capital, goods and services would move freely, without any internal tariffs. A common external tariff would ensure that irrespective of where goods entered the common market from non-common market countries, the tariff would be the same. The common market was perceived as a way to increase the standard of living of all those living within the area and to make Europe one of the most powerful trading blocs in the world.

1 France, Germany, Italy, Belgium, Luxembourg and the Netherlands.

THE EVOLUTION OF THE EUROPEAN COMMUNITY AND UNION[2]

1951	Treaty of Paris	Creates the European Coal and Steel Community
1957	Treaty of Rome (the EC Treaty)	Creates the European Economic Community
1957	Treaty of Rome	Creates the European Atomic Energy Community 1965
1965	The Merger Treaty	Merges the institutions of the three Communities
1986	The Single European Act	Expands the powers of the European Parliament; extended areas of competence of Community beyond economic issues
1992	The Treaty on European Union (Maastricht)	Establishes the European Union; sets timetable for introduction of single European currency; further extends powers of the European Parliament
1997	Treaty of Amsterdam	Alters EU pillar structure; introduces framework decisions
2001	Treaty of Nice	Makes arrangements for enlargement of EU membership
2004	The Draft Constitution Treaty	Rejected by France and Netherlands and therefore not ratified
2007	Treaty of Lisbon	When approved, replicates most of the provisions of the rejected Constitution Treaty; makes major reforms to powers and working of institutions; increases Parliament's powers and introduces new system of voting in Council and provides for reduction in the size of the Commission

Figure 6.1

While some of the founding fathers of the 'new Europe' dreamed of a United States of Europe, others were more sceptical. Not least of all the British government, with trading ties to Commonwealth countries and a keen sense of national independence and sovereignty.

As the common market developed and its membership expanded, so too did its goals. As noted above, the Treaty on European Union 1992 (TEU) established the EU, with the Community as one of three pillars, the second being the ambitious objective of a Common Foreign and Security policy, the third relating (as amended in 1997) to cooperation in judicial and criminal matters. The Union has as its objectives:

2. Further details on the Treaties can be found on the companion website at www.routledge.com/textbooks/9780415552554

- to promote economic and social progress and a high level of employment; to achieve balanced and sustainable development. . .;
- to assert its identity on the international scene, particularly through its common foreign and security policy;
- to strengthen the rights and interests of nationals of Member States;
- to maintain and develop the Union as an area of freedom, security and justice.

In relation to the Common Foreign and Security policy, Article 11 of the TEU provides that the objectives of this policy are:

- to safeguard the common values, fundamental interests, independence and integrity of the Union in conformity with the principles of the United Nations Charter;
- to strengthen the security of the Union in all ways;
- to preserve peace and strengthen international security;
- to promote international cooperation; and
- to develop and consolidate democracy and the rule of law, and respect for human rights and fundamental freedoms.

On police and judicial cooperation, the TEU, Article 29, states that its objectives are 'to provide citizens with a high level of safety', achieved by preventing and combating crime, including terrorism and trafficking in persons, arms and drugs, and offences against children and offences of corruption and fraud through:

- the closer cooperation between police forces, customs authorities and other relevant bodies;
- closer cooperation between judicial and other authorities; and
- approximation, where necessary, on rules on criminal matters.

The 1992 Treaty also set the timetable for the achievement of a complete 'single market' and the free movement of capital throughout the Union. The TEU also provided for the introduction of a common currency for all Member States, their eligibility to join being dependent upon certain 'convergence criteria' being met by their economies.

Membership of the Union (with dates of accession)

1957	Belgium, France, Germany, Italy, Luxembourg and the Netherlands
1972	Denmark, Ireland and the United Kingdom

1981	Greece
1986	Spain and Portugal
1995	Austria, Finland and Sweden
2004	The Czech Republic, Cyprus, Estonia, Hungary, Latvia, Lithuania, Malta, Poland, Slovenia and Slovakia
2007	Bulgaria and Romania
	Croatia and Turkey[3]

PRINCIPLE INSTITUTIONS OF THE EUROPEAN UNION

The European Council (Heads of Government and Foreign Secretaries, President of the Commission and two Commissioners.)
The Council of the EU (One Minister from each Member State, membership determined by subject matter under discussion. Ministers defend national interests.)
The Commission (Currently one Commissioner per Member State. Commissioners act in the interests of the European Union.)
The European Parliament (785 members [MEPs], the number per Member State being proportionate to the population. MEPs are directly elected. Parliament acts in the interests of the citizens of the European Union.)
The European Court of Justice (ECJ) and Court of First Instance (One judge per Member State. The ECJ interprets the Treaties, ensures the supremacy of EU law, rules on references from Member State courts, rules on the legality of acts of the EU institutions, makes binding judgments and has the power to impose penalties.)

Figure 6.2

The European Council[4]

Twice a year the heads of state/government and foreign secretaries meet to discuss the most pressing political issues. Formally recognised under the Single European Act 1986, the Council came into being as a result of political need rather than by treaty.

The European Parliament[5]

Originally the Parliament (known as the Assembly) comprised representatives of national Parliaments and had only advisory and supervisory – rather

3 Croatia is due to become a member in 2010. Turkey remains a candidate for membership.

4 Article 4, TEU. Not to be confused with the Council, formerly known as the Council of Ministers.

5 Articles 189–201 EC Treaty.

than law-making – power. Members of the European Parliament (MEPs) have been elected since 1979 and gradually the powers of the Parliament have been increased. Seats in the 785-member Parliament are allocated according to the populations of Member States, and MEPs sit for a five-year term.

The Council of the EU (formerly the Council of Ministers)[6]

The Council has both law-making and executive powers. The Council is made up of one member from each Member State. The composition of the Council depends on the subject matter under discussion. For example, when the subject matter is agriculture, the membership will be made up of agriculture ministers; when the subject matter is transport, it will be transport ministers. It is in Council that the national interests of Member States are defended.

The Council is headed by a President, the office being held in turn by Member States for a six-month period. This rotating presidency will come to an end once the Lisbon Reform Treaty comes into effect, whereupon a more permanent office will be created.

Article 202 of the EC Treaty provides that the functions of the Council are to:

- ensure the coordination of the general economic policies of the Member States;
- take decisions;
- confer on the Commission powers for the implementation of decisions taken by Council.

Decisions are reached by voting, as specified by the Treaties. Voting may be unanimous, by a simple majority or by a 'qualified majority'. In order that the Union can make progress and not be restricted by a minority of Member States, the qualified majority voting system has been increasingly used. The Treaty of Nice revised the system and for a qualified majority to be reached there must be:

- 255 of the 345 possible votes in favour of the proposal;
- 62 per cent of the EU population must be represented by the vote; and
- a majority of the 27 Member States must support the proposal.[7]

The ongoing work of the Council is assisted by a Committee of Permanent Representatives of the Member States (COREPER), members of which are drawn from the Member States' diplomatic service, which in turn is sup-

6 Articles 202–210 EC Treaty.

7 The Treaty of Lisbon 2007 further revises the system.

ported by a secretariat under the direction of a secretary general and his or her deputy.

The Commission[8]

Each Member State appoints one commissioner. Once appointed a commissioner is under a duty to act in the interests of the EU and s/he must not take instructions from his or her appointing government. Commissioners act for a renewable five-year term. The Commission lies at the heart of the EU, its central function being defined as being to 'ensure the proper functioning and development of the common market'. The Commission is divided into Directorates-General, each responsible for a particular aspect of the EU's activities.

The functions of the Commission are:

- to ensure that the provisions of the Treaty are applied;
- to formulate recommendations or deliver opinions;
- exercise its own power of decision and participate in the legislative process;
- exercise powers conferred on it by the Council.

It can be seen from the above that the Commission has administrative and legislative functions, as well as the power of enforcement. This latter power is regulated by Article 226 of the EC Treaty, which provides that if the Commission considers that a Member State has failed to fulfil a Treaty obligation, the Commission must deliver a 'reasoned opinion' on the matter, having given the Member State the opportunity to explain its position. Should the Member State then fail to act in accordance with the Commission's opinion within the time specified, the Commission may refer the matter to the Court of Justice for a formal ruling.

In its legislative capacity, it is the Commission that puts forward the majority of proposals for law-making. The legislative process is complex, and defined in detail in the Treaties. In essence, the process involves a proposal from the Commission, which is then adopted by the Council of the EU, usually with the approval of the Parliament that has the power of 'co-decision' with the Council.

The Court of Justice[9]

Judges are appointed by common agreement of the governments of Member States. Each Member State nominates one judge. Judges are appointed for a

8 Articles 211–219 EC Treaty.
9 Articles 220–245 EC Treaty.

once-renewable three-year term of office. The Court is presided over by a President who holds office for a three-year term. The judges are assisted by Advocates-General. Their task is to act with impartiality and independence and present the legal arguments to the Court for its decision. A Court of First Instance (CFI) was introduced under the Single European Act 1986 to relieve the pressure on the ECJ.

Sources of EC law

EC law has both primary and secondary sources. The primary sources are the Treaties. Secondary sources include Regulations, Directives and Decisions. There are also non-legal sources such as Recommendations and Opinions. In addition there are what are known as 'soft law' provisions – framework decisions, guidance and declarations by the European Council.

The treaties

In order for a new treaty to be introduced and come into effect there must be common agreement among the Member States. Negotiations and agreements will take place in an Intergovernmental Conference (IGC). Once the provisions are finalised they must be ratified (approved) by all Member States according to their own constitutional requirements. To come into effect every Member State must ratify the treaty: the failure by one Member State to ratify will prevent the treaty coming into effect.

Once the treaty is ratified it will come into effect on the date agreed. All Member States must amend their laws to the extent necessary to bring it in line with the treaty.

Regulations

Article 249 of the EC Treaty provides that:

> A regulation shall have general application. It shall be binding and directly applicable in all Member States.

The meaning of this Article is that a Regulation applies throughout the EU, providing for uniformity of law in all Member States. As noted in *Key Words and Phrases* 'direct applicability' means that a Regulation comes into effect automatically on the specified date without the need for Member States to take any measures to implement it.

Directives

Article 249 provides that:

> A directive shall be binding, as to the result to be achieved, upon each Member State to which it is addressed, but shall leave to the national authorities the choice of form or methods.

From this it can be seen that (unlike a Regulation) a Directive does not have 'general application' throughout the EU – it may be addressed to one or more Member States. A further difference from a Regulation is that the Member State is left with a degree of discretion as to the methods used to achieve the required objective. The Directive will specify the date by which the objective must be achieved. Once that date is reached, a Directive is capable of having 'direct effect' (on which see below).

Decisions

Article 249 provides that:

> A decision shall be binding in its entirety upon those to whom it is addressed.

Decisions may be addressed to Member States and to natural and legal persons. Decisions are directly applicable: they do not require any law-making on the part of the Member States' legislatures to come into effect. Like a Regulation, a Decision is absolutely binding on those to whom it is addressed.

Recommendations and opinions

Article 249 provides that:

> Recommendations and opinions shall have no binding force.

Although Recommendations and Opinions have no 'binding force' (are not legally binding) they are of persuasive authority and must be taken into account by national courts when interpreting the requirements of EC law. Recommendations and Opinions form part of the 'soft law' of the EC. Also included in 'soft law' are framework decisions, codes of conduct, guidelines and policy statements.

Basic principles in law-making

In order to avoid the criticism that the EU institutions are overactive in law-making, to the detriment of the Member States, two main principles have been developed, which are employed in relation to the question of whether law should be made at the EU level or domestic level. These are 'subsidiarity' and 'proportionality'.

Subsidiarity is designed to ensure that the decision is taken at the level closest to the consumer. The concept is now formally recognised in the Treaties.[10] In terms of law-making, it has been interpreted as meaning (in relation to the European Community) that the Community should only act:

- where the objective cannot be achieved at national level;
- where the objective can be better, or more effectively, achieved by action at Community level;
- where the matter in question can be more effectively regulated at Community level.[11]

The related concept of proportionality, in the law-making context, requires that when the institutions of the EU are to legislate, they should do so only to the extent that is strictly necessary to achieve the stated objective.

The law-making process

It should be noted at the outset that the law-making process differs between the European Community, explained below, and the EU. While the law-making process in relation to Community law is set out in detail in the treaties and has the Council and European Parliament as key actors in the process, decision-making in relation to EU matters relies far more heavily on intergovernmental cooperation and the consent of Member States.

All power to make new Community law derives from the Treaties, the individual Articles of which will specify the procedure to be followed. Unlike the position in the UK where there is a uniform procedure for enacting primary or secondary legislation, in the EU there are a number of law-making procedures – as specified in the Treaties – which may be followed. In order to ascertain the relevant procedure it is necessary to consult the appropriate Treaty Article. In general it should be noted that while the European Parliament originally had a limited role and little power in relation to legislation, the movement over the years has been to enhancing its powers to the point where the dominant procedure is now that of Co-decision with Council. In summary, there are six legislative procedures, namely:

1. The Commission acting alone;
2. Council and Commission acting alone;
3. Council, Commision and Consultation with the European Parliament;
4. The Council and Commission acting under the Cooperation Procedure with the European Parliament: Article 252;

10 See EC Treaty, Article 5; the Lisbon Reform Treaty 2007.
11 Steiner, J, 'Subsidiarity under the Maastricht Treaty', in O'Keefe and Twomey, 1994.

5. The 'Article 251 Procedure': Co-decision;
6. Council, Commission and the European Parliament: Assent.

1 The Commission acting alone – This is unusual, and confined to the power to enact Directives relating to public bodies.[12]

2 The Council and Commission acting alone – A small number of areas permit the Council to enact legislation following a proposal from the Commission.[13]

3 The Council, Commission and Consultation with Parliament – Where the Treaty specifies that consultation is required, the Council will make a decision based on a Commission proposal and then await the opinion of the Parliament. Failure to comply with the consultation procedure will result in a measure being annulled. However, while consultation must be undertaken, there is no requirement for Council to accept Parliament's opinion.

4 The Council, Commission and Cooperation Procedure with Parliament: Article 252 – The Cooperation Procedure was introduced by the Single European Act 1986,[14] and represented the single greatest increase in Parliament's role in legislation. Where the Treaty states that the Article 252 procedure is to be employed, the following stages apply:

- Council acts by a qualified majority on a proposal from the Commission, and after obtaining the Opinion of the Parliament, adopts a common position.
- The common position is communicated to Parliament, with reasons as to why it was adopted.
- If, within three months, the Parliament approves the common position or fails to take a decision on it, the Council shall adopt the act in accordance with its common position.
- Within the three-month period, the Parliament may – provided that a majority of its Members agree – propose amendments to the common position. Parliament may also reject the common position.
- If Parliament has rejected the common position, Council is required to act by unanimity.
- Where Parliament has proposed amendments, the Commission shall re-examine the proposal within a period of one month.
- The Commission shall forward to Council the re-examined proposal and the amendments of the Parliament, which it has not accepted. Council may adopt these amendments unanimously.

12 See for example, Article 86(3) and also Article 39(3).
13 See for example, Articles 26, 45, 55, 57, 60, 96, 99, 104, 133(2).
14 See, now, Article 252 EC Treaty.

- Council, acting by a qualified majority, shall adopt the proposal as re-examined by the Commission.
- If Council intends to amend the proposal as re-examined by the Commission it must act unanimously.

5 Council, Commission and Parliament: Co-decision: Article 251

- The Commission submits a proposal to the Parliament and the Council.
- Council acts by a qualified majority after obtaining the opinion of Parliament:
  - if it approves all the amendments proposed by Parliament it may adopt the proposed act as amended;
  - if Parliament does not propose any amendments, Council may adopt the proposed act;
  - if it shall otherwise adopt a common position which must be communicated to Parliament with reasons for its adoption.

If, within three months, the Parliament:

- approves the common position or has not taken a decision, the act is deemed to be adopted in accordance with the common position.
- rejects, by an absolute majority of its Members, the common position, the proposed act shall not be adopted;
- proposes amendments to the common position by an absolute majority of its Members, the amended text shall be forwarded to Council and the Commission which shall deliver an opinion on the amendments.

6 Council, Commission and the European Parliament: Assent – If, within three months, the Council – acting by a qualified majority – approves all the amendments the act shall be deemed to be adopted. If the Commission has delivered a negative opinion on the amendments, Council must act unanimously. If Council does not approve all the amendments it must, within six weeks, convene a meeting of the Conciliation Committee.

The Conciliation Committee comprises equal numbers of members or their representatives of Council and the Parliament. It has the task of reaching agreement on a joint text, by a qualified majority of members of Council or their representatives and by a majority of representatives of the Parliament. The Commission participates in the proceedings, with a view to reconciling the positions of Council and the Parliament. The Committee considers the text in light of the amendments proposed by Parliament.

If, within six weeks of being convened, the Conciliation Committee approves a joint text, the Parliament – acting by an absolute majority of votes case – and the Council – acting by a qualified majority – have a period of six weeks in which to adopt the act in accordance with the joint text. If either institution fails to adopt the act, it shall be deemed not to have been adopted.

Where the Conciliation Committee does not approve a joint text, the proposed measure is deemed not to have been adopted.

The periods of three months and six weeks may be extended by a maximum of one month and two weeks, respectively, at the initiative of the Parliament or the Council.

Ensuring the uniform application of EU law

In order to ensure that EU law operates in a uniform way within the legal systems of all 27 Member States, the European Court of Justice (ECJ) has applied and developed a number of concepts. These are:

- direct applicability;
- direct effect;
- indirect effect;
- state liability.

Direct applicability

This concept is provided for in the EC Treaty, Article 249 stating that Regulations are '. . . directly applicable in all Member States'. The meaning of this is that once the Regulation comes into force, it automatically takes effect within all Member States without the Member States having to take any law-making action.

Direct effect

This concept is one developed by the ECJ. Direct effect means that a provision of EC law – whether a Treaty Article, Regulation or Directive – automatically confers legal rights and duties on individuals, which must be enforced by the domestic courts, without the Member State taking any law-making action. This differs from direct applicability in that a measure may become applicable within a Member State without conferring any enforceable rights, whereas the essence of direct effect is that it confers rights. Direct effect may occur in two ways: vertically and horizontally.

The principle of vertical direct effect

Vertical direct effect means that a right is enforceable against all state – or public – bodies. The duty imposed moves downwards from the government to its agents, which are deemed to be 'emanations of the state'.

THE VERTICAL EFFECT OF EU LAW

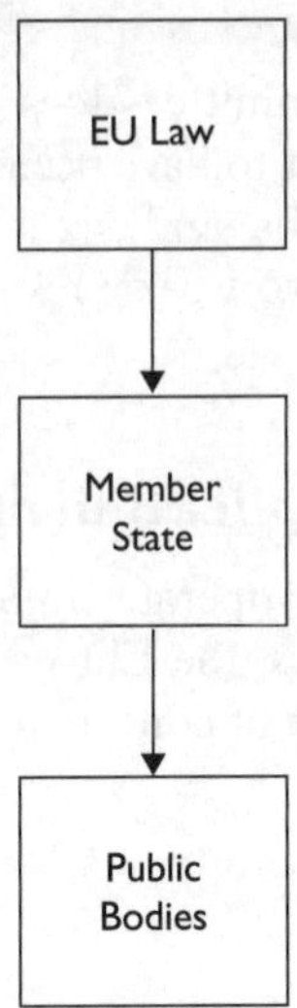

Figure 6.3

However, many government functions are undertaken not by nationalised, publicly owned bodies, but private bodies. In order to ensure the uniform application of EC law, therefore, the courts interpret state or public bodies according to the function that body undertakes.

- In *Foster v British Gas* (1991)[15] the Court of Appeal ruled that British Gas – a denationalised industry – was a public body for the purposes of EU law. If British Gas did not provide the service it did, the government would be obliged to provide it. By contrast, in:
- *Doughty v Rolls-Royce* [1992][16] the Court of Appeal ruled that the Rolls-Royce company was a private body. The company produced engines for the British Royal Airforce, which suggested that it should be defined as a public body. However, it also manufactured cars for sale to private individuals and this was held to be its dominant role or function: accordingly, it was categorised as a private body.

15 [1991] 2 AC 306.
16 [1992] IRLR 126.

Note that Treaty Articles, Regulations and Directives may all have direct vertical effect. Whether or not a particular EC law has direct vertical effect will depend on the nature of the measure. Only a provision that is 'clear and unconditional' will be interpreted as being capable of direct vertical effect. The provision must also be designed 'to create enforceable legal rights'.

For example, in:

- *Marshall v Southampton Area Health Authority* (1986)[17] a woman employee challenged the legality of the requirement that women retire at the age of 60, arguing that the Sex Discrimination Act 1975 was contrary to the EC Equal Treatment Directive (76/207/EEC). Could an individual rely on the Directive to challenge the Health Authority? Yes: the Health Authority was a public body, and the Directive clear and unconditional and intended to create enforceable rights. A Directive could not, however, operate horizontally (i.e. against private bodies: see below).

The principle of horizontal direct effect

If EC law only applied to state bodies, or 'emanations' of the state, there would be a considerable gap in the protection of EC law and this is not permitted by the ECJ. It has therefore developed the concept of horizontal direct effect to extend the scope of the law to cover private as well as public bodies.

A Treaty Article and a Regulation may have horizontal direct effect, a Directive may not (but see Indirect Effect below). For example in:

- *Defrenne v SABENA* (1978)[18] a woman employee was paid less than male employees, contrary to Article 119, which provided for equal pay.[19] She successfully took action against her employer. The matter being referred to the ECJ, the ECJ ruled that Article 119 (now renumbered Article 141) was directly effective against both public and private sector employers, even where the state had failed to act to implement the equal pay provision.

17 [1986] 1 CMLR 688.

18 [1978] ECR 1365.

19 There were also issues relating to the discriminatory retirement age and pension entitlement.

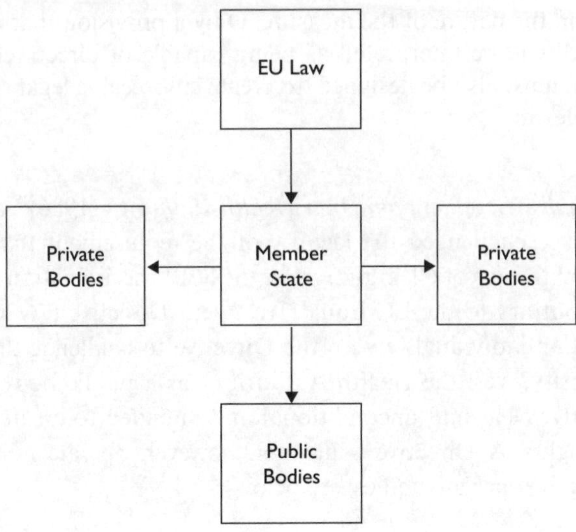

Figure 6.4

In relation to Directives, the ECJ re-examined its position in:

- *Faccini Dori v Recreb srl* (1994).[20] The ECJ confirmed that Directives could only be enforced vertically – that is, against state/public bodies. However, the Court also noted that Directives could be 'indirectly effective' and/or that they might be enforceable under the principle of 'state liability'. Both of these concepts are considered below.

Indirect effect

Article 10 of the EC Treaty sets out the basic duty of Member States. It provides that:

> Member States shall take all appropriate measures, whether general or particular, to ensure fulfilment of the obligations arising out of this

20 [1994] ECR I-3325.

> Treaty or resulting from action taken by the institutions of the Community. They shall facilitate the achievement of the Community's tasks.
> They shall abstain from any measure which could jeopardise the attainment of the objectives of this Treaty.

The Court of Justice has employed Article 10 creatively to expand the scope of Community law. It does this by interpreting Article 10 in a way that imposes a duty on national courts to apply EU law – the courts being public bodies and therefore under the same duty as a Member State government. Two cases illustrate its use:

- *Von Colson v Land Nordrhein-Westfalen* (1984).[21] In this case Ms Von Colson had applied for a job in the prison service. Her application was rejected on the grounds of her sex. The only compensation available to her under German law was her travelling expenses. The ECJ used Article 10 (then Article 5) to impose a duty on the courts to give effect to EC law.
- *Marleasing SA v La Comercial Internacional de Alimentacion SA* (1992).[22] In this case, the ECJ confirmed that a Directive could not have horizontal effect, but employed Article 10 to ensure that the courts interpreted national law – irrespective of whether it was passed before or after the relevant Directive – in a way to make it compatible with the provisions of the Directive. The failure of the Member State to implement the Directive could not frustrate the application of EC law.

State liability

Where a Member State fails to comply with its obligations under EC law, the ECJ has been willing to hold the state liable for any direct loss suffered as a result of its failure. The concept of state liability diminishes the importance of direct effect – whether vertical or horizontal. The case law clarifies the position.

- *Francovich and Bonifaci v Italy* (1991).[23] The Italian government had failed to implement a Directive designed to protect workers'

21 [1984] ECR 1891.
22 [1992] 1 CMLR 305.
23 [1991] ECR I-5357.

wages in the event of their employer becoming insolvent. The ECJ ruled that the Directive was not sufficiently clear to be directly effective. Article 10, however, imposed a duty to comply with EC law. Accordingly the state was under a duty to compensate those who had suffered loss as a result of its failure.

- *Brasserie du Pêcheur SA v Federal Republic of Germany* (1996).[24] In this case, the ECJ laid down the principles governing the concept of state liability. Member States are under an obligation to compensate individuals for loss suffered when:
  - the national legislature, executive or judiciary is responsible for the breach;
  - the rule of law breached is intended to confer rights on individuals;
  - the breach is sufficiently serious, defined as a 'manifest and grave disregard' of the limits on the Member State's discretion; and
  - there is a direct causal link between the breach of the obligation and the damage suffered.

Establishing the supremacy of EU law

With a membership of 27 very different States, each with its own legal system, it is essential that EC law be applied in a uniform manner throughout the Union. Central to achieving the harmonisation and uniform application of EC law has been the Court of Justice of the EU (ECJ). From its earliest case law it can be seen that – although the Treaties are silent on the matter – that the ECJ has regarded the supremacy of Community law as a natural and necessary concept. The following cases represent the development of the idea of the supremacy of EC law.

- *Van Gend en Loos v Nederlandse Tariefcommissie* (1963).[25] The Court of Justice expressed the view that by signing the Treaties, Member States had created a new legal order, the effect of which was to limit their independent, sovereign rights.

24 [1996] ECR I-1029.
25 Case 26/62; [1963] ECR 1; [1963] CMLR 105.

- *Costa v ENEL* (1964).[26] Here, the ECJ stated that where EC law and national law conflict, EC law must prevail over any incompatible national law. Member States had 'transferred' rights and obligations arising out of the Treaties and this represented a 'permanent limitation of their sovereign rights'.
- *Internationale Handelsgesellschaft mbH v EVST* (1970).[27] Here, the ECJ ruled that Community law must take precedence even over fundamental rights guaranteed under a Member State's written constitution.
- *Amministrazione delle Finanze dello Stato v Simmenthal* (1982).[28] The ECJ ruled that Community law must take precedence over conflicting domestic law and that a domestic court is obliged to set aside its own law in order to give effect to Community law.
- *R v Secretary of State for Transport ex parte Factortame (No 2)* (1990).[29] Here, the House of Lords for the first time disapplied an Act of Parliament in order to give effect to Community law.

EU law and domestic UK law

Monism and dualism

The means by which international law – of which EC law is an example – enters into the domestic legal system of Member States depends on the approach of that State to international law. There are many countries – the majority of European states – that take the view that once a Treaty is signed and ratified, its laws automatically enter into domestic law, without the need for any action on the part of the domestic legislature. This approach is known as monism: the idea being that international law and domestic law are conceptually part of the same order, with international law taking priority. A dualist state, by contrast, takes the view that international law and domestic law are conceptually separate and distinct entities, and that international law cannot enter into the domestic legal system unless and until the domestic Parliament enacts a law that makes provision for its entry. The UK is a dualist state.

26 Case 6/64. [1964] ECT 585; [1964] CMLR 425.
27 Case 11/70; [1970] ECR 1125; [1972] CMLR 255.
28 Case 119/82; [1983] ECR 3595; [1985] 2 CMLR 658.
29 Case C-213/89; [1990] ECR 1-2433; [1990] 3 CMLR 1.

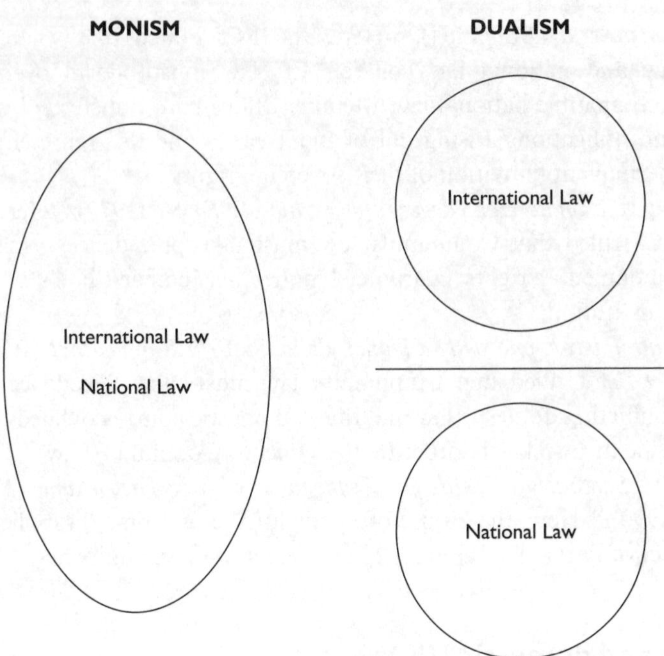

Figure 6.5

The European Communities Act 1972

The European Communities Act 1972 enables Community law to take effect within the domestic legal system. Section 2 is the most important section. Section 2(1) provides, in part, that:

> All such rights, powers, liabilities, obligations and restrictions from time to time created or arising by or under the Treaties, and all such remedies and procedures from time to time provided for by or under the Treaties, as in accordance with the Treaties are without further enactment to be given legal effect or used in the United Kingdom shall be recognised and available in law, and be enforced, allowed and followed accordingly; and the expression 'enforceable Community right' and similar expressions shall be read as referring to one to which this subsection applies.

Section 2(2) of the Act provides that delegated legislation may be used to implement EU law, while section 2(4) directs the courts to interpret domestic law in line with EU law. As a result of these provisions, when the judges in the

UK give effect to EU law they do so as a result of an ordinary Act of the UK Parliament: the European Communities Act 1972. The courts, however, have adopted a more purposive approach than usual to Community law – that is to say, the court looks less at the exact wording of the statute and more towards the objective being sought by that statute.

In order to see how the courts have approached the issue of supremacy, it is again necessary to refer to case law.

- *Macarthys v Smith* (1979).[30] Article 141 of the EC Treaty provides for equal pay for men and women. The relevant domestic law was the Equal Pay Act 1970. The Act was silent as to whether equal pay applied not only to men and women doing equal work at the same time but also to situations where a woman takes over a job previously done by a man. The Court referred the matter to the ECJ. The ECJ ruled that Article 141 required equal pay irrespective of whether they were employed at the same time or in succession.

  Lord Denning in the Court of Appeal stated that it was the court's duty to give effect to Community law because of the effect of section 2 of the 1972 Act. However, he also commented that if Parliament at some future time chose expressly to go against Community law, the judges would be obliged to give effect to Parliament's will and follow the inconsistent statute.
- *Garland v British Rail Engineering Ltd* (1983).[31] In this case the House of Lords endorsed the view that Community law must be given effect as a result of the European Communities Act 1972.
- *Pickstone v Freemans plc* (1989).[32] The House of Lords upheld the right to equal pay guaranteed by Article 119 and Directive 75/117 on the basis that the Equal Pay Act 1970, as amended, had been enacted to give effect to Community law. Accordingly, the Act should be interpreted in such a way as to ensure that domestic law complied with the obligation undertaken by membership of the European Community.

30 [1979] 2 All ER 32; [1980] 2 CMLR 205.
31 [1983] 2 AC 751.
32 [1989] AC 66.

- An exception to this approach can be seen in *Duke v GEC Reliance Ltd* (1988).[33] This case concerned unequal retirement ages for men and women. The applicant argued that domestic law (the Equal Pay Act 1970 and Sex Discrimination Act 1975) should be interpreted to give effect to the EC Equal Treatment Directive 76/207. The House of Lords, however, ruled that both Acts had intentionally retained difference retirement ages and that there was no breach of domestic law. Nor was there a breach of EC law, in that the Directive was not horizontally effective. This case is explainable in that it was a pre-*Marleasing* case (discussed above at page 79), which introduced the notion of indirect effect via Article 10 of the EC Treaty.
- *Litster v Forth Dry Dock and Engineering Co Ltd* (1990).[34] Here the House of Lords again adopted a purposive – rather than literal – approach, interpreting domestic Regulations in a manner which gave effect to an EC Directive.
- *R v Secretary of State for Transport ex parte Factortame (No 2)* (1991), discussed above. The House of Lords, having sought the opinion of the Court of Justice, ruled that the Merchant Shipping Act should be set aside in order to give preference to Community law.
- *Webb v EMO Air Cargo (UK) Ltd* (1992, and No. 2 1995).[35] In the 1992 case the House of Lords made a reference to the ECJ relating to the lawfulness of dismissal on grounds of pregnancy. Having received the ruling from the ECJ the House of Lords held in the 1995 case that, contrary to its original interpretation of the law, a woman could not be dismissed on grounds of pregnancy.

Summary

The original three European Communities have evolved into the EU, with far broader aims and objectives than originally envisaged. Constitutionally, the EU is not yet a state, but is far more than a cooperative venture based on the sovereignty of individual Member States. The Community and Union has its own system of governance and law-making, which binds all Member States. From the perspective of the ECJ, from the earliest days Member States have transferred their sovereign power in relation to matters regulated under the Treaties.

33 [1988] AC 618.
34 [1990] 1 AC 546.
35 [1992] 2 All ER 43; [1995] 4 All ER 577.

The Court of Justice has used its jurisdiction creatively to ensure the uniform, harmonious application of Community law. With its concepts of direct and indirect effect (vertical and horizontal) and that of the liability of the state, the ECJ has expanded the application of Community law.

Community law is supreme over domestic law and such domestic law as conflicts with Community law must be set aside. For the ECJ the sovereignty of the Community law derives from the Treaties. From the perspective of the judges in the UK courts, Community law is given priority because section 2 of the European Communities Act 1972 directs the judges to give it effect.

Further reading

Craig, P, 'Directives: Direct Effect, Indirect Effect and the Construction of National Legislation' (1997), 22 EL Rev 519.

Craig, P, 'Britain in the European Union', in J Jowell and D Oliver (eds), *The Changing Constitution* (6th edn, 2007), Oxford: OUP.

Harlow, C, 'European Governance and Accountability', in M Bamforth and P Leyland (eds), *Public Law in a Multi-Layered Constitution*, 2003, Oxford: Hart Publishing.

Harlow, C and Rawlings, R, 'Accountability and law enforcement: the centralised EU enforcement procedure' (2006), 31 EL Rev 447.

Hartley, TC, *The Foundations of European Community Law* (6th edn, 2007), Oxford: OUP.

Klamert, M, 'Judicial Implementation of Directives and anticipatory indirect effect: connecting the dots' (2006), 43 CML Rev 1251.

Lenaerts, K and Van Nuffel, P, *Constitutional Law of the European Union* (2005), Sweet & Maxwell.

Lenzl, M, 'Horizontal what? Back to Basics' (2000), 25 EL Rev 509.

Mathijsen, PSRF, *A Guide to European Union Law* (9th edn, 2007), Sweet & Maxwell.

Munro, CR, *Studies in Constitutional Law* (2nd edn, 1999), London: Butterworth, Chapter 6.

Ross, M, 'Beyond Francovich' (1993), 56 MLR 55.

Shaw, J, 'Europe's Constitutional Future' [2005] PL 132.

Steiner, J, 'From Direct Effects to Francovich: shifting means of enforcement of Community Law' (1993), 18 EL Rev 3.

Steiner, J, 'The Limits of State Liability for Breach of European Community Law' [1998] EPL 69.

Walker, N, 'European Constitutionalism and European Integrations' [2005] PL, 266.

? *SELF-ASSESSMENT QUESTIONS*

1. Name the Treaty that brought about the European Economic Community and the Treaty that introduced the European Union (EU).

Continued

? SELF-ASSESSMENT QUESTIONS *(continued)*

2. Name the four principal institutions of the EC and EU.
3. List the primary and secondary sources of EC law.
4. Write a brief sentence defining 'direct effect' and 'indirect effect'.
5. Write a definition of 'monism' and 'dualism'.
6. Name at least three major cases in which the European Court of Justice proclaimed the supremacy of Community law over national law.

SAMPLE EXAMINATION QUESTIONS

1. Critically examine the means by which the European Court of Justice ensures the supremacy of EC Law.
2. 'Membership of the European Union requires a fundamental reassessment of the traditional theory of parliamentary sovereignty.'
   Do you agree? To what extent does the case law support such a view?
3. Outline the role and powers of the European Commission, the Council of Ministers and the European Parliament of the European Union. To what extent is the European Union 'democratic'?

Chapter 7

Central, regional and local government

CONTENTS

KEY WORDS AND PHRASES

Cabinet	The group of senior Ministers at the heart of government
Collective ministerial responsibility	The convention that members of Cabinet keep discussions confidential and that all Ministers are bound by Cabinet decisions
Devolution	The granting of self-rule to a regional or national legislature
Individual ministerial responsibility	The convention that Ministers are accountable for their personal conduct and the conduct of their Department
Motion	A parliamentary request
Official Opposition	The political party with the second largest number of seats in Parliament
Votes of confidence	A vote in Parliament indicating support for the government

Introduction

The United Kingdom has as its Head of State, the Queen.

Heading the central executive government is the Prime Minister and Cabinet, made up of senior Ministers who form the inner core of government. Central government is located in Westminster, a short walk from the Houses of Parliament, and the major Departments of State. However, while the focus of media attention falls on central government, much of the work of government is carried out elsewhere.

The UK is made up of four nations: England, Wales, Scotland and Northern Ireland. Since 1998, Wales, Scotland and Northern Ireland have had their own parliament or assembly, with varying degrees of law-making powers. Below this level of devolved government is local government – the system of localised democracy closest to the people.

The Crown

The hereditary monarch is Head of State and all acts of government are carried out 'in the name of the Crown'. The executive acts in the name of the

Crown. Parliament comprises the Crown, House of Lords and House of Commons and the Crown must assent (agree to) all Acts of Parliament. In addition, the courts are commonly referred to as the Queen's courts, and the Crown as the 'fountain of justice'.

Theoretically, the executive (Prime Minister and Ministers), legislature (Parliament) and judiciary (courts) are united under the Crown. However, although the Crown holds wide-ranging legal powers,[1] these are in fact exercised by others. The monarchy today is a 'constitutional' or limited monarchy: the Queen reigns but does not rule – rather she acts on the advice of her government. However, this does not mean that the Queen has no influence: having reigned since 1952 Queen Elizabeth II has a wealth of knowledge and experience – as a number of former Prime Ministers have acknowledged. Walter Bagehot, the nineteenth-century political journalist and author wrote that the Crown has the 'right to be consulted, the right to advise and the right to warn'.[2] The formal opportunity to exercise these rights occurs weekly in the Queen's meeting with the Prime Minister.

Queen Elizabeth II is also the Head of the Commonwealth – colonies, former colonies and dependent territories, which form a voluntary association of some 54 states for their mutual benefit.

The office of Prime Minister

As with so much of the British Constitution, the office of Prime Minister came into being when the need arose for one Minister to advise the Crown. While references can be found to the office in Acts of Parliament, there is no formal legal source of power for the office. The first Prime Minister was Sir Robert Walpole who held office from 1721 to 1742.

The Monarch formally appoints the Prime Minister. Until the 1960s the Queen had some discretion as to who should be appointed. However, once the major political parties had established a formal system for the selection of the leader of their party, that discretion came to an end. It is now the convention that the Crown will appoint the office of Prime Minister to the leader of the political party that wins the largest number of seats in Parliament in a general election and forms a government. The only possible (and extremely unlikely) scenario for the Crown to have any choice in the matter would be where the two major political parties won the same number of seats in Parliament.

By convention the Prime Minister is always a member of the House of Commons rather than the House of Lords. As such s/he is an ordinarily elected constituency Member of Parliament (MP).

1 See, further, Chapter 2.

2 *The English Constitution*, 1867, London: Fontana, 1993.

Once inaccurately described as *primus inter pares* 'first among equals', the role and functions of the Prime Minister include the following:

- the Prime Minister holds office as Prime Minister and First Lord of the Treasury;[3]
- the Prime Minister as First Lord of the Treasury has responsibility for the Civil Service and assumes the title of Minister for the Civil Service;
- by convention the Prime Minister must be a Member of the House of Commons; and is an elected constituency Member of Parliament;
- the Prime Minister usually has control over the timing of a general election and formally requests the Queen to dissolve Parliament in order for the general election to be held: by convention this request is never denied;
- by convention, if the Government loses the support of the House of Commons over an important matter of policy, the Prime Minister must request a dissolution of Parliament;
- the Prime Minister has powers of appointment and dismissal of Ministers (formally this is undertaken by the Crown);
- the Prime Minister determines the size of the Cabinet;
- the Prime Minister determines which Ministers sit in the Cabinet;
- the Prime Minister controls the agenda for the Cabinet;
- the Prime Minister controls the number and role of Cabinet Committees;
- the Prime Minister has special responsibility for national security and receives intelligence data from the security services
- the Prime Minister has the power to declare war and peace and to send troops to war;
- the Prime Minister has a weekly audience with the Queen;
- the Prime Minister represents the Crown in foreign affairs;
- the Prime Minister exercises many of the formal powers of the Crown, for example Treaty-making powers;
- the Prime Minister, together with the Secretary of State for Foreign Affairs, participates in European Union Heads of State Summit (the European Council) Meetings;
- the Prime Minister is accountable to Parliament through weekly Prime Ministerial Question Time and the convention that the government must maintain the confidence of the House of Commons.

The Cabinet

The Cabinet is the heart of government: the 20 to 24 most senior Ministers who meet weekly. As with the office of Prime Minister, the existence of

3 Prime ministers may assume other offices. For example, Ramsey MacDonald held office as Foreign Secretary and Winston Churchill was also Minister of Defence.

the Cabinet is explained by political practice rather than by law – there is no statutory source of power or definition of the size, role and function of the Cabinet. By convention, certain offices of state are always in the Cabinet: the Chancellor of the Exchequer, the Foreign Secretary, Defence Secretary, Home Secretary, Minister for Justice and Leader of the House of Commons.

Collective ministerial responsibility

Collective ministerial responsibility is one of the key constitutional conventions. The essence of the convention is that it gives to the country the impression of a strong and united government. It does this through two basic rules. The first is that there should be no public disclosure of Cabinet discussions: they are absolutely confidential. The second rule is that all Ministers – whether they have a place in Cabinet or not and irrespective of whether they participated in the decision-making process – are obliged to support the decision taken. Any Minister not able to support a Cabinet decision is expected to resign.

Cabinet Committees

Much of the work of the Cabinet is carried out in Committees. If a matter cannot be resolved in Committee it will be taken to a meeting of the whole Cabinet. Decisions taken in Committee will bind the whole government – the doctrine of collective ministerial responsibility dictating that there be no disclosure of the discussions and no public dissent from the decision.

Ministers of the Crown

The operation of central government is organised through government departments, headed by a ministerial team and staffed by civil servants (see below). Major departments are headed by a Secretary of State and will usually have a number of junior Ministers with particular responsibilities for aspects of the department's work.

Ministerial appointments are formally made by the Crown, although as noted above it is the Prime Minister who in fact appoints and dismisses Ministers.

The Home Office

STRUCTURE OF THE HOME OFFICE

Secretary of State for the Home Department (Home Secretary): Head of the Home Office
Minister of State responsible for Policing, Crime and Security
Minister of State for Borders and Immigration
Parliamentary Under-Secretary of State for Security and Counter-Terrorism
Parliamentary Under-Secretary for Identity
Permanent Secretary: senior civil servant responsible for implementing policy

Located within the Home Department:
Office for Security and Counter-Terrorism
Crime and Policing Group
Strategic Centre
Professional services, including legal advice and communications support and programme and project management support

Three agencies provide directly managed frontline services from within the Home Office:
The UK Border Agency (immigration and asylum)
The Identity and Passport Service
The Criminal Records Bureau

Figure 7.1

The Civil Service

The Civil Service is regulated under the royal prerogative, not by Act of Parliament.[4] As such, the terms and conditions of employment differ from those of other employees. A civil servant holds office 'at Her Majesty's pleasure' and does not enjoy the same legal protection as other employees. Appointment is on merit.

Three main principles apply to the Civil Service: anonymity, permanence and political neutrality. The Civil Service is permanent in the sense that there is no change of personnel when there is a change of government: civil servants must serve governments of all political persuasions. This also explains the principle of political neutrality. The principle that civil servants are 'anonymous' is also linked. In terms of political accountability, it is the Minister in charge of the Department who is responsible to Parliament – not his or her staff in the Department. While civil servants may be called upon

4 There has long been a call for a Civil Service Act to regulate the service and provide greater clarity and employment protection.

to give evidence before parliamentary Select Committees, they are obliged to take instructions from their Minister and not to disclose any information that might be damaging to the government of the day.

A Civil Service Code regulates the service. The Code states that the core values of the Civil Service are integrity, honesty, objectivity and impartiality.

The Opposition

The Official Opposition is the political party with the second highest number of Members of Parliament (MPs): it is the 'government in waiting', ready to assume the office of government should the government of the day fall through loss of confidence or fail to be re-elected at a general election. The structure of government is mirrored by the structure of the Opposition. In addition to the Opposition in the House of Commons, there is a Leader of the Opposition in the House of Lords.

The importance of the Opposition lies in its ability to probe and question the government and ensure that the government is accountable to the people through Parliament.[5] Reflecting this importance is the fact that the Leader of the Opposition is a salaried position in both the House of Commons and the House of Lords.

To ensure that the Opposition has adequate opportunities to call government to account there are 20 days per parliamentary year (session) on which the Opposition determines the subject-matter for debate.

Confidence votes

If a government is seen to be failing in a key area of its policy, the Opposition may propose to Parliament that it take a 'vote of no confidence'. If this vote is successful, the Prime Minister must, by convention, seek a dissolution of Parliament in order that a general election be held. Votes of no confidence are rare, and rarely successful.

The other side of the coin is that a government may test its support in Parliament by seeking a 'vote of confidence'. Prime Minister John Major adopted this ploy towards the end of his premiership when faced with a significant number of rebellious MPs. He held a vote, forcing them to support him or risk the loss of their seats in a general election.

Devolution: regional government

The UK comprises England and Wales, Scotland and Northern Ireland. Part of the 1997 government's policy was to devolve law-making and

5 On parliamentary procedures, see Chapter 9.

administrative powers away from central government and the UK Parliament at Westminster and to confer these powers on assemblies in the nations of Scotland, Wales and Northern Ireland. Northern Ireland had experienced its own law-making Assembly (Stormont) from 1922 to 1972 when the Assembly was suspended as a result of the troubles in that country. The governance of Northern Ireland was once again returned to London until a resolution of the political troubles could be reached.

In order to test whether the idea of devolution had the support of the people, referendums were held in the three nations. All supported the proposal. The Government of Wales Act 1998 (as amended by the Government of Wales Act 2006), the Scotland Act 1998 and the Northern Ireland Act 1998 were the statutory means by which powers were devolved.

In addition to statute, there is a memorandum of understanding (MOU) – a non-legal agreement between the UK government and the devolved administrations in Scotland and Wales.[6] The memorandum expressly states that the UK Parliament has the right to legislate for the devolved nations. However, it also states that the convention that the UK Parliament will not legislate in respect of devolved matters will be respected.

The UK government retains responsibility for foreign affairs. In respect of the EU, however, the devolved administrations are to be 'involved as fully as possible' in formulating the UK's policy on all EU and international issues that are relevant to devolved matters.

In order to facilitate cooperation there is a Joint Ministerial Committee comprising the UK government, Scottish, Welsh and Northern Ireland Ministers.

Northern Ireland

Northern Ireland had enjoyed a large degree of law-making independence from the 1920s until 1972 when, as a result of the civil unrest and terrorist activity in the province, power was recalled to London and the Northern Ireland Assembly suspended. In 1998, negotiations between the British and Irish governments and the major political parties in Northern Ireland finally succeeded. The resulting Belfast (or Good Friday) Agreement became the basis for the re-devolution of power.

The Northern Ireland Act 1998, section 1 provides that Northern Ireland shall not cease to be part of the UK unless and until the people of Northern Ireland, voting in a referendum, vote for change.

The devolution of power to the Assembly was conditional upon the terms of the Belfast Agreement being complied with. While devolution took place in 1999, power was recalled to London in 2002. The Northern Ireland

6 See Cm 4444 1999; Cm 4806 2000, Cm 5240 2001.

(St Andrews Agreement) Act 2006 provided for the re-devolution of power once again, subject to conditions. Power was restored once more in 2007.

The Assembly has 108 elected members, six from each of the Westminster constituencies. Elections are held every four years, and the voting system used is the single transferable vote.

Law-making powers

The Northern Ireland Act 1998 provides that the Assembly may make Acts, but reserves for the UK Parliament the right to legislate for Northern Ireland – subject to the right of the Assembly to amend those Acts. The 1998 Act defines the law-making competence of the Assembly and provides that no law that is outside the Assembly's competence is valid.

Certain Acts of the UK Parliament are not subject to amendment by the Northern Ireland Assembly. Such Acts include the European Communities Act 1972, the Human Rights Act 1998 and part of the Northern Ireland Act 1998.

The executive

Because of Northern Ireland's history of religious conflict and sectarian violence, the Belfast Agreement included the requirement that former bitter political enemies, the Ulster Democratic Party and Sinn Fein, the political wing of the Irish Republican Party, work together. The First Minister and Deputy First Minister are elected by the Assembly and hold office jointly: if one resigns so must the other. The number of other ministerial offices must not exceed ten.

Ministers take office subject to the requirement that they affirm the 'pledge of office'. This reflects the particular difficulties in Northern Ireland and includes the commitment to non-violence – the requirement to serve all the people of Northern Ireland equally to promote equality and prevent discrimination.

Scotland

The Scotland Act 1998 established a 129-seat Scottish Parliament, based in Edinburgh. The Parliament is unicameral (has one house, not two) and sits for a fixed four-year term of office.

Members of the Scottish Parliament (MSPs) are elected in two ways. The majority are elected from individual constituencies. The remaining members are selected from party lists drawn up for each of the current European Parliament constituencies.

There is continued representation of Scottish constituencies in the UK

Parliament at Westminster, although the number of seats has been reduced from 72 to 59.

Law-making powers

The Scottish Parliament has the power to make Acts of Parliament within the areas of competence laid down in the 1998 Act. Any Act passed that is not within the scope of Parliament's power is void. The Act reserves some major categories of law-making power to the UK Parliament. Principal among these are the Constitution, the registration of political parties, foreign affairs, the Civil Service and defence.

In relation to taxation, the Scottish Parliament has the power to increase or decrease the rate of income tax set by the UK Parliament by up to three pence in the pound.

The Scottish executive

The Scottish Executive comprises the First Minister, an MSP appointed by the Crown, such Ministers as the First Minister appoints, the Lord Advocate and the Solicitor General for Scotland.

Wales

The country of Wales has the longest association with England of the three nations and has been subject to English law since the thirteenth century.

The Government of Wales Act 1998 devolved limited powers to a directly elected body corporate known as the National Assembly for Wales (Cynulliad Cenedlaethol Cymru). The Assembly has 60 members, 40 that represent Assembly constituencies (the constituencies are the same for the Assembly and for the Westminster Parliament) and 20 that represent five Assembly regions.

Constituency members are elected on the simple majority voting system. Members representing Assembly regions are elected on the basis of proportional representation.

The Assembly sits for a fixed four-year term.

Law-making powers

As originally established, the Assembly had no power to pass Acts and was restricted to passing secondary legislation. Acts of Parliament continued to be made for Wales by the UK Parliament. The Government of Wales Act 2006 confers potentially more wide-ranging power. The Assembly may make 'Measures', a form of subordinate legislation, in relation to 20 specified matters ('fields' in the Act).

In the future, and subject to a successful referendum, the Assembly will be entitled to make Acts over the same range of issues as it currently makes Measures. The procedure for making Measures and Acts mirrors that of the House of Commons.

The executive

Under the 1998 Act there was no formal distinction between the Assembly and the executive, and hence no formal separation of powers. The Government of Wales Act 2006 remedies this by providing for the National Assembly for Wales and for a Welsh Assembly Government. The First Minister and other Ministers form the government. There is a limit of 12 on the number of Ministers. The First Minister is nominated for appointment by the Assembly, and s/he appoints the other Ministers from among the Assembly members.

The London Assembly and Mayor

The Greater London Authority Act 1999 established the London Assembly and the office of Mayor of London.

Elections

Elections are held every four years. Every eligible elector has one vote for a mayoral candidate, one vote for an Assembly member and one vote for a registered political party – the 'London vote'.

The simple majority system is used for the mayoral election unless there are three or more candidates. If there are more than three candidates, the Mayor is elected under the supplementary vote system, a vote that indicates the voter's first and second preferences from among the candidates.

Assembly members are elected by the simple majority system. 'London members' are elected under the party list system.

Powers and functions

The Assembly

The general power of the Assembly is to do anything that furthers its principal purposes, namely:

- promoting economic development;
- promoting social development; and
- promoting the improvement in the environment.

The Assembly has no law-making powers, but may promote a Bill in Parliament or oppose a Bill that affects Greater London.

The Assembly reviews the work of the Mayor, and may make proposals to the Mayor.

The Mayor

The Mayor of London has a duty to keep under review and develop strategies in relation to:

- the London Development Agency;
- transport;
- planning;
- biodiversity
- waste management;
- air quality and 'ambient noise'; and
- culture.

The Mayor reports to the Assembly and must attend every meeting of the Assembly. The Mayor publishes an annual report on his activities.

Local government

In England and Wales there are 410 local authorities, having 19,000 elected councillors and employing over two million people in the task of delivering over 700 different services.

There are five main types of local authority: county councils, district councils, metropolitan districts (or boroughs), unitary councils and London borough councils. In Northern Ireland there are 26 councils and in Scotland 32 unitary councils.

Local government pre-dates central government. It represents democracy at the level closest to the people. The powers of local authorities are all laid down by an Act of Parliament. Parliament can alter local authority boundaries as well as their powers and functions. Local authorities have a range of responsibilities in relation to education, housing, welfare, waste management and the provision of leisure facilities.

Elections

Councillors are elected for a four-year term of office and represent 'wards' within the local government area. The simple majority system is used for elections.

Candidates for election must be able to demonstrate a 'close local connection' with the area.

Management

Three different models of management were introduced under the Local Government Act 2000. These are:

1. The Mayor and Cabinet Executive: a democratically elected mayor who then appoints two or more councillors to the executive. The number of members may not exceed ten.
2. Leader and Cabinet Executive: all members of council elect the leader of the council. There are then two options: the leader will appoint an executive drawn from the council, or the council itself appoints the executive.
3. Mayor and Council Manager Executive: under this system there is a democratically elected mayor and an officer of the authority appointed as council manager.

Revenue

Approximately 50 per cent of local government revenue comes from central government. The remaining money comes from local taxes and in addition local authorities may borrow money, subject to strict control by the Treasury.

Expenditure

Local authorities are required to operate on a 'best value' basis, adopting the most cost-effective way of delivering services to its area, either by undertaking the tasks themselves or through agreements with private bodies or through partnership agreements with other local bodies.

Each financial year the local authority prepares a 'best value performance plan'. The Audit Commission carries out inspections and if an authority is failing in its duties, the Commission can recommend that the Secretary of State give directions to the authority.

Summary

Government in the UK is conducted at several different levels. Key policy decisions and legislation affecting the whole country are made by central government – the Prime Minister, Cabinet and Civil Service – based in Westminster, in central London.

Since 1998, Northern Ireland, Scotland and Wales have each had powers devolved to their national assembly (in Scotland the Parliament). By convention the UK Parliament will not legislate for these nations unless requested to do so. However, the UK Parliament retains the ultimate power to legislate for the whole of the UK.

Local government is the level of government closest to the people, enabling particular local conditions and concerns to be dealt with in a local manner. The powers of local government are entirely statutory and local government is partly dependent upon central government for finance.

Further reading

Bogdanor, V, *Devolution*, 1979, Oxford: OUP.
Bogdanor, V, 'Our New Constitution' (2004), 120 LQR 242.
Brazier, R, 'The Scottish government' [1998] PL 212.
Hadfield, B, 'The Belfast Agreement' [1998] PL 599.
Hadfield, B, 'Devolution, Westminster and the English Question' [2005] PL 286.
Hazell, R, 'Reinventing the Constitution: Can the State Survive?' [1999] PL 84.
Jones, T and Williams, J, 'The Legislative Future of Wales' (2005), 68 MLR 642.
Jones, T, Turnbull, J and Williams, J, 'The Law of Wales or the Law of England and Wales?' [2005] Stat LR 135.
McCrudden, C, 'Northern Ireland and the British Constitution since the Belfast Agreement', in J Jowell and D Oliver (eds), *The Changing Constitution*, 6th edn, 2007, Oxford: OUP.
Rawlings, R, 'The New Model Wales' (1998), 25 *Journal of Law and Society*, 461.
Wicks, E, 'A New Constitution for a New State? The 1707 Union of England and Scotland' (2001) 117 LQR 109.

? *SELF-ASSESSMENT QUESTIONS*

1. To what extent is it accurate to describe the office of Prime Minister as 'first among equals'?
2. What are the two principal rules relating to collective Cabinet responsibility?
3. Does devolution to national assemblies affect the supremacy of the UK Parliament?
4. List three advantages of local government.

 *SAMPLE EXAMINATION QUESTIONS*

1. With the devolution of power, the UK's constitution now operates as different levels – central, regional/national and local.

   Discuss.
2. To what extent, if at all, does devolution diminish the sovereignty of the UK Parliament?

Chapter 8

Electoral law

CONTENTS

KEY WORDS AND PHRASES

By-election	an election in a single constituency caused by death/resignation of incumbent representative
Constituency	district or body of voters returning an elected representative to a legislature
Democracy	government by the people or their elected representatives
Franchise	the right to vote
General election	a country-wide election of all Members of Parliament
Mandate	the approval of a policy by the people in an election or referendum
Proportional representation	a voting system resulting in the number of parliamentary seats won being proportionate to the number of votes cast
Simple majority system	a voting system under which the winner must only secure one more vote than the other candidates

Introduction

The Head of State in Britain is the Monarch: an inherited position. However, while kings and queens in centuries past wielded vast power, since the Bill of Rights 1689 those powers have been residual – powers that remain at Parliament's will. While the history of political parties and elections is beyond the scope of this work, for the sake of brevity this history may be described as the gradual 'democratisation' of Britain.

It was the nineteenth century that produced the most extensive reform of the electoral system, with many of the restrictions and prohibitions on voting being gradually removed. The greatest historical discrimination in the right to vote related to the property-less working class and to women. Despite legal challenges and political campaigns in the nineteenth and early twentieth centuries, women only won the right to vote on equal terms with men in 1928.

With the right to vote being extended to the working class, working-class representation in Parliament was demanded. The birth of the Labour Party in 1896 was to transform the political landscape, which had formerly been dominated by the Conservative and Liberal parties. With the rise of the Labour Party, the Liberal Party declined, and today the Liberal Democratic Party is the smallest of the three main political parties.

There are a number of different elections in the UK. In addition to general elections, which by law must take place at least once every five years, there are elections to the Northern Ireland, Scottish and Welsh national assemblies, elections to local government and elections to the European Parliament. It is likely that in the future there will be elections for members of the House of Lords. While a rational system would provide for a consistent voting system to be employed for all of these elections, this is in fact not the case and the differing voting systems used for differing elections need to be considered.

The franchise

The right to vote is the hallmark of citizenship. By law, those entitled to vote are:

- citizens over the age of 18 who are registered on the Electoral Register and have legal capacity to vote;
- Commonwealth citizens with the right to remain in the UK indefinitely;
- a citizen of the Republic of Ireland, resident in the UK.

Those who are not eligible to vote include:

- persons under the age of 18;
- aliens;
- Commonwealth citizens with no right of permanent abode;
- non-British EU citizens;
- Members of the House of Lords;
- convicted prisoners in detention;
- mental patients detained under statutory authority;
- persons convicted of corrupt or illegal practices at elections.

Constituencies

There are currently 646 constituencies in the UK.

In charge of regulating the size of constituencies is the Electoral Commission established under the Political Parties, Elections and Referendums Act 2000. If the electoral system is to respect the principle of equality in voting power, it is important that there are approximately the same number of voters in each constituency. With population shifts and children reaching the voting age, regular reviews are necessary. These are conducted by the Boundary Committees for England, Northern Ireland, Scotland and Wales, which undertake reviews between eight and twelve years, following a general election.

The Parliamentary Constituencies Act 1986 lays down the rules to be followed in reviewing boundaries.[1] First, the Committees are to attempt to reach approximate equality in the number of voters in each constituency. The target

1 See Schedule 5.

number will be the number of eligible voters divided by the number of constituencies. However, equality may be departed from if necessary to ensure that local authority boundaries are respected. Also, in areas where there are special geographical considerations – for example, the Scottish highlands – equality may be departed from. The effect of these factors is that the Committees are striving to achieve boundaries, which include voters within 20 per cent of the target figure.

General elections and by-elections

Under the Parliament Act 1911, no Parliament may last more than five years. Accordingly, while there is no minimum period a Parliament must sit, a general election must be held within five years of the date of the previous general election. It is for the Prime Minister to determine when to hold a general election, giving the governing Party the benefit of being able to hold an election at a time when it is politically advantageous to do so. By convention, the assent of the Crown must be given to a prime ministerial request for a dissolution of Parliament, which is the trigger for a general election.[2]

Once Parliament is dissolved there is a campaign period of, usually, just three weeks before the date of the election.

The Representation of the People Act 1983, as amended, regulates the conduct of election campaigns. In order to be able to put up candidates for election, political parties must be formally registered with the Electoral Commission.[3] To ensure a 'level playing field' between candidates, the amount that can be spent on the campaign is strictly controlled and there are a number of criminal offences relating to the conduct of the campaign.

Financial limits

In each constituency, a candidate for a political party may spend a specified amount of money. This sum is made up of a lump sum plus a certain amount of money per voter, the amount of which will vary depending on whether the constituency is rural or urban. Candidates for election to Parliament or the European Parliament are entitled to free postage for one election communication and to the free use of a public building for an election meeting.

In order to ensure financial transparency, a candidate is required to appoint an agent who is responsible for keeping records of expenditure and submitting the accounts for scrutiny following the election. A candidate may appoint

2 It is thought that the Crown would have the right to refuse a dissolution if the request represented an abuse of power on the part of the government and granting the request would undermine the constitution.

3 Under the Political Parties, Elections and Referendum Act 2000.

him/herself to act as agent. It is unlawful for any person to provide money in contravention of the Act.

At the national level, political parties are permitted to spend up to a maximum limit, which is linked to the number of constituency seats they are contesting. In the 2005 general election the actual amounts spent by the three major parties were:

The Labour Party	£17,939,617
The Conservative Party	£17,852,240
The Liberal Democrat Party	£4,324,574

Election broadcasts

Political parties are allocated television time for election broadcasts according to the number of seats won at the previous general election. No party political broadcast may be made unless the political party is registered under the Political Parties, Elections and Referendums Act 2000.[4]

Corrupt practices

Bribery, treating and undue influence are unlawful. Bribery is defined as the giving of money or the making of gifts to or for any voter in order to induce that voter to vote or refrain from voting or to induce a person to procure, or attempt to procure, the election of a person at an election.[5]

Treating is the corrupt giving or provision or payment for any 'meat, drink, entertainment or provision' to any person for the purpose of influencing that person to vote or refrain from voting.[6] A person is guilty of undue influence if s/he directly or indirectly uses or threatens to use violence in order to induce or compel a person to vote or refrain from voting.[7]

Challenging an election result

If, following an election, a candidate suspects that the winning candidate is guilty of overspending the allowable amount or is guilty of corrupt practice, the matter goes to the election court, a division of the High Court. If found guilty, the election court may invalidate the winning candidate's election and award the seat to the runner-up. Exceptionally, the court may order a fresh election to be held. If there are irregularities in the vote counting, the court may order a recount.

4 Political Parties, Elections and Referendums Act 2000, s 37.

5 Representation of the People Act 1983, s 113.

6 *Ibid.* s 114.

7 *Ibid.* s 115.

The case law illustrates the approach taken to allegations of electoral wrongdoing.

In *R v Tronoh Mines Ltd*[8] it was alleged that a newspaper advertisement urging voters not to vote socialist, had an adverse impact on the election of the Labour Party candidate, and contravened the expenditure rules. The court disagreed: the advertisement was general in nature and did not have an impact on the particular candidate standing for election.

In *Grieve v Douglas-Hume*[9] it was alleged that the election of Douglas-Hume was void on the basis that he had participated in a national televised broadcast on behalf of the Conservative Party and had not declared the cost of this broadcast in his election expenses. The court held there had been no wrongdoing: the broadcast was not designed to promote Douglas-Hume's candidacy but to provide information about the Conservative Party as a whole.

An election result was set aside in *Re Parliamentary Election for Bristol South East* (1964). In this case the winning candidate who stood for re-election to Parliament had recently succeeded to a peerage and was accordingly ineligible to stand. His election was declared void and awarded to the runner up.

In *Ruffle v Rogers* (1982)[10] irregularities in the counting of votes which had an effect on the outcome of the election led to the election being set aside. The court made it clear, however, that had the irregularities not affected the result, the election would have been upheld.

Voting systems

General elections and local council elections

The simple majority vote

The system used to elect Members of Parliament (MPs) is the simple majority system. The country is divided into 646 constituencies, each of which is

8 [1952] 1 All ER 697.
9 1965 SLT 186.
10 [1982] 3 WLR 143.

represented in Parliament by one Member of Parliament. In order to be elected the winner needs only to secure one more vote than any of the other candidates. There is no fixed proportion of the vote (i.e. 40 or 50 per cent), which needs to be achieved. For example:

Brown	4,001 votes
Jones	4,000 votes
Smith	3,000 votes

The winner is Brown, having the largest number of votes when compared to Jones and Smith, but having a minority of votes when considered against the total number of votes cast in the election (4,001 + 4,000 + 3,000 = 11,001). Or differently expressed, 7,000 voters voted for an alternative candidate.

If this result is extended across all 646 constituencies, the result would be a government elected with a majority of parliamentary seats won, but a minority of the popular vote. A look at the 2005 election result confirms this effect:

Labour	355 seats	54.9% of seats	35.2% of vote
Conservative	198 seats	30.6% of seats	32.3% of vote
Lib Dem	62 seats	9.6% of seats	22.5% of vote
Other	31 seats	4.8% of seats	10.4% of vote

As can be seen from the above, the percentage of seats won bears no relationship to the percentage of the vote overall. In other words, there is no 'proportionality'. A voting system will reflect the principle of proportionality if it produces the result that a party winning 50 per cent (say) of the popular vote will win 50 per cent of the seats in Parliament.

The additional member system

This system employs the single member constituency but also attempts to ensure overall proportionality between votes and seats. If the additional member system was used in relation to general elections, three-quarters of MPs (484) would be elected in single-member constituencies. The remaining quarter (162) would be elected from lists of candidates prepared by the political parties on a regional basis, using a formula based on the largest average of votes cast between the parties.

The system is used for elections to the Scottish Parliament, the Welsh Assembly and the Greater London Authority.[11]

11 Scotland Act 1998, ss 1–8; Government of Wales Act 1998, ss 1–8; Greater London Authority Act 1999, s 4.

The single transferable vote[12]

The single transferable vote offers both proportionality and a constituency-based system. Constituencies are large and each return several members. Votes are cast for candidates in order of preference. To be elected a candidate must achieve the electoral quota. If a candidate achieves the quota based on the count of first preferences s/he is elected. Any votes over and above the quota are redistributed among the other candidates according to the voters' second preferences. This process continues until the number of seats is filled. If no candidate reaches the electoral quota, the candidate with the smallest number of votes is eliminated and his or her votes redistributed among the other candidates according to the expressed preferences.

The alternative vote

The alternative vote is a majoritarian, rather than proportional representation, system. The system retains individual constituencies. It requires multiple votes. Candidates are voted for in order of preference. After each round the candidate with the lowest number of votes is eliminated and his votes redistributed according to stated preferences. The process continues until a candidate with a clear majority is elected.

The system is criticised on the basis that potentially candidates with no clear support will be elected. However, it does ensure that within each constituency the candidate with the most support overall is elected.

The Commission established in 1998 to review the electoral system, chaired by Lord Jenkins, recommended a mixed system involving the alternative vote and party list system. The majority of members would be constituency members elected on the alternative vote system. A minority of members would be regional members, elected on the party list system. The advantages of this would be that it would be constituency-based, but also offer a greater degree of proportionality between the votes cast and seats won.[13]

The party list system

Under this system the political parties draw up a list of candidates. The voter casts his or her vote for the preferred party. The system is widely used throughout Europe. However, the party list system gives political parties complete control over who is on the list and who should represent which constituency. The close link between a Member of Parliament and the constituency is lost.

12 Used for elections to the Northern Ireland Assembly and Northern Ireland elections to the European Parliament.

13 *Report of the Independent Commission on the Voting System*, 1998, Cm 4090, London: HMSO.

The funding of political parties

Political parties receive state funding for their parliamentary work, but not for their election expenses. Accordingly, they are dependent upon contributions from individuals or organisations. Membership subscriptions make up a portion of a party's income, but donations are essential. The law has been slow to regulate this issue. The Registration of Political Parties Act 1998 required political parties to be formally registered in order to put candidates up for election. That was followed by the Political Parties, Elections and Referendums Act 2000 (PPERA), which achieved a number of objectives.

The PPERA established the Electoral Commission, which assumed responsibility for the registration of political parties. The Act also defined permissible and impermissible donors to political parties and required the disclosure and recording of donations. Anonymous or unidentifiable donors are not allowed.

The Political Parties Elections and Referendums Act 2000, section 54, provides that permissible donors include:

- an individual on the electoral register;
- a company registered under the Companies Act 1985 or the Companies (Northern Ireland) Act 1986; and
  incorporated within the UK or another Member State, which carries on business in the UK;
- a registered party;
- a registered trade union;
- a building society;
- a registered limited liability partnership;
- a registered friendly society;
- any unincorporated association of two or more persons not falling within the above, but which carries on business or other activities wholly or mainly in the UK and whose main office is there.

Political parties are under a duty to ensure that donations are only received from permissible donors. Any donations from impermissible donors must be returned. If a donation is received from a person other than the donor, where the donor is unidentifiable, the donation must be returned to that third party. Any entirely unidentifiable donation must be sent to the Commission and shall be paid into the Consolidated Fund. If a political party accepts a donation that is prohibited, the Commission may apply to the court for an order forfeiting the donation.[14]

14 Political Parties, Elections and Referendums Act 2000, ss 56, 57, 57A, respectively.

State funding

As noted above, political parties receive state money to assist with their parliamentary work. In the House of Commons this is known as 'Short money' (after the minister who introduced it) and in the House of Lords 'Cranbourn money'. They do not, however, receive any public funding for election purposes.

In Austria, Denmark, France, Germany Greece, Italy, Portugal and Spain, political parties are publicly funded. In Britain, however, the issue is controversial. The benefits of state funding include getting rid of the dangers associated with donations from individuals, companies or trade unions, and so on. The system would be transparent and a matter of public record and thereby increase public confidence in the political process. However, set against that argument is the objection that state funding could encourage the growth of small extremist parties. The argument is also made that individual taxpayers would resent being forced to pay for a political system in which they have little or no interest and for parties with which they have no sympathy.

Referendums

Referendums have been held in the UK in the 1970s in relation to continuing membership of the European Union (then European Economic Community). More recently in 1997 referendums have been held in Scotland and Northern Ireland over devolution.

Referendums are regulated under the Political Parties Elections and Referendums Act 2000. Under section 101, a referendum is defined as a:

> '. . . referendum or other poll held, in pursuance of any provision made by or under an Act of Parliament, on one or more questions specified in or in accordance with any such provisions.'

The Act imposes restrictions on expenditure and makes it an offence to exceed the prescribed limit.

Summary

The electoral system comprises several different aspects. For the system to reflect democratic principles, it should, as far as possible, ensure that each person's vote is of equal value. In turn, that requires that constituency sizes be approximately equal, having an equal number of voters. Further, it requires that the law controls expenditure both during individual candidate's election campaigns and the income and expenditure of political parties. Equality is also a factor in the voting system used for elections.

It has been seen above that the system used for general elections and local authority elections is one that fails to ensure that the number of votes cast for a political party is translated into the number of seats won by that party. Moreover, no political party has been elected to government with a majority of the popular vote for over 50 years.

Further reading

Marriot, J, 'Alarmist or Relaxed: Election Expenditure Limits and Freedom of Speech' [2005] PL 764.

Report of the Independent Commission on the Voting System (Jenkins Report), 1998, Cm 4090, London: HMSO.

Rowbottom, J, 'The Electoral Commission's Proposals on the Funding of Political Parties' [2005] PL 168.

The Party Funding Review Report: 'Strengthening Democracy: Fair and Sustainable Funding of Political Parties', March 2007.

Webb, P, 'Parties and Party Systems: Modernisation, Regulation and Diversity' (2001), 54 Parliamentary Affairs, 308.

www.partyfundingreview.gov.uk

SELF-ASSESSMENT QUESTIONS

1. List the categories of persons who are not qualified to vote.
2. Name the voting system used for the following elections:

   general elections
   elections to the Scottish Parliament
   elections to the European Parliament
   elections to the Northern Ireland Assembly
   elections to the Welsh Assembly

3. Name the Act that regulates the conduct of elections campaigns and the Act that regulates donations to party political funds and controls expenditure at national level.
4. Name the court that adjudicates on disputed elections.

SAMPLE EXAMINATION QUESTIONS

1. To what extent does electoral law in the UK reflect the principle of 'one person, one vote, one value'? What reforms, if any, would you advocate?

Continued

SAMPLE EXAMINATION QUESTIONS *(continued)*

2. 'The simple majority voting system's sole merit is that of simplicity.'

   Discuss.

3. 'It is undeniable that electoral reform is required in order to ensure truly representative government. However, detailed consideration of the constitutional consequences of such reform is necessary before such reform is undertaken.'

   Discuss

Chapter 9

Parliament

CONTENTS

KEY WORDS AND PHRASES

Backbencher	Member of Parliament not holding ministerial office
Bill	A proposed Act of Parliament

Committee of the Whole House	The House of Commons as a whole sitting to scrutinise a Bill
Crown	The monarch in whose name all Acts of government are undertaken
Dissolution of Parliament	The formal ending of a Parliament in order that a general election may be held
Frontbencher	Member of Parliament holding ministerial office in government or shadow ministerial office in Opposition party
Hansard	The Official Report of both Houses of Parliament
House of Commons	The elected House
House of Lords	The unelected House
Members of Parliament	Elected members of the House of Commons
Motion	Request
Parliament	Crown, House of Commons and House of Lords
Parliamentary privilege	The immunities and rights that Parliament and its members have to protect its independence
Peers	Members of the House of Lords
Public Bill Committee	The committee established to consider a Bill
Royal Assent	The Crown's formal agreement to an Act of Parliament, without which it cannot come into effect
Select Committee	A permanent subject Committee, which scrutinises the work of a related government department
Standing Orders	Formal rules of procedure of both Houses
The Speaker	The Member of Parliament or Peer (in the Lords) who controls parliamentary proceedings, acting as chairperson

Introduction

The United Kingdom Parliament is made up of three components: the Crown, the House of Commons and the House of Lords. Parliament is the highest law-making body within the UK (see Chapter 5). In addition to its law-making role, Parliament also scrutinises government administration and calls government to account for its actions. In this chapter we examine Parliament's structure, composition and powers.

Structure and composition

The Crown

The role of the Crown nowadays is formal. The Queen attends the State Opening of Parliament, which takes place each autumn, signifying the start of the new parliamentary year, and her agreement must be sought and given to a request by a Prime Minister to dissolve Parliament in order that a general election may be held. When a proposal for legislation has passed its parliamentary stages, it must be approved by the Crown through the Royal Assent.

The House of Commons

The elected 'lower' House comprising 646 Members of Parliament, each of whom represents a constituency (voting area). By convention, the Prime Minister must be a member of the House of Commons and most of his or her government will be Members of the Commons. The maximum length of time between general elections is laid down in the Parliament Act 1911 as five years, but the Prime Minister can ask the Crown for a dissolution in order to hold a general election at any time within the five-year period.

Most Bills will be introduced in the Commons and scrutinised and approved before going to the House of Lords for consideration.

The House of Lords

The unelected 'upper' House, comprising over 700 Members (peers). The undemocratic composition of the Lords has long been a source of concern and there have been several attempts – none of which has been totally successful – to reform its membership. This will be considered later in this chapter.

The House of Lords must approve Bills. However, if the Lords refuse to agree to a Bill there is a statutory procedure that will be used to resolve the conflict, discussed below.

The legislative (law-making) process

Proposals for law-making come from a number of sources. First and foremost will be the policies of the government of the day, which will have been put to the people at a general election or which are adopted during the government's term of office. The government may also propose legislation to deal with a particular event in society, which indicates a need for legal regulation. Proposals will also come from law reform bodies such as the Law Commission, which has a statutory duty to keep the law under review and recommend reform. There also exist numerous bodies such as trade unions, which represent their members' interests and pressure groups that focus on particular concerns. Examples of these include: Greenpeace, the environmental campaigners; the Wetland and Wildfowl Trust; the Royal Society for the Protection of Birds.

Whatever its origins, a proposal for legislation must first be translated into the language of an Act of Parliament and presented to Parliament in the form of a Bill. There will then follow several formal stages at which the Bill is scrutinised by Members of Parliament in the House of Commons and then by members of the House of Lords. It is also possible for a Bill to be introduced first in the House of Lords and to be sent to the Commons for scrutiny, once the proceedings in the Lords are completed.

Bills are classified as follows:

Public Bill	A Bill that applies to all in society
Private Bill	A Bill relating only to a particular person or group in society
Hybrid Bill	A Bill having both public and private application
Private Members' Bill	A Bill introduced by an individual Member of Parliament
Consolidation Bill	A Bill re-enacting the law previously contained in different statutes, with or without amendments

The scrutiny of Bills

Pre-legislative scrutiny

Since 1997, it has become the practice to publish draft Bills in order that Members of Parliament and others have an opportunity to consider the Bill and suggest changes before the formal scrutiny process begins.

In 2007, the Government announced that it would publish its proposed legislative programme before the start of the forthcoming parliamentary session.[1]

Public Bills

In order to become an Act of Parliament a Public Bill must complete all its parliamentary stages within the same session. If it does not, the Bill is

1 Green Paper: *The Governance of Britain: The Government's Draft Legislative Programme* Cm 7175, 2007.

lost. In order to prevent the loss of Bills, it is possible for the Commons to agree to the Bill being 'carried over' to the next session.

A Public Bill will be scrutinised in the following stages.

First reading: the formal presentation of the Bill to Parliament when a date is set for the first debate on the Bill.

Second reading: the first debate on the Bill, which is confined to a discussion of the principles of the Bill. If a majority of Members of Parliament vote against the Bill at this stage it is defeated and will be withdrawn from Parliament. If the Bill passes second reading it will be sent to a Committee for detailed consideration.

Committee stage: a Bill may be sent to (committed to) different types of parliamentary Committees. It may be considered by a *Committee of the Whole House*, which means that it will be scrutinised in the Commons' chamber by all attending Members of Parliament. This procedure is usually reserved for Bills of constitutional importance. It may be sent to a *Select Committee*, which is a Committee of (usually) 11 members, who specialise in a particular subject-matter. This procedure is fairly rare. The most normal process is for the Bill to be sent to a *Public Bill Committee* (formerly known as *Standing Committees)*.

A Public Bill Committee is made up of 16 to 50 Members of Parliament (usually around 20). Because the Committee is acting on behalf of the Commons it will reflect the political party composition of the Commons as a whole. Accordingly, if a government has a strong majority in the Commons overall, the Committee membership will reflect this with a majority of members being government supporters.

Public Bill Committees are established to consider a particular Bill and then disbanded: they are not permanent Committees established according to subject matter. It is considered that if there were permanent specialist subject Committees, these would become too inward-looking and too familiar with the subject and with the relevant minister who is steering the Bill through Committee.

Committee proceedings are very formal. The Committee will examine the Bill from start to finish, deciding which clauses will stand and which will be amended. The Committee is confined to the Bill before it: it has no power (unlike Select Committees) to call for documentary evidence to assist its work, nor is it allowed to appoint specialist advisers or call for specialists to give evidence.

Report stage: once the Bill has been scrutinised in committee, the Bill returns to the Commons. Usually there is little debate at this stage, although if a Bill is controversial it may be debated for up to three hours and a vote taken. Amendments may be made at this stage.

Third reading: this is the final stage of the Bill in the Commons. There is usually little debate and the only amendments that may be made are grammatical.

House of Lords: the Bill will now be sent to the Lords, which will undergo a similar process of scrutiny. Proceedings in the Lords are less formal, and less use is made of scrutiny committees than in the Commons, although increasingly, Bills are being considered by a Public Bill Committee.

Royal Assent

The Royal Assent is required in order for a Bill to become an Act. The Royal Assent has not been personally granted by the monarch since 1854 and last refused in 1708. However, the right to refuse the Assent remains a prerogative power. In practice, the Royal Assent is either announced by the Speaker in the House of Commons and House of Lords or given by members of the House of Lords who have been appointed as Commissioners to give the Royal Assent, which is then notified to the Commons.[2]

Curtailing debate

One of the principal problems with scrutiny lies in the shortage of parliamentary time. Bills must generally complete all stages of scrutiny within the same parliamentary session (year). As a result there are various ways in which debate can be cut short in order to ensure that a Bill succeeds.

Selection of amendments

This is uncontroversial and simply allows amendments to be grouped together for more efficient discussion.

Closure motion

This is a means of stopping debate, usually with the agreement of government and opposition, at a particular time. To apply, the Speaker must approve the motion and at least 100 Members of Parliament must vote in favour of closure.

Allocation of time motion

The government may request the Commons to approve the timetabling of a Bill. If approved, all stages of a Bill may be subject to strict time

2 Royal Assent by Commission Act 1541; Royal Assent Act 1967.

limits. Because this can result in parts of a Bill not being scrutinised in the Commons, it is a controversial device that is now only used where a Bill's passage is being obstructed by the opposition.

Programming of Bills

Since 2001, standing orders of the House of Commons have provided for Programme Orders. Immediately after Second Reading, a request is made for the order which, if approved, allows the remaining stages of a Bill to be timetabled.

'Carry over' of Bills

To prevent the loss of a Bill, standing orders now provide that, subject to agreement, a government Bill may be carried over from one session to another. A Bill may only be carried over once.

Post-legislative scrutiny

The Law Commission has recommended that there be a Joint Committee established to undertake systematic post-legislative scrutiny to ascertain whether an Act is achieving its purpose and working in practice.[3]

Private Bills

A Private Bill starts its parliamentary passage by way of a formal petition. The Bill will then follow the same stages as a Public Bill. At the Committee stage, however, if the Bill is controversial the Committee may hear representations from legal counsel.

Hybrid Bills

Hybrid Bills are Bills affecting both the public and also certain private interests. For example, the Channel Tunnel Bill was hybrid in that it provided for the construction of the Channel Tunnel Rail Link, but also affected the interests of property owners whose homes would be compulsorily purchased to make way for the rail track.

A Hybrid Bill follows the same stages as other Public Bills. If the Bill is opposed the Committee stage may be held in Select Committee. Otherwise it will be scrutinised by a Public Bill Committee or considered by a Committee of the Whole House.

3 Law Com No 302, 2006, Cm 6945, *Post-Legislative Scrutiny*.

Private Members' Bills

Members of Parliament have the opportunity to propose Bills. Between ten and 13 days a year are set aside specifically for the consideration of Private Members' Bills, with the first six Fridays reserved for the second reading of Private Members' Bills. However, unless the government – which controls the parliamentary timetable – is prepared to make additional time available for the Bill to complete its stages the Bill is unlikely to become law. The majority of Private Members' Bills relate to sensitive social or moral issues. Successful Private Members' Bills include the Abortion Act 1967, the Sexual Offences Act 1967, the Female Genital Mutilation Act 2004 and the Human Fertilisation and Embryology Act 2004.

Private Members' Bills may be introduced in the following ways.

By ballot

At the beginning of each parliamentary session, a ballot is held. The first 20 to be drawn out have the opportunity to propose a Bill. The 'winner' may agree to give up his or her opportunity in favour of an unsuccessful Member's proposed Bill.

The Bill will follow the same stages as a public Bill.

Ten-minute rule Bills

Immediately after Question Time on Tuesdays or Wednesdays, having given five days notice, a Bill may be introduced by a Member who may make a ten-minute speech in support of it. These are rarely successful, but provide the opportunity to raise a matter in Parliament.

Presentation Bills

Any Member of Parliament may introduce a Bill under the Ordinary Presentation process. Notice is required. The Clerk of the House reads the short title of the Bill, which is then deemed to have had its first reading. However, most Bills fail due to lack of time.

Bills from the House of Lords

A Bill may be introduced in the House of Lords, complete its stages there and then be sent to the House of Commons for scrutiny.

Consolidation Bills

Consolidation Bills are Bills that bring together a number of Acts of Parliament on the same subject, without amending the law, or introducing minor corrections or improvements.[4] Consolidation Bills are normally introduced in the House of Lords. After Second Reading they are referred to a Joint Committee on Consolidation Bills, which has 12 members from each House.

Following consideration by the Joint Committee, Report stage and Third Reading take place in the Lords, without debate.

The Parliament Act 1911

Before 1911, the House of Lords had equal powers with the Commons in relation to legislation. However, *by convention*, the House of Lords would always give way to the wishes of the Commons in relation to financial matters. In 1908, however, the House of Lords defied this convention and tried to block the government's budget proposals. The outcome of this prolonged constitutional crisis was that an Act of Parliament – the Parliament Act 1911 – was passed (with the approval of both Houses) to regulate future relations.

The Parliament Act 1911 (which, as amended by the Parliament Act 1949, is still in force) provides that in relation to a Money Bill (a Bill dealing 'solely' with finance section 1(2)), if the Bill has been passed by the Commons and sent to the Lords at least one month before the end of the session (parliamentary year) and is not passed by the Lords without amendment within one month, the Bill shall be presented for the Royal Assent and become an Act. In relation to non-money Public Bills, if the Bill has passed the Commons in two parliamentary sessions and is sent to the Lords at least one month before the end of each session, and is rejected by the Lords in each session, it can be sent for the Royal Assent and become an Act.

Section 2(3) of the Parliament Act 1911 defines the meaning of 'rejected' as being:

> '. . . not passed by the House of Lords either without amendment or with such amendments only as may be agreed to by both Houses.'

The Parliament Act procedure does not apply to a Bill extending the maximum duration of Parliament beyond five years or to Bills introduced into the House of Lords.

The Parliament Act 1949

The Parliament Act 1949 was passed by the House of Commons and the Crown under the Parliament Act procedure. This gave rise to academic

4 Consolidation of Enactments (Procedure) Act 1949.

debate concerning the validity of the 1949 Act. The argument centred on the principle that a body to which power is delegated may not expand its own powers without express authority. The Parliament Act 1949, being passed under the 1911 Act, expanded the power of the Commons and Crown by further restricting the amount of time the House of Lords could delay a Bill. The issue was finally resolved in the case of *Jackson v Attorney General* (2005).[5] In this case, there was a challenge to the validity of the Hunting Act 2004, which had been passed under the Parliament Act procedure. It was argued that the Parliament Act 1949 was invalid (because it breached the principle concerning a delegate extending its powers) and that accordingly the Hunting Act 2004 must also be invalid. The House of Lords rejected the argument: both the Parliament Act 1949 and the Hunting Act 2004 were valid.

A further argument tested in *Jackson* concerned the scope of the power to legislate under the Parliament Acts. Section 2 of the 1911 Act specifically excludes Bills that aim to extend the life of a Parliament, and Money Bills, from its procedures. In the Court of Appeal it was argued that there was an additional, implied, restriction, namely Bills that seek to give effect to fundamental constitutional reform. In the House of Lords this view was firmly rejected. There could be no implied restrictions read into the Act. Even fundamental constitutional reform could therefore be brought about without the consent of the House of Lords.

Coming into effect

An Act may come into effect on the date the Royal Assent is given. Alternatively, some of the Act may come into effect on that date and other parts come into effect at a later date, usually on a date decided by the relevant minister.

Example: The Companies Act 2006

1300 Commencement

(1) The following provisions come into force on the day this Act is passed –

(a) Part 43 (transparency obligations and related matters), except the amendment in paragraph 11(2) of Schedule 15 of the definition of 'regulated market' in Part 6 of the Financial Services and Markets Act 2000 (c.8),

(b) Part 44 (miscellaneous provisions) –
section 1274 (grants to bodies concerned with actuarial standards etc), and
section 1276 (application of provisions to Scotland and Northern Ireland),

5 [2005] UKHL 56; [2005] 3 WLR 733.

(c) Part 46 (general supplementary provisions), except section 1295 and Schedule 16 (repeals), and
(d) this Part.

(2) The other provisions of this Act come into force on such day as may be appointed by order of the Secretary of State or the Treasury.

Delegated (secondary) legislation

The function of delegated, or secondary, legislation is to fill in the detailed rules of law that are needed to implement a particular policy. To have all of these details in the Act of Parliament would make the Act overly complex, long and unwieldy. Accordingly, the Act will confer on the relevant public authority (a minister, a local council, a public body such as British Airports Authority) the power to draft detailed rules.

Delegated legislation takes several forms:

- Order in Council: orders of the Privy Council relating to the prerogative;
- Bye-laws: the rules made by local authorities and public authorities;
- Remedial orders under the Human Rights Act 1998;
- Regulatory reform orders: under the Legislative and Regulatory Reform Act 2006, orders reducing the burden on businesses, professions etc.;
- Statutory Instruments under the Statutory Instruments Act 1946.

To be valid, delegated legislation must fall within the scope of power granted by the Act of Parliament. Whereas the validity of an Act of Parliament cannot be challenged in court, the courts will scrutinise delegated legislation, and should it fall ouside the power granted, invalidate it.

Delegated legislation is not subject to the same parliamentary scrutiny as Bills. Three forms of scrutiny exist.

The affirmative resolution procedure

Under this procedure, a statutory instrument will be laid before Parliament and must be approved by both Houses of Parliament before coming into effect. The normal period for approval is 28 days following the laying of the instrument.

The negative resolution procedure

This is the most common form of procedure. A statutory instrument will come into effect 40 days (usually) after it has been laid before Parliament, unless either House passes a motion for its annulment within that period.

Note that statutory instruments cannot be amended by either House. They must be approved or rejected as they are.

Scrutiny by parliamentary committees

The House of Commons and House of Lords each has a Select Committee, which examines statutory instruments. In addition, there is a Joint Select Committee on statutory instruments, made up of members of both Houses. The Joint Committee examines all delegated legislation on the following grounds:

- that the instrument imposes a tax or charge;
- that the parent Act excludes review by the courts;
- that the instrument is to operate retrospectively;
- that there has been an unjustifiable delay in publication or laying;
- that the instrument has come into effect in convention of the required procedure;
- that there is doubt as to whether the instrument is *intra vires*;
- that the instrument requires clarification;
- that the instrument's drafting is defective.

The scrutiny of government administration

In the UK, the people elect Members of the House of Commons to represent their interests. The Prime Minister will be the leader of the political party that wins the largest number of seats in the House of Commons. The Prime Minister will select a majority of government ministers from the Members of Parliament in his party (a minority will be appointed from members of the unelected House of Lords). The majority of government ministers (the executive) are accordingly ordinary elected Members of Parliament.

In order to ensure that the government is accountable to the people, it is essential that Parliament as a whole has adequate procedures to scrutinise the manner in which the government implements its policies. Scrutiny takes place in both Houses of Parliament, but as the majority of government ministers sit in the House of Commons, the main focus is on procedure in the Commons.

Debates

The House of Commons was once described as the 'sounding board of the nation'.[6] Reflecting this, much parliamentary time is spent in debate. While the government controls the subject-matter for debate most of the time, there are 21 days in each parliamentary session (year) on which the opposition parties can decide what will be debated. This is important in

6 By John Stuart Mill, the nineteenth-century liberal philosopher and for a brief time Member of Parliament.

ensuring that the government is unable to avoid discussion of various matters that it would prefer to remain undiscussed.

In addition to general debates on matters of current interest, there are daily adjournment debates. These take place for 30 minutes at the close of business and enable an individual MP to raise an issue with a particular minister. The discussion will be formally recorded in *Hansard*.

Emergency debates of up to three hours duration will take place on matters requiring urgent attention. A request for an emergency debate is made to the Speaker. If granted, the debate will take place after Prime Minister's Question Time.

Early Day Motions

These are written requests for a debate 'at an early day'. They act as a way of testing the strength of feeling in the House over a particular matter. The EDM will remain throughout the parliamentary year and other MPs may add their names to it in support. As the number of MPs' names increases, so too does the pressure on the government to provide a debate.

Question Time

All ministers, including the Prime Minister, face Question Time. Prime Ministerial Question Time takes place once a week for 30 minutes. Other ministers face Question Time about once a month. Question Time takes place on three days a week, for approximately one hour during which two or three ministers will normally answer questions relating to their departmental responsibilities.

An MP wishing to ask a question must give up to three days' notice in order to enable the relevant minister to research the issue. Answers may be oral or written. In all cases the answers will be published in the official journal of the House of Commons, *Hansard*. Questions to the Prime Minister are not specific: rather the questioner asks the Prime Minister to 'list his or her engagements for the day'. Once this has been done, the real – or supplementary – question is asked, and this can be on any aspect of government policy. This means that the Prime Minister must be able to demonstrate that s/he is fully prepared and able to answer questions on almost every aspect of policy.

By convention, a number of issues are not subject to parliamentary questions. These include:

- questions relating to the Crown;
- questions relating to advice given to the Crown on matters falling under the Royal prerogative;
- questions not relating to a matter directly within a minister's individual responsibility;

- defence and national security;
- Cabinet business;
- questions relating to the internal affairs of another country;
- questions aimed at criticising judges;
- matters which are *sub judice*;
- questions phrased in 'unparliamentary language'.

Questions that avoid the normal requirement of notice and require an urgent response, known as urgent questions, require the permission of the Speaker. If given the question will be discussed after Question Time, thereby disrupting the rest of the day's scheduled business. For this reason, very few requests for urgent questions are granted.

Select committees

The most in-depth scrutiny of government takes place in select committees. There are different forms of select committees, which include the following:

- *ad hoc* committees established to enquire into a particular matter, which is not subject to scrutiny elsewhere;
- domestic committees: select committees such as Accommodation and Works, the Catering Committee, Finance and Service Committee;
- committees dealing with procedural matters: the Procedure Committee, Modernisation Committee, Liaison Committee, Information Committee;
- finance: the Public Accounts Committee;
- delegated legislation: the Committee on Statutory Instruments.

Of major importance in relation to scrutiny are the departmental select committees, with each major department of state having its own committee. There are usually 11 Members, representing the party political composition of the Commons as a whole. Proceedings are generally open to the public. The committees have the power to call for witnesses and documents and to appoint specialist advisers.

Once appointed to a committee, a Member will remain on that committee for the life of the Parliament (on average about four years). The committee may be chaired by a Member from any political party, although by convention certain chairs are reserved for the government of the day.

Select committees act as committees of inquiry. They determine what topics to examine. Under the standing orders of the House, the committee is empowered to examine the 'policy, administration and expenditure' of the relevant government department. The committees try to operate in a non-party political manner, setting aside any political differences in the interests of in-depth scrutiny. They aim to produce a unanimous Report, which will have greater authority than one that might reflect political disagreement within the committee.

Select committees can take evidence from anyone deemed necessary, including ministers. However, although successive governments consent to cooperate with select committees, if a minister should refuse to attend, the committee has no power to force the minister to appear. Such a lack of cooperation is rare. The *Ministerial Code*, drafted by the Prime Minister and published by the Cabinet Office, states that:

> Ministers have a duty to Parliament to account, and be held to account, for the policies, decisions and actions of their departments and agencies;
>
> It is of paramount importance that Ministers give accurate and truthful information to Parliament, correcting any inadvertent error at the earliest opportunity. Ministers who knowingly mislead Parliament will be expected to offer their resignation to the Prime Minister.[7]

House of Lords committees

The House of Lords does not have the same structure of select committees as the House of Commons. There are, however, a number of important committees. These include the European Union Committee, the Science and Technology Committee and the Economic Affairs Committee. In addition there is the Select Committee on the Constitution. There is also a Joint Committee on Human Rights, having six members from the House of Lords and six from the House of Commons. There is also a Joint Committee on Delegated Legislation, having seven members from the House of Lords and seven from the Commons.

House of Lords reform

The Preamble to the Parliament Act 1911 envisaged a fully elected House of Lords. This, however, has yet to be achieved and reform of the House of Lords is fraught with difficulties. In addition to the Parliament Acts 1911 and 1949, which regulate relations between the Commons and Lords, there have been other reforms to the Upper House. What has not been achieved is a fully elected House.

Life Peerage Act 1958

This Act enabled individuals to be appointed to the House of Lords for their lifetime. The peerage is not hereditary and does not pass down to the next in line once the life peer dies.

7 Ministerial Code, Cabinet Office, 2007, para 1.2.b and c.

Peerage Act 1963

This Act provided that those who succeed to a hereditary peerage may disclaim that peerage within one year, or one month if already a member of the House of Commons.

House of Lords Act 1999

The Labour Government elected in 1997 had intended to exclude all hereditary peers from the House of Lords as the first stage in reforming the composition of the House to a fully elected House. For political reasons, however, the House of Lords Act 1999 excluded all but 92 hereditary peers from the House.

The Royal Commission on the House of Lords

This Commission, chaired by Lord Wakeham, was established to examine further reform and to make recommendations. The Report, *A House for the Future*,[8] recommended that:

- the size of the House should be about 550;
- there should be a majority of nominated members;
- there should be a minority of elected members;
- the powers of the House of Lords should remain as they are.

In relation to the proportion of nominated/elected members the Report put forward three models.

1. Model A proposed that there should be 65 members selected on a regional basis in proportion to each political party's share of the vote in a general election.
2. Model B proposed that there should be 87 directly elected members, with elections coinciding with elections for the European Parliament.
3. Model C proposed 195 directly elected regional members, with elections coinciding with elections for the European Parliament.

On 14 July 2008 the Government published its White Paper, An Elected Second Chamber, further reform of the House of Lords, Cm 7438. The White Paper is the result of cross-party discussions designed to reach wide-ranging consensus on the issue of reform.

8 Cm 4534, London: HMSO.

The major provisions include:

- a 100 or 80 per cent elected chamber;
- the voting system for elections will be either first-past-the-post, alternative vote, single transferable vote or a list system;
- the primacy of the House of Commons is to be maintained;
- the powers of the House of Lords will remain substantially the same as at present;
- Members would normally serve a non-renewable term of 12–15 years;
- the size of the chamber will be reduced, possibly to around 430;
- new Members will be elected in thirds coinciding with general elections;
- existing Members will continue until the new membership is achieved;
- the link between a peerage and a seat in Parliament will finally be broken;
- the right of the remaining hereditary peers to sit will be removed;
- if there is to be an appointed element, a statutory Appointments Commission will be established;
- appointments would be made on the basis of an individual's willingness to take part in the work of the chamber;
- the name of the second chamber will change, possibly to the Senate.

Parliamentary privilege

In order that Parliament may carry out its functions without interference from elsewhere, both Houses enjoy certain legal immunities and privileges. These privileges are a unique form of common law, the 'law and custom of Parliament', which are recognised and respected by the judges. Privilege can be divided into two main aspects: the collective privileges of both Houses and the individual privileges enjoyed by all Members of Parliament (both Commons and Lords).

Privileges are interpreted and enforced by both Houses of Parliament. If a matter of parliamentary privilege arises before the courts, the courts will determine whether a privilege in fact exists, and if it does will decline to rule on the matter – leaving it to Parliament. An illustration of this process is seen in the case of *Rost v Edwards* (1990).[9]

In *Rost v Edwards* a newspaper article alleged that an MP had failed to register certain interests. The MP sued for libel. The MP wanted to admit in evidence correspondence between himself and a Clerk of Parliament and also the Register of Members' Interests. Before the

9 [1990] 2 WLR 1280; [1990] 2 All ER 641.

court could proceed to determine the issue of libel it had to decide the preliminary issue of privilege and whether these items were admissible in a court of law. The Court ruled that the correspondence was not admissible, being a matter solely within Parliament's domain. The Register, however, being a public document, was admissible.

If there is an allegation that privilege has been breached in the House of Commons, the matter goes initially to the Speaker who decides whether to refer the matter to the Parliamentary Commissioner for Standards for investigation or to the Committee on Standards and Privileges for a ruling.

Collective privileges

Parliament determines its own composition, powers and procedures. This power is an integral part of Parliament's sovereignty and is reflected in the courts refusal to look 'behind' an Act and enquire into the procedure by which it was passed (see *Pickin v British Railways Board*[10] discussed in Chapter 5).

Other cases that illustrate this power include:

Ashby v White[11] in which a qualified voter had been denied the right to vote and sought and was granted damages. Other voters, also denied their rights, instituted legal proceedings but were imprisoned by the House of Commons. The courts refused to interfere to release the detainees, deferring to Parliament.

Bradlaugh v Gosset[12] in which a newly elected Member of Parliament refused to take the oath as required by the Parliamentary Oaths Act of 1866, offering instead to affirm allegiance. He was excluded from the House of Commons. Seeking a declaration and injunction from the courts, the court ruled that the issue was a matter for Parliament and that the court had no jurisdiction.

This last case has echoes in relation to the two elected MPs from Northern Ireland, Gerry Adams and Martin McGuinness, each of whom as supporters

10 [1974] AC 785.
11 (1703) 2 Ld Raym 938; 14 St Tr 695.
12 (1884) 12 QBD 271.

of the reunification of Ireland, refused to swear allegiance to the Crown. They have not been permitted to take their seats in the Commons.

> *R v Graham-Campbell ex parte Herbert*[13] in which the High Court ruled that magistrates had been right to decide there was no jurisdiction to prosecute Members of Parliament for selling alcohol in the Members' Bar without a licence.

In 1960 an MP, Tony Benn, inherited the title of Viscount Stansgate. He was then excluded from the Commons. The law was subsequently changed to enable a peerage to be relinquished (the Peerage Act 1963).

Individual privileges

Members of Parliament enjoy freedom from arrest in relation to civil (not criminal) matters, and freedom of speech in parliamentary proceedings.

Freedom from arrest

This anachronistic privilege derives from the need for the King to have Members of Parliament available to advise him. Accordingly, to detain a Member deprives Parliament of his or her attendance and thereby breaches privilege. The privilege still applies for 40 days before and after a parliamentary session, reflecting the slow speed of travel in former times.

If an MP is suspected of criminal activities, s/he is subject to the law in the same way as anyone else. However, if the police intend to enter Parliament for the purpose of an arrest, they must seek the permission of the Speaker.

Freedom of speech

The need for full and frank discussion in Parliament – without which democracy would be damaged – provides the justification for this privilege. Members of Parliament have total immunity from the law of defamation (libel and slander) in relation to words spoken during the course of parliamentary proceedings. This privilege is protected by Article 9 of the Bill of Rights 1689, which states:

> That the freedom of speech, and debates or proceedings in Parliament ought not to be impeached or questioned in any court or place out of Parliament.

13 [1935] 1 KB 594.

Members' interests

Becoming a Member of Parliament does not require a person to end his or her existing forms of employment outside Parliament. In the nineteenth century, being a Member of Parliament was regarded as a privilege and a public duty and was unpaid. With the birth of the Labour Party at the turn of the twentieth century and the election of MPs to represent the working class, it became necessary to introduce salaries for MPs (members of the House of Lords are still unsalaried and receive only a daily attendance allowance and expenses).

The fact that MPs have outside interests – whether as in employment, or holding directorships or acting as consultants – requires that there are procedures that ensure that an MP's parliamentary work is not affected by these interests. Accordingly, there is a requirement that all interests be formally recorded and that all interests are declared when an MP is participating in parliamentary debate. The **Register of Members' Interests** was introduced in the House of Commons in 1974. There is a similar Register for the House of Lords. The Register requires that the following matters are recorded:

- paid directorships of companies, public or private;
- paid employment, trade, professions, offices or vocations;
- names and details of clients of lobbying companies in relation to which an MP plays a role;
- gifts, benefits or hospitality;
- financial sponsorship related to election expenses or parliamentary work;
- overseas visits;
- any payments or benefits received from overseas governments, organisations or persons;
- land or property of substantial value (excluding the MPs home) or from which a substantial income is derived;
- names of companies or other bodies in which the Member has a beneficial interest of a value greater than a hundredth of the issued share capital;
- miscellaneous and unpaid interest which a Member considers should be recorded.

In the 1990s it was revealed that a few MPs had been accepting payment for asking parliamentary questions. The 'Cash for Questions' saga led to the enquiry into Standards in Public Life, chaired by Lord Nolan. The Report, *Standards in Public Life*,[14] found that while many MPs had substantial

14 Cm 2850-I, London: HMSO 1995.

outside interests, there was no evidence of widespread wrongdoing. However, in order to improve the regulation of interests the Committee recommended, and the Commons accepted, that there should be established an office of Parliamentary Commissioner for Standards, responsible for the Register of Members' Interests and for investigating and reporting of allegations of financial impropriety.

Where an allegation is made that an MP has broken the rules, the matter goes first to the Speaker of the House of Commons who may refer the matter to the Parliamentary Commissioner. Following investigation, the Commissioner will report to the Committee on Standards and Privileges, which may recommend that an MP is punished by the House of Commons. Such punishment includes:

- suspension from the Commons for a defined period;
- loss of salary for the period of suspension.

Should there be suspected criminal conduct, the Commissioner may refer the matter to the Commissioner of Police for the Metropolis for further investigation. If there is sufficient evidence of criminal conduct, the Crown Prosecution Service may institute prosecution proceedings.

The Parliamentary Standards Act 2009

The Parliamentary Standards Act 2009 was passed in order to establish a reformed system for regulating Members of Parliaments' pay, allowances and expenses. The need for the Act arose out of damaging disclosures concerning the abuse of the allowances and expenses system by MPs which were revealed following a request under the Freedom of Information Act 2000. Before details of MP's claims were published officially, details of individual expenses were leaked to a national newspaper, leading to widespread condemnation of those who abused the system, and a perceived loss of public confidence in Parliament and its ability to regulate itself.

Several Ministers and Members of Parliament tendered their resignation, and many of those accused of abusing the system have been ordered to repay sums wrongly claimed. Many of the wrongful allowances and expenses claims had been approved by the Commons Department of Resources, the 'Fees Office', further fuelling the demand for parliamentary reform. The resignation of Ministers prompted a wide-scale Cabinet reshuffle, and threats to the leadership of the Prime Minister.

A further casualty of the scandal was the forced resignation of the Speaker of the House of Commons, Michael Martin, who had lost the confidence of MPs. The Speaker is chairman of the Members Estimates Committee which oversees the *Green Book*. This sets out the principles to which MPs are to adhere when making claims against allowances. He became the first

Speaker to be forced out of office since 1695. He resigned office following unprecedented cross-party calls for his resignation.

The allowances and expenses scandal led to the rapid introduction and passage of the Bill, which had the support of all political parties. The Act creates an Independent Parliamentary Standards Authority (IPSA) to regulate the system of pay and allowances, to formulate rules to deal with financial interests and to prepare a code of conduct on financial interests. The Act also provides for a Commissioner for Parliamentary Investigation who will investigate allegations of financial wrongdoing (section 9). Members' rights are protected under section 9(11) and (12) which provide for the right to make representations to the Commissioner, including the right to be heard in person and the opportunity, where the Commissioner considers it appropriate, to call and examine witnesses. The Commissioner will report to the Committee on Standards and Privileges which will make recommendations on appropriate sanctions to the House of Commons.

As originally presented to Parliament, the Bill introduced three new criminal offences, namely knowingly providing false or misleading information in a claim, failing to comply with the rules on the registration of financial interests and breaching the rules which prohibit paid advocacy. Concerns were expressed in both Houses that the offence of knowingly providing false or misleading information, carrying a maximum sentence of 12 months imprisonment, was an offence already covered by the Fraud Act 2006. The Fraud Act carries a far higher penalty, giving rise to allegations that Parliament was providing a 'softer' regime for MPs than that applying to the general public. Section 10 of the Act, however, retains the offence, with liability on conviction to a fine or a term of imprisonment not exceeding 12 months.

The offences relating to paid advocacy and of failing to declare financial interests were abandoned. The original Bill also contained a clause permitting evidence relating to parliamentary proceedings to be admissible in a court of law – removing the protection of privilege from MPs accused of an offence. This measure attracted serious concerns over the protection of parliamentary privilege under Article IX of the Bill of Rights 1689, and caused the clause to be withdrawn. Section 1 of the Act provides that:

> Nothing in this Act shall be construed by any court in the United Kingdom as affecting Article IX of the Bill of Rights 1689.

The Bill received the Royal Assent on 21 July 2009, having completed all its parliamentary stages in a month. The Act, following major amendments during its passage, is very different from the Bill, the government being forced to make concessions and accept amendments in order to get the Bill through before the parliamentary recess beginning on 21 July.

Constitutionally the Parliamentary Standards Act raises a number of issues. The Act for the first time establishes a body outside Parliament to regulate Parliament's affairs. Questions relating to Parliament's sovereignty and privilege inevitably arise. The question of who will oversee the working of the Independent Parliamentary Standards Authority and the Commissioner for Investigation also arises. The government's view is that the new Commissioner is not protected by parliamentary privilege. Would this, as Lord Mackay suggested in debate, mean that the Commissioner would be subject to judicial review? And would such a situation give rise to a difficulty in the relationship between Parliament and the courts?

Concerns over the working of the Act, so hastily drafted and passed by Parliament, led to the insertion of a 'sunset clause' – a provision stating that sections of the Act will cease to have effect at the end of a period of two years beginning on the date on which section 8 (relating to the code of conduct) comes into force (see section 15).

Summary

Parliament is made up of the elected House of Commons and the unelected House of Lords. The Prime Minister and a majority of ministers sit in the Commons. The law-making process involves both Houses, with the House of Commons having the power to override the objections of the House of Lords under the Parliament Act procedure. Both the Houses exercise scrutiny of legislation and scrutiny of government administration.

Much of the work of the Commons is undertaken by committees. Public Bill Committees scrutinise bills while Select Committees scrutinise government administration.

The composition of the unelected House of Lords has been the subject of debate for decades and further reform is expected – probably in the form of a fully elected House.

Both Houses of Parliament enjoy privileges and immunities designed to protect their proceedings from outside interference. Where an issue of privilege is raised, it is for Parliament – not the courts – to adjudicate upon the matter. Individual Members of both Houses also enjoy privileges. The most important of these is freedom of speech in the course of parliamentary proceedings.

Further reading

House of Commons: legislation

Blackburn, R and Kennon, A, *Parliament: Functions, Practice and Procedures*, 2nd edn, 2003, London: Sweet & Maxwell.

Brazier, A, Flinders, M and McHugh, D, *New Politics, New Parliament? A Review of Parliamentary Modernisation since 1997*, 2005, London: Hansard Society.

Cowley, P and Stuart, M, 'Parliament: A Few Headaches and a Dose of Modernisation' (2001), 54(3) Parliamentary Affairs, 442.

Oliver, D, 'Improving the Scrutiny of Bills: the Case for Standards and Checklists', [2006] PL 219.
Oliver, D, 'The Modernization of the United Kingdom Parliament', in *The changing Constitution*, J Jowell and D Oliver (eds), 6th edn, 2007, Oxford: OUP.

House of Commons: scrutiny

Judge, D, 'Whatever Happened to Parliamentary Democracy in the United Kingdom? (2004), 57(3) Parliamentary Affairs.
Leopold, P, 'Standards of Conduct in Public Life', in J Jowell and D Oliver (eds), *The Changing Constitution*, 6th edn, 2007, Oxford: OUP.
Maer, L and Sandford, M, *Select Committees under Scrutiny*, 2004, London: the Constitution Unit, UCL.
Oliver, D, 'The Challenge for Parliament, [2001] PL 666.
Tomkins, A, 'What is Parliament For?' in M Bamforth and P Leyland (eds), *Public Law in a Multi-Layered Constitution*, 2003, Oxford: Hart Publishing.

House of Lords

Bogdanor, V, 'Reforming the Lords: a Sceptical View', [1999] 70 Political Quarterly 375.
Hansard Society, *The Future of Parliament: Reform of the Second Chamber*, 1999, London: Hansard Society.
Royal Commission on Reform of the House of Lords, *A House for the Future*, Cm 4534, 2000, London: HMSO.
Russell, M, *Reforming the House of Lords: Lessons from Overseas*, 2000, OUP.
Russell, M and Cornes, R, 'The Royal Commission on the House of Lords: A House for the Future?', [2000] 64 MLR 82.

Parliamentary privilege

Geddis, A, 'Parliamentary Privilege: Quis Custodiet Ipsos Custodes?' [2005] PL 696.
Leopold, P, 'Free Speech in Parliament and the Courts' [1995] Legal Studies 15: 204.

? SELF-ASSESSMENT QUESTIONS

1. What is meant by the terms 'backbench' and 'front bench'?
2. Write a sentence explaining the constitutional importance of the Opposition and state who represents the Opposition.
3. List at least three functions of the House of Commons.
4. What are the principal functions of:

   (a) Public Bill Committees
   (b) Select Committees?

Continued

?

SELF-ASSESSMENT QUESTIONS (continued)

5. List four categories of persons who sit in the House of Lords.
6. List at least four functions of the House of Lords.
7. List at least four Acts of Parliament, which have reformed the House of Lords since the beginning of the twentieth century.
8. Name the constitutional source that provides for freedom of speech.
9. Write a brief definition of parliamentary privileges.
10. In addition to freedom of speech, list three other privileges.
11. Write a brief sentence explaining the meaning of the term 'proceedings in Parliament'.

SAMPLE EXAMINATION QUESTIONS

1. 'Parliamentary procedures provide adequate opportunities for backbenchers to scrutinise government policy.'

   Do you agree?
2. 'Paradoxically, the House of Lords is an essential and valuable second chamber.'

   Critically assess this statement.
3. Is parliamentary privilege an entirely anachronistic concept in a modern, democratic legislature?

Chapter 10

The protection of human rights

CONTENTS

KEY WORDS AND PHRASES

Convention on Human Rights and Fundamental Freedoms	The treaty setting out rights and freedoms to be protected by High Contracting Parties
Council of Europe	The body formed in 1949 to further the protection of human rights in Europe
Derogation	The suspension of a right in times of national emergency
High Contracting Parties	States that have signed the Convention
Margin of appreciation	The area of leeway, or discretion, left to governments
Proportionality	The action taken must be no more than necessary to achieve the objective
Reservation	A formally recorded limitation on the guarantee of a right

Introduction

The idea that individuals have rights that no government can violate has a long history, and is a key element in most written constitutions. In the United Kingdom, with its uncodified Constitution, the traditional approach to human rights has been rather different. Here, individuals are free to do whatever they please, provided that they do not contravene the law. Freedoms and rights exist but may be limited by what Parliament may enact. For example, in order to understand the scope (and limits) of the right to freedom of speech it is necessary to know that defamation (making wrongful and damaging falsehoods about another person) is actionable; that expression which threatens a breach of the peace or speech, which stirs up racial hatred, is a criminal offence. The 'right' is what remains once all the restrictions are considered.

This conventional approach must now be seen in light of both the European Convention on Human Rights and the Human Rights Act 1998, which makes the majority of Convention rights enforceable in the domestic courts. Before looking at these in detail, a brief overview of the history of rights is required.

The origins of rights

In Western societies Christian natural law has historically been highly influential. Natural law thought pre-dates Christianity and may be traced to the ancient Greek philosophers. Natural law theory in essence claims that there is a higher source of authority than the government. That higher source is – for Christian natural law theorists – God. For secular theorists, the higher source of authority is man's rationality, which enables humans to understand what is morally required for the law of the State to be valid and to require the obedience of its citizens. In either case – religious or secular – natural law sets moral standards with which the law must comply. Failure to comply with this essential morality would make the law of the State invalid. Furthermore, according to some theorists, if the law of the State (the positive law) fails to match up to moral standards, citizens are not obliged to follow that law. An immoral law is no law and creates no obligation of obedience. This, in turn, leads to questions about the obligation to obey law and the 'right' to be civilly disobedient in order to raise awareness about a morally repugnant law.[1]

Echoes of this natural law approach can be seen in *Dr Bonham's case*, in which Coke CJ declared that:[2]

> It appears in our books that in many cases the common law will control Acts of Parliament and sometimes adjudge them to be utterly void; for

1 The literature on civil disobedience is extensive. See Further reading at the end of this chapter.

2 (1610) 8 Co Rep 114a; 77 ER 646; 2 Brown 255.

> when an Act of Parliament is against the common right or repugnant or impossible to be performed the common law will control it and adjudge such Act to be void.

Sentiments such as these could not, however, survive the establishment of Parliament's sovereignty under the Bill of Rights 1689,[3] since which time it has been the duty of the courts to apply the will of Parliament.

In addition to natural law theory, there is the idea of the social contract, which has been discussed in Chapter 4. Essentially, social contract theory – of which there are many versions – provides that citizens enter into a contract to establish an ultimate power in the State. In return, the sovereign body is under a duty to protect its citizens and not to violate their rights. If the sovereign breaches the terms of the contract, citizens may overthrow that power and establish one that will comply with the contract.

It was not until the twentieth century that the international movement towards the better protection of rights began. Two world wars and the devastation and human suffering inflicted prompted the establishment of the United Nations (UN) and in 1948 the International Convention on Civil and Political Rights and the International Convention on Social and Economic Rights. The UN International Covenant on Civil and Political Rights became the basis for the introduction of regional Conventions, the European Convention on Human Rights and the Fundamental Freedoms being established under the Council of Europe.

The Council of Europe

In Europe, the Council of Europe was established in 1949 and, under its authority, the European Convention on Human Rights and Fundamental Freedoms came into being in 1951. The Council of Europe has a wider membership than the European Union (EU) and it has its own institutional structure.

The institutions

The Committee of Ministers

The Committee of Ministers is made up of the foreign secretaries of the High Contracting Parties (States). The Committee of Ministers receives all of the Court's judgments. The Committee may request the Court to give an advisory opinion on the interpretation of the Convention and its protocols.

3 On which see Chapter 5.

The Parliamentary Assembly

The Parliamentary Assembly comprises representatives from the 47 Member countries, which together debate rights issues.

The Human Rights Commissioner

The Human Rights Commissioner investigates rights' issues and reports to the Assembly.

The European Court of Human Rights

The Court of Human Rights sits in Strasbourg, France. Each High Contracting Party has one judge. The Court sits in Committees of three judges and Chambers of seven judges.[4] Above these Chambers is the Grand Chamber, a Court comprising 17 judges.

Qualifications for appointment include the requirement that a person be of 'high moral character' and possess the qualifications required for appointment to high judicial office in their own State or to be 'jurisconsults of recognised competence'.

The Parliamentary Assembly of the Council of Europe elects judges to office, by a majority vote cast from a list of three candidates nominated by the High Contracting Party. Judges are elected for a renewable six-year term of office.

The European Convention on Human Rights and Fundamental Freedoms

The European Convention on Human Rights (the ECHR) protects civil and political (as opposed to economic and social) rights. Some of these rights are absolute, others are subject to restrictions on various grounds. The rights protected are:

Article 1	imposes a duty on 'High Contracting Parties' to protect the Convention rights of everyone within their jurisdiction;
Article 2	provides the right to life;
Article 3	is an absolute prohibition against torture, inhuman or degrading treatment;
Article 4	prohibits slavery and forced labour;
Article 5	provides the right to liberty and security of the person;
Article 6	provides the right to fair trial;
Article 7	prohibits the retrospective imposition of criminal liability;
Article 8	protects the right to private and family life;

4 Article 27 ECHR.

Article 9	protects freedom of thought, conscience and religion;
Article 10	provides for freedom of expression;
Article 11	protects the right to freedom of peaceful assembly and association;
Article 12	protects the right to marry;
Article 13	provides the right to an effective remedy for the violation of rights;
Article 14	provides that there should be no discrimination in the enjoyment of the rights listed above.

The impact of the Convention prior to the Human Rights Act 1998

The Convention is an agreement under international law. As such, according to British constitutional theory, the Convention could not be directly applied under domestic law without an Act of Parliament to give it effect. Accordingly, the Convention could only have influential effect. Two cases that illustrate this are:

R v Secretary of State for the Home Department ex parte Brind (1991).[5] In this case, the Home Secretary had exercised a discretionary power to issue a notice prohibiting the broadcasting of the voices of any person speaking on behalf of a terrorist organisation. In a challenge primarily based on the UK government's duties under Article 10 of the Convention, the House of Lords accepted that there was a presumption that Parliament intended to comply with its obligations under international law, and to make law which complied with the Convention. However, since at the time Convention rights were not incorporated into domestic law, the House of Lords took the view that where a domestic Act of Parliament permitted two interpretations, the interpretation to be preferred was that which was in line with Convention requirements.[6]

Derbyshire County Council v Times Newspapers Ltd (1993). In this case, which involved the question whether a local authority could sue in defamation, the Court of Appeal had stated that where there was ambiguity in English law the court was obliged to consider Article 10 of the Convention. The House of Lords, however, while agreeing with the

5 [1991] 1 AC 696; [1991] 1 All ER 720.
6 See also *Derbyshire County Council v Times Newspapers* [1993] AC 534.

decision of the Court of Appeal, ruled that it had come to its decision relying on the common law, not the Convention.

Convention protocols

Since the Convention was drafted there have been a number of protocols drawn up, which confer additional rights to those rights protected under the main Convention.

These rights are as follows:

The right to property

The right is to the 'peaceful enjoyment of possessions.' The right does not impair the right of the State to make laws regulating the use of property or the raising of taxes.

The right to education

This Article provides that no one shall be denied the right to education. It also confers on parents the right to ensure that their children's education is in conformity with their own religious and philosophical convictions.

The right to free elections

The right to regular elections 'at reasonable intervals' is provided for. The right includes the right to a secret ballot.

Prohibition of imprisonment for debt

This provides that no one shall be imprisoned because of their inability to fulfil a contractual obligation.

Freedom of movement

The right confers on everyone lawfully within a country to move freely within it and to choose his or her place of residence. The right also includes the right to leave any country, including one's own. The rights are subject to such restrictions as are in accordance with law and necessary in a democratic society in the interest of national security or public safety, the maintenance of public order, the prevention of crime or for the protection of rights and freedoms of others.

Freedom from expulsion

No citizen of a country may be expelled from his or her own country. Furthermore, no one may be deprived of the right to enter into the country of which s/he is a citizen.

Protection is also given to non-citizens, in that the collective expulsion of aliens is prohibited.

Abolition of the death penalty

The death penalty is abolished. There can be no derogations from or reservations made in relation to this protocol.

Procedure

Applicants

Applications may be made by individuals or by 'any High Contracting Party' to the Convention alleging that another Member State has violated the Convention. The latter are known as 'inter-state applications'.

Admissibility criteria

In order to have a complaint considered by the European Court of Human Rights the following requirements must be adhered to:

- the applicant must have exhausted all domestic remedies: that is, if there is any remedy available in domestic law, it must be pursued.
- the application must be made within six months from the date on which the final decision was made.
- the Court may not deal with an individual application that is:

  (a) anonymous;
  (b) substantially the same as a matter that has already been considered by the court;
  (c) incompatible with the provisions of the Convention;
  (d) manifestly ill-founded;
  (e) an abuse of the right of application.

The court's decision

Once an application has been declared admissible the Court will examine the facts of the case, with the assistance of the representatives of the parties. Note that the individual applicant does not appear in person before the Court.

The Court will attempt to achieve a *friendly settlement* with the State concerned.[7] If a friendly settlement is achieved the case will be struck out of the list by a decision that is confined to the facts and the solution reached.[8]

The decisions of the Grand Chamber are final: there is no further appeal available. Parties to the proceedings may request that a decision of a Chamber be referred to the Grand Chamber 'in exceptional cases'. The request must be made within three months of the Chamber's decision. A panel of five judges of the Grand Chamber examine the request and will accept it if the case:

> 'raises a serious question affecting the interpretation or application of the Convention or the protocols thereto, or a serious issue of general importance.'[9]

Decisions of a Chamber become final when:

(a) the parties declare that they will not request that the case be transferred to the Grand Chamber;
(b) three months after the date of judgment, if reference of the case to the Grand Chamber has not been made;
(c) when a panel of the Grand Chamber rejects the request to refer the case.[10]

States undertake to abide by the final judgment of the Court.[11]

Derogations and reservations

Where a State finds it impossible to comply with specific Articles, it is possible to enter a derogation. No derogation is permitted in respect of Article 2 (the right to life) other than in wartime, and no derogation is permitted from Articles 3 (freedom from torture, etc), 4 (freedom from slavery) and 7 (non-retrospectivity).

In order to lodge a derogation, there must be a situation amounting to 'war or other public emergency threatening the life of the nation'. Furthermore, the derogation must be no greater than strictly required in the circumstances. The Secretary General of the Council of Europe must be kept informed as to the measures taken and also informed of when such measures cease to

7 Article 38 ECHR.
8 Article 39 ECHR.
9 Article 43 ECHR.
10 Article 44 ECHR.
11 Article 46 ECHR.

operate.[12] It is for the Court of Human Rights to rule on the legality of a derogation.

A reservation is a limitation on a right. The First Protocol to the Convention provides the right to education. In 1952, the British government entered a reservation in respect of this right, providing that it is guaranteed in the UK 'only so far as it is compatible with the provision of efficient instruction and training, and the avoidance of unreasonable public expenditure.'[13]

Under the Human Rights Act, section 16, both Houses of Parliament must approve a derogation within 40 days of the order being made. There is no such requirement in relation to reservations, which are within the discretion of the executive. The Human Rights Act, section 17, requires that these be reviewed by the relevant minister every five years.

The Human Rights Act 1998

The Human Rights Act 1998 incorporates most of the substantive rights protected under the European Convention. It also ends decades of debate as to how best to protect Convention rights within the domestic legal system.

The Human Rights Act is an 'ordinary' Act of Parliament insofar as no special procedures needs to be employed to amend or repeal it. However, in *R v Secretary of State for the Home Department ex parte Simms* (1999)[14] Lord Hoffman in the House of Lords stated that the Act had 'constitutional status', the effect of which is that the courts will not allow the doctrine of implied repeal to operate to undermine the Act, and if Parliament intends to amend the Act it must do so expressly.[15]

The Act extends the protection of the European Convention of Human Rights to all those present within the UK. It also extends to those territories outside the UK, which are under the effective control of the UK government. This 'extra-territorial' application is exceptional. In *R (Al-Skeini and Others) v Secretary of State for Defence* (2007),[16] the House of Lords ruled that the Convention operates extraterritorially in circumstances where the State is in military occupation of another country and has effective control. It will also operate in relation to diplomatic embassies/consulates abroad and also on ships and vessels registered as flying the UK flag.

The Act was drafted with the intention that the normal constitutional relationship between Parliament and the judges should be preserved. Whereas under written constitutions it is usual for judges to be able to invalidate legislation that conflicts with fundamental rights, the Human Rights Act

12 Article 15 ECHR.
13 See now the Human Rights Act 1998, Schedule 3, Part II.
14 [2000] 2 AC 115.
15 On implied repeal see Chapter 5.
16 [2007] UKHL 26; [2007] 3 WLR 33.

preserves Parliament's sovereign law-making power and expressly states that when a breach of Convention rights is found by the courts the validity or continuing application of the offending law is not affected. This will become clearer as we examine the individual sections of the Act.

The Act in outline

Section 1	Incorporates Articles 2 to 12 and 14 (and specified Protocols) of the Convention into domestic law.
Section 2	Requires courts to 'take into account' decisions taken by the ECHR institutions.
Section 3	Directs the courts to interpret domestic legislation in line with the Convention 'so far as it is possible to do so'.
Section 4	Enables the High Court and higher courts to grant 'Declarations of Incompatibility'. This does not affect the validity or continuing operation of the incompatible legislation (section 4(6)).
Section 5	Enables ministers to become parties to proceedings.
Section 6	Provides that it is unlawful for public bodies to act in a way that is incompatible with Convention rights. 'Public bodies' includes the courts but excludes Parliament.
Section 7	Entitles 'victims' or potential victims to bring proceedings against public bodies, within one year of the act complained of.
Section 8	Provides that a court or tribunal may grant remedies for breaches of Convention rights.
Section 9	Restricts actions relating to judicial acts to exercising rights of appeal or to judicial review and prevents damages being granted in respect of judicial acts.
Section 10	Enables a minister to make a 'remedial order' rectifying defective legislation if there are 'compelling reasons' to do so.
Section 11	Provides that Convention rights do not restrict any other right existing under domestic law.
Section 12	Prevents courts making orders restraining freedom of expression unless certain conditions are met.
Section 13	Provides that courts must have 'particular regard' for the importance of the right to freedom of thought, conscience and religion in deciding any question which might affect its exercise.
Section 14	Regulates derogations.
Section 15	Regulates reservations
Section 19	Requires ministers to certify, before second reading of a Bill, whether the Bill complies with Convention rights or not.

Making an application

The requirement is that only a victim or potential victim of a breach of a Convention right may apply. This is a more restricted test than that of 'sufficient interest' in judicial review proceedings (See Chapter 13).

The proceedings must be brought within one year of the act in question, although the court or tribunal may extend this period.

Public authorities

It was Parliament's intention that only agents of the State should be required to comply with Convention rights. However, public authorities are not defined under the Act, other than to state that a public authority includes courts and tribunals, excludes Parliament, and includes 'any person certain whose functions are of a public nature'. In other words, it is not the ownership – public or private – which determines whether a body is a public authority or not, but whether the functions it performs are of a public nature. This has led to difficulties, as best illustrated by the case of *YL v Birmingham City Council*.[17]

> The applicant was living in a private residential home for elderly people. She had been placed there by the local authority which paid her fees, save for a small 'top up' amount paid by her relatives. The company which ran the home sought to terminate its contract with the local authority for her care, and have her removed from the home. The applicant sought the protection of the court, arguing that the care home was exercising public functions and therefore obliged to protect her Convention rights (in this case Article 8, the right to respect for private and family life). The matter went to the House of Lords.
>
> The House of Lords ruled that the care home was private, not public. Accordingly, while the applicant had rights against the local authority, she had none against the care home. The Court said that there was a distinction to be made between the local authority which had a statutory duty[18] to arrange for care and accommodation, and the care home which was a private company, providing care and accommodation under a contract with the local authority and on a commercial profit-making basis rather than by a subsidy from public funds.

17 [2007] UKHL 27; [2007] 3 WLR 112.
18 Under the National Assistance Act 1948.

Two judges – Lord Bingham of Cornhill and Baroness Hale of Richmond – dissented from the majority, both arguing that the situation in *YL* was exactly the sort of situation which Parliament intended to be covered by the Human Rights Act 1998.

In *Billesley Parochial Church Council v Wallbank* (2001)[19] the House of Lords ruled that a church council, which had statutory duties to enforce parish church repairs was not a public authority. Although the Church of England had special links with central government and performed certain public functions it was not a core public authority for the purposes of the Human Rights Act.

A restrictive approach to 'public authority' was also taken in *R (Heather) v Leonard Cheshire Foundation* (2002).[20] This again involved a residential care home. The Foundation was a private charity that provided accommodation for disabled people, some of which was funded by the local authority. The Court ruled that apart from the public funding, there was nothing about the Foundation, which had a public nature: it did not 'stand in the shoes of the local authority'.

The interpretative duty: sections 2 and 3

Section 2 of the Human Rights Act requires the judges to 'take into account' decisions made under the European Convention by the institutions in Europe 'so far as, in the opinion of the court or tribunal, it is relevant to the proceedings . . .'. Note that this falls far short of a direction to follow the decisions of the Court of Human Rights and gives to the judges a degree of freedom in relation to the binding nature of those decisions.

A degree of flexibility is also evident in section 3. The interpretative duty is to read and give effect to domestic legislation (primary and secondary) in a way that is compatible with Convention rights 'so far as it is possible to do so'. This clearly envisages situations where the judges find it impossible to interpret domestic law in a compatible manner, as the case law below illustrates. Furthermore, section 3 makes it clear that the validity, continuing operation or enforcement of any incompatible primary legislation is not affected by interpretation. In relation to secondary legislation, its validity and continuing operation and enforcement is not affected in situations where the relevant primary legislation prevents removal of the incompatibility.

19 [2001] 3 All ER 393.
20 [2002] TLR 8 April.

Limits to the interpretative duty

Re W and B (Children: Care Plan) (2002).[21] In this case the Court of Appeal had ruled that there should be implied into the Children Act 1989 a system whereby local authorities with responsibilities towards children in their care should operate a 'starred milestones' system for monitoring a child's progress. On appeal to the House of Lords, the Court ruled that section 3 of the Human Rights Act preserved the boundary between interpretation by the courts and the enactment of statutes by Parliament. The Court of Appeal's ruling went beyond the boundary of interpretation and exceeded its judicial jurisdiction.

Pearce v Governing Body of Mayfield School (2001) and *Secretary of State for the Home Department v Wainwright* (2002).[22] In the Mayfield School case, the Court of Appeal ruled that since the conduct complained of was before the coming into effect of the Human Rights Act, there could be no remedy. The Human Rights Act is not retrospective in effect. Similarly, in the *Wainwright* case, the Court of Appeal ruled that since there was no common law tort of invasion of privacy, and since the conduct complained of preceded the Human Rights Act there could be no remedy.

Vertical and horizontal effect

It was Parliament's intention that the duty to comply with Convention rights should be imposed only on those public bodies carrying out functions for which the government has responsibility. That is vertical effect: the duty imposed on government moving downwards to its agents or institutions. It was not intended that private non-governmental bodies should be required to be Convention-compliant.

However, as a result of section 6(3) of the Act, which includes courts and tribunals within the definition of 'public authority', the courts have felt obliged to protect Convention rights against private bodies – introducing horizontal effect. This is the natural consequence of the combination of sections 6(3) and 6(1), which provides that:

> It is unlawful for a public authority to act in a way which is incompatible with a Convention right.

21 [2002] 2 All ER 192.
22 [2001] IRLR 669; [2004] 2 AC 406; [2003] 3 All ER 969.

The case law on freedom of expression and privacy illustrates this horizontal effect.

Venables v News Group Newspapers (2001).[23] In this case the court granted an indefinite injunction restraining newspapers from publicising the identity or whereabouts of two young men who had been convicted, while children, of killing a toddler. The court recognised that newspapers were not public authorities but decided that the court itself had to protect Convention rights. Accordingly, the court protected the rights of the former prisoners against the right to freedom of expression of newspapers.

Freedom of expression of the press was again at issue in *Douglas v Hello! Ltd.* (2001).[24]

In this case, the actors Michael Douglas and Catherine Zeta-Jones had granted *OK!* Magazine exclusive rights to publish photographs of their wedding. *Hello!* magazine obtained photographs and were subjected to an injunction restraining them from publishing them. It was accepted that the actors had lessened their right to privacy by allowing another magazine to publish photographs. Accordingly, the injunction was lifted – freedom of expression winning over the right to privacy.

A rather different result was reached in *Campbell v Mirror Group Newspapers* (2002). (See also Chapter 11.)

The Mirror Group disclosed information about the model Naomi Campbell and published photographs of her leaving a particular venue. The court once again had to balance the right to privacy and the right to freedom of expression. Awarding damages to Ms Campbell, the court ruled that the intrusion into her privacy was exacerbated by the photographs – the right to privacy here prevailed over the newspaper's right to freedom of expression.

23 [2001] 1 All ER 908.
24 [2001] 2 All ER 289; (2000) 9 BHRC 543.

Declarations of Incompatibility

The High Court and higher courts may grant Declarations of Incompatibility; courts lower in the court structure may not, although they have the power to grant other remedies for the breach of rights. A Declaration of Incompatibility acts as a signal to the government and Parliament that a law is contrary to the requirements of the Convention.

Section 4(6) makes it clear that a Declaration of Incompatibility does not affect 'the validity, continuing operation or enforcement of the provision in respect of which it is given.' Accordingly, the incompatible law remains in force and in operation unless and until it is reformed.

Amending the law

There are two principal ways of changing the law to make it compatible with Convention rights. The first is through the ordinary legislative process, discussed in Chapter 9. This, however, can be time-consuming. The Human Rights Act 1998, section 10, accordingly makes it possible for the relevant minister to amend the law by order.

The conditions under which a remedial order can be made are first that a Declaration of Incompatibility has been made and secondly that if there is an appeal available that it has been made or the relevant person states in writing that they do not intend to appeal, or that the time for an appeal has passed and no appeal made in that time.

A further criterion for the making of a remedial order is where there is a finding of the Court of Human Rights, which necessitates a change in the law. In addition to the above, the minister must consider that there are 'compelling reasons' for proceeding under section 10. Where these criteria are satisfied the minister may, by order, amend both primary and secondary legislation.

The power to make remedial orders is subject to the requirement that Parliament approve the changes made.[25]

Statements of compatibility: section 19

In order to ensure that the law complies with Convention rights, section 19 of the Human Rights Act 1998 requires that the relevant minister must, before second reading of a Bill, state whether the Bill is Convention-compatible. However, preserving Parliament's sovereign law-making right, section 19(1)(b) provides that if the minister does not consider the Bill to be Convention-compatible he must make a statement to the effect that although

25 If an Order has been made without prior approval (because of urgency), it will cease to have effect if a Resolution is not passed by each House of Parliament at the end of a period of 120 days following the making of the Order: Human Rights Act 1998, Schedule 2, para 4.

the Bill is not Convention-compatible, the government nevertheless wishes to proceed with the Bill.

The effect of this is that the government is intentionally breaching a Convention right, thereby setting the scene for a future challenge before the courts.

Derogations and reservations

Derogations and reservations are regulated under sections 14 and 15, respectively, and Schedule 3 to the Act.

Case law under the Human Rights Act 1998

Since coming into effect in Scotland in 1998 and England and Wales in 2000, there have been numerous cases brought under the Act. In this section a few illustrative cases are presented so that we can begin to evaluate the effectiveness of the Act.

Article 2: the right to life

In *National Health Service Trust A v M* (2001)[26] the court applied the principle established in *Airedale National Health Service Trust v Bland* (1993),[27] namely that the lawful withdrawal of treatment in a case where a patient was in a permanent vegetative state does not infringe the right to life.

In *R (Pretty) v Director of Public Prosecutions* (2001)[28] the House of Lords ruled that Article 2 was designed to protect life and did not include the right to terminate one's own life. Mrs Pretty was seeking to protect her husband from prosecution for aiding her suicide. She subsequently lost her case before the Court of Human Rights.

In *Van Colle v Chief Constable of Hertfordshire Constabulary* (2007)[29] the Court of Appeal ruled that the failure of the police to protect a vulnerable prosecution witness violated the right to life and the right to family life (Article 8). However, on appeal to the House of Lords, the Court overturned the Court of Appeal's decision, ruling that for a breach of Article 2 to occur the police knew or ought to have known that there was a real and immediate risk posed to the life of an individual. In this case, on the facts, it could not reasonably have been anticipated that there was such a risk.[30]

26 [2001] 1 All ER 801.
27 [1993] AC 789.
28 [2001] UKHL 61; [2001] 3 WLR 1598.
29 [2007] 1WLR1821.
30 [2008] UKHL 50; [2008] 3 WLR 593.

Article 2 includes a procedural duty to hold a public enquiry into situations where a person is seriously injured or killed while in the custody of the State.[31]

Article 3: freedom from torture, inhuman and degrading treatment and punishment

The failure of the State to provide the bare necessities of life to an asylum seeker is capable of violating Article 3.[32]

However, the House of Lords ruled in *N v Secretary of State for the Home Department* (2005)[33] that returning a seriously ill illegal immigrant to her country of origin where it was alleged that her life expectancy would be reduced, would violate Article 3 only in exceptional circumstances.

Article 5: the right to liberty

R (H) v Mental Health Review Tribunal, North and East London Region (2001).[34] In this case the applicant was detained under the Mental Health Act 1983. The Act provided that it was up to the patient to prove that he or she was no longer suffering from a mental disorder warranting detention. The Court of Appeal ruled that this provision (section 72) which reversed the burden of proof, could not be read in a manner compatible with the Convention. A Declaration of Incompatibility was granted and the Secretary of State made a remedial order under section 10 of the Human Rights Act 1998.

The independence of the Parole Board – the body which determines whether a prisoner is eligible for being released on licence – is coming under increasing challenge. The issue was raised in:

R (Girling) v Parole Board (2005).[35] The Home Secretary was under a duty to refer matters regularly to the Board, and his or her failure

31 See for example *R (Amin) v Secretary of State for the Home Department* [2003] UKHL 51.

32 See *R (Limbuela) v Secretary of State for the Home Department* [2005] UKHL 66; [2005] TLR 4 November.

33 [2005] UKHL 31; [2005] 2 AC296; [2005] 2 WLR 1124.

34 [2001] 1 FCR 206; [2001] All ER 429.

35 [2005] EWHC 546; [2006] 1 WLR 1917.

to do so would be corrected by judicial review. The Home Secretary's power to issue directions to the Board was to be confined to the Board's administrative functions, not its judicial functions. Although there was some trespass to the Board's independence it was not sufficiently serious to deprive the Parole Board of its character as a judicial body.

Article 6: the right to fair trial

The overall approach of the courts is to look at the overall fairness of a trial, rather than focus on alleged detailed irregularities.

- Where there has been a defect in proceedings which is remedied through the appeal process or through judicial review, the courts will be slow to make a finding that Article 6 has been violated;
- Article 6 has been employed to assess whether an oral hearing must always be allowed;
- whether a hearing is free from bias, whether the presence of temporary judges who have been appointed by the executive can be 'fair and impartial';
- whether evidence which has been unlawfully obtained may be used in court;
- whether a delay between charges being made and a trial violates Article 6;
- whether the presumption of innocence is harmed by a statutory requirement that a driver disclose to the police the name of the driver.

The House of Lords issued a Declaration of Incompatibility in:

R (Anderson) v Secretary of State for the Home Department (2002).[36] The Declaration related to section 29 of the Crime (Sentences) Act 1997, which conferred on the Home Secretary the power to determine the time to be served for punitive purposes by defendants convicted of murder and sentenced to life imprisonment. The provision was incompatible with the right to have one's sentence imposed by an independent and impartial tribunal.

36 [2002] UKHL 46.

Article 7: freedom from retrospectivity

The most significant case under this provision remains *R v R* (1991),[37] the marital rape case in which the House of Lords ruled, and the Court of Human Rights affirmed, that a husband should no longer have a legal immunity from the law in relation to the rape of his wife. The Court of Appeal applied the precedent of *R v R* in *R v C*, ruling that the conviction for a rape committed some 30 years previously did not violate Article 7.

Article 8: the right to respect for private and family life

Article 8 protects privacy in relation to a person's 'private and family life, his home and correspondence'.

> In *R (Daly) v Secretary of State for the Home Department* (2001)[38] the House of Lords ruled that the Home Office policy of requiring prisoners to leave their cells while officers conducted searches – which included privileged legal correspondence – was unlawful.

As the case law discussed above at page 153 shows, Article 8 has been used successfully by people in the public eye to protect their privacy. *Campbell* was considered in *Murray v Express Newspapers plc* in which it was held by the House of Lords that a child of a famous parent was entitled to privacy when going about their ordinary daily activities such as walking down the street or shopping.

The Court of Appeal also extended the right to privacy – through its interpretation of the scope of confidence – in *McKennitt v Ash.*[39] Buxton LJ stated that the first question for the court to ask was whether the information was 'private in the sense that it was in principle protected by Article 8. If it was not, that was the end of the case.' However, if the answer was 'yes', then the court had to consider whether, in all the circumstances, the interests of the owner of the private information had to give way to the right of freedom of expression conferred by Article 10. It was the balance between these two Articles that was crucial.[40]

37 [1991] 2 WLR 1065.

38 [2001] UKHL 26; [2001] 2 AC 532.

39 *Times LR* 20 December 2006; [2007] 3 WLR 194.

40 The Court rejected the argument that it would be a defence to establish that the information disclosed was in fact untrue.

In *HRH Prince of Wales v Associated Newspapers Ltd* (2007),[41] a former member of the Prince's staff disclosed to the defendant copies of travel journals written by the Prince. These were intended to remain confidential and not intended for publication. Lord Phillips of Worth Matravers CJ stated that the courts 'have extended the law of confidentiality so as to protect Article 8 rights in circumstances which do not involve a breach of a confidential relationship.'[42]

The Court of Appeal returned to its analysis of breach of confidence and privacy in *Lord Browne of Madingley v Associated Newspapers* (2007). The chief executive of a major international company, had obtained an interim injunction restraining the defendant newspaper from publishing information concerning his private life and business activities. The Master of the Rolls stated that the Court should first decide whether Article 8 is engaged; then consider whether Article 10 is engaged and then proceed to decide whether the applicant '. . . has shown that he is likely to establish at a trial that publication should not be allowed within the meaning of section 12(3) . . . '[43]

Article 8 has also been invoked in relation to:

- whether planning laws infringe a Gypsy's right to a home;
- whether the sale of the electoral register without permitting an individual to remove his name infringes the right to privacy;
- whether deportation orders violate the right to family life.

Article 9: freedom of religion and conscience

Article 9 has been used to challenge a school's uniform policy. In *R (Shabina Begum) v Denbigh High School* (2006)[44] the House of Lords ruled that the refusal to allow a pupil to wear a jilbab did not violate Article 9. The school offered a choice of uniforms and had been sensitive to the religious requirements of pupils.

Article 9 has also been used – unsuccessfully – to challenge a school policy not to use corporal punishment on pupils[45] and equally unsuccessfully to challenge the prohibition on cannabis, which it was claimed was needed for religious worship.[46]

41 [2006] EWHC 522 (Ch); [2006] EWCA Civ 1776; [2007] 3 WLR 222.

42 The Court ruled that Prince Charles had 'an unanswerable claim for breach of privacy. When the breach of a confidential relationship is added to the balance, the case is overwhelming': paragraph 74.

43 See also *Lord Browne of Madingley v Associated Newspapers Ltd.*

44 [2006] 2 WLR 719.

45 *R v Secretary of State for Education ex parte Williamson* [2005] unreported.

46 *R v Taylor (Paul Simon)* [2001] 98 9450 LSG 25.

Article 10: freedom of expression

Article 10 has to be considered in its own right, but also in relation to Article 8, the right to privacy. Section 12 of the Human Rights Act requires a court to have particular regard for freedom of expression when considering whether to grant an interim injunction restraining publication. The court should not make such an order unless it is satisfied that when the issues are fully considered at a trial, the person seeking to restrain publication would be likely to succeed.

For the manner in which the courts balance the right to privacy and freedom of expression see further Chapter 11.

Article 11: freedom of association

The right to peaceful demonstration and protest is inextricably linked to the powers of the police to control demonstrations in the interests of public order. The case law is accordingly focused on whether the actions of the police in relation to protesters have been reasonable or proportionate to the requirements of public order.

For example, in *R (Laporte) v Chief Constable of Gloucestershire Constabulary* (2004)[47] the police had ordered coaches carrying demonstrators to an airbase where they intended to protest against the Iraq war, to return to London and provided an escort to ensure that they did not stop. The court ruled that the police action violated the demonstrators right to liberty (Article 5).

By contrast, in *Austin v Commissioner of the Metropolitan Police* (2007)[48] the court ruled that the police had acted lawfully when confining some 3,000 protesters within an area. The police argued that they feared unrest and that it had been impossible to arrest them all.

Article 12: the right to marry

Article 12 has been used to challenge a discriminatory statutory scheme, which required those who are subject to immigration control to apply to the Home Secretary for permission to marry. See *R (Baiai) v Secretary of State for the Home Department* (2007).[49]

47 [2005] 2 WLR 789.
48 [2008] 2 WLR 415.
49 [2007] 3 WLR 573.

Summary

The European Convention on Human Rights has provided invaluable protection for citizens against the power of the State. The case law has led to many changes in the law. However, the procedure of applying to Strasbourg has always been complex and time-consuming. The incorporation of Convention rights into domestic law was a logical step forward for a government seriously committed to individual rights and freedoms and represents a significant extension of the rule of law. Incorporation of Convention rights may also change the traditional public conception of individual freedoms in favour of rights, and brings a greater clarity to the law relating to both civil liberties and human rights.

Further reading

Allan, TRS, 'Human Rights and Judicial Review: A critique of "due deference"' [2006] CLJ 671.

Bamforth, N, 'The True "Horizontal Effect" of the Human Rights Act 1998' (2001), 117 LQR 34.

Beyleveld, D and Pattinson, S, 'Horizontal Applicability and Horizontal Effect' (2002), 118 LQR 623.

Craig, P, 'The Courts, the Human Rights Act and Judicial Review' (2001), 117 LQR 589.

Edwards, R, 'Judicial Deference under the Human Rights Act' [2002] 65 MLR 859.

Fredman, S, 'Human Rights Transformed: Positive Duties and Positive Rights' [2006] PL 498.

Gearty, C, 'Reconciling Parliamentary Democracy and Human Rights [2006] LQR 118: 248.

Gearty, C, *Can Human Rights Survive?* (2006), Cambridge University Press (Hamlyn Lectures).

Harris, DJ, 'Human Rights or Mythical Beasts' [2004] LQR 120.

Harvey, C, 'Talking about Human Rights [2004] EHRLR 500.

Hickman, TR, 'Between Human Rights and the Rule of Law: Indefinite Detention and the Derogation Model of Constitutionalism [2005] MLR 655.

Irvine of Lairg (Lord), 'The Impact of the Human Rights Act: Parliament, the Courts and the Executive [2003] PL 308.

Jowell, J, 'Judicial Deference and Human Rights: a Question of Competence, in P Craig and R Rawlings (eds), *Law and Administration in Europe*, 2003, Oxford University Press.

Jowell, J, 'Judicial Deference, Servility, Civility or Institutional Capacity?' [2003] PL 592.

Klug, F, 'A Bill of Rights: Do we need one or do we already have one?' [2007] PL 701.

Klug, F and Starmer, K, 'Standing Back from the Human Rights Act: How Effective is it Five Years On?' [2005] PL 716.

Lester, A, 'The Utility of the Human Rights Act: a Reply to Keith Ewing' [2005] PL 249.

Lester, Lord and Clapinska, L, 'Human Rights and the British Constitution', in J Jowell and D Oliver (eds), *The Changing Constitution* (6th edn, 2007) Oxford: OUP.
Nicol, D, 'Law and Politics after the Human Rights Act' [2006] PL 722.
Oliver, D, 'Functions of a Public Nature and the Human Rights Act' [2004] PL 329.
Sedley, Sir Stephen, 'The Rocks or the Open Sea: Where is the Human Rights Act Heading?' (2005), 32 J Law & Soc. 3.
Steyn, Lord, 'Deference: a Tangled Story' [2005] PL 346.
Steyn, Lord '2000–2005: Laying the Foundations of Human Rights Law in the United Kingdom' [2005] EHRLR 349.
Wade, Professor Sir William 'Horizons of Horizontality' (2000) 116 LQR 217.
Young, A, 'A Peculiarly British Protection of Human Rights [2005] 68 MLR 858.

? *SELF-ASSESSMENT QUESTIONS*

1. Under which organisation was the European Convention on Human Rights (ECHR) introduced?
2. List at least six rights protected under the ECHR.
3. List at least three criteria for an application under the ECHR to be admissible.
4. What do you understand by the word 'derogation'?
5. What is the definition of a 'public body' under the Human Rights Act 1998 (HRA)?
6. Who may make an application under the HRA? May interest/pressure groups apply?
7. Write a sentence explaining the status and effect of a 'declaration of incompatibility'.
8. Is the Human Rights Act 1998 entrenched? Or is it an 'ordinary statute'?

SAMPLE EXAMINATION QUESTIONS

1. 'Incorporation of the Convention rights through the Human Rights Act 1998 ensures the supremacy of Parliament over the rights of individuals.'

   Discuss.
2. With the Human Rights Act 1998, rights and freedoms have moved centre stage in the Constitution.

   Discuss.

Chapter 11

Freedom of expression and privacy

CONTENTS

KEY WORDS AND PHRASES

Breach of confidence	the unauthorised disclosure of information imparted in a confidential situation or relationship
Defamation	the wrongful publication (oral or written) of a falsehood that is damaging to the reputation of another
Incitement	to stir up or provoke to action
Privilege	the legal protection conferred on certain circumstances or material that provides a defence in a legal action. Privilege may be absolute or qualified.
Qualified privilege	the material is privileged, provided that the person publishing it did not do so maliciously.

Introduction

Freedom of expression is an essential feature of a free and democratic society. Without freedom of expression, there could be no exchange of ideas, no political debate. A free press is equally essential. In this chapter we will consider the law relating to freedom of expression and its limitations. We will also consider privacy of the individual. At first glance it might seem curious to link freedom of expression with the 'right' to privacy – not least because there is, under domestic law as usually understood, no 'right' to privacy. The justification for linking these two concepts lies in the way in which an aspect of freedom of expression – its limitation under the law relating to confidential disclosures – has led to the protection of privacy by the courts. This development is recent and in strict contradiction of the intention of the government when introducing the Human Rights Act 1998.

Freedom of expression

The right to freedom of expression is guaranteed by the European Convention on Human Rights, Article 10 which provides that:

> Everyone has the right to freedom of expression. This right shall include freedom to hold opinions and to receive and impart information and ideas without interference by public authority and regardless of frontiers. This article shall not prevent States from requiring the licensing of broadcasting, television or cinema enterprises.
>
> The exercise of these freedoms, since it carries with it duties and responsibilities, may be subject to such formalities, conditions, restrictions

> or penalties as are prescribed by law and are necessary in a democratic society, in the interests of national security, territorial integrity or public safety, for the prevention of disorder or crime, for the protection of health or morals or for the protection of the rights and freedoms of others. This article shall not prevent the imposition of lawful restrictions on the exercise of these rights by members of the armed forces, of the police or of the administration of the State.

Before considering the impact of Article 10, it is necessary to discuss domestic law. The starting point for this exercise is to remember that under domestic law, the traditional approach to civil liberties is that everything is allowed provided that it is not prohibited by law. In other words, 'rights' are more accurately defined in a negative way as 'freedoms under the law'. In order, therefore, to understand the scope of freedom of expression it is necessary to consider those aspects of the law that restrict it.

Restrictions on freedom of expression

Defamation: slander and libel

It is a civil wrong (a 'tort'), actionable at law, to damage the reputation of another by publishing a falsehood. The 'publication' may be in oral or written form: slander or libel. There are a number of defences to an action for defamation, which include the following:

> **Truth** If the damaging publication is true, then there can be no remedy for defamation.
>
> **Fair comment** This is rather more vague, but in essence it will be a defence to an action in defamation if the damaging publication represents what a reasonable person would regard as 'fair comment'.

In addition to the above offences, an action for defamation may not succeed because the situation in which it took place attracts privilege – absolute or qualified.

Absolute privilege means that there is a situation that is completely immune from legal proceedings. A prime example of this is parliamentary privilege, discussed in Chapter 9. When a Member of Parliament (MP) participates in parliamentary proceedings, s/he is absolutely protected by the law, and cannot be sued even where a clear defamatory statement has been made. The justification for this exemption from the law lies in the need for a full and frank debate on matters of public interest, debate that might be inhibited by the threat of legal proceedings.

Absolute privilege also protects information provided to the police, and to those who act as witnesses in legal proceedings.[1]

Qualified privilege, on the other hand, provides protection from the law of defamation on the condition that the damaging publication has not been made maliciously. Malice will remove the protection of privilege. Newspaper reports of parliamentary proceedings are covered by qualified privilege.[2]

Sedition, incitement to disaffection

It is a criminal offence to use freedom of expression in such a way as to undermine the security of the State.

Sedition is a common-law offence, which may involve the spoken word or written materials. The words used must be intended to bring the Crown or government 'into hatred or contempt' or 'incite disaffection against the Crown or government. The words used must be such that they are intended to promote violence or public disorder.

The Incitement to Disaffection Act 1934 provides that it is an offence intentionally to attempt to dissuade members of the armed forces from complying with their duty. The same offence applies to intentionally attempting to dissuade police officers from complying with their duty.[3]

Incitement to racial or religious hatred

Freedom of expression is also restricted by the need to protect minority groups from demeaning and discriminatory speech. The Public Order Act 1986, sections 17–23 regulates incitement to racial hatred. It is a criminal offence to use language – spoken or written – which is 'threatening, abusive or insulting', and which is intended to incite racial hatred.

The need to protect minorities from religious hatred is recognised under the Racial and Religious Hatred Act 2006, which amends the Public Order Act 1986. To use 'threatening words or behaviour' is unlawful if the person intends to stir up religious hatred. The publication and distribution of material, or the public performance of a play is also unlawful if the material involves the use of threatening words or behaviour and is intended to stir up religious hatred.

In order to protect freedom of speech and prevent the law being used oppressively, section 29J of the Public Order Act 1986 provides that the Act shall not be used in a way that 'prohibits or restricts discussion, criticism or expressions of antipathy, dislike, ridicule, insult or abuse of particular

1 See *Taylor v Director of the Serious Fraud Office* [1999] 2 AC 177; *Buckley v Dalziel* (2007) Times LR 7 June.

2 Defamation Act 1996, s 15, and Sched I, Pt I.

3 Police Act 1997, s 91.

religions or the beliefs or practices of their adherents . . .'. The Act also provides that the prohibition does not apply to fair and accurate reports of parliamentary proceedings or judicial proceedings.[4]

Obscenity and indecency

The Obscene Publications Act 1959 makes it an offence to publish an obscene article. An article is defined as obscene if 'its effect . . . is . . . such as to deprave and corrupt persons who are likely to read, see or hear the matter contained or embodied in it.'[5]

What must be proved is not that the article is obscene, but that it is capable of 'depraving' or 'corrupting' a significant proportion of persons likely to read or see the article.

The law is little used.

Conspiracy to corrupt public morals

This is a common-law offence first recognised in *Shaw v Director of Public Prosecutions*[6] in which the House of Lords upheld the conviction of the publisher of a directory, giving details of prostitutes' services (at a time when prostitution was unlawful). The House of Lords ruled that it had a residual power to protect the 'moral welfare of the state'.

Blasphemy and blasphemous libel

Blasphemy is a common-law offence that protects the Christian faith – but not other faiths – from abuse. The Law Commission – the body with a duty to keep the law under review – recommended in 1985 that the offence be abolished but the government has not acted on it. The leading case remains *R v Lemon* (1979).[7] In this case a gay magazine published a poem and illustration depicting Christ at the crucifixion. The House of Lords upheld the conviction, ruling that a publication calculated to outrage and insult a Christian person's religious belief amounted to blasphemy – even though there was no intention to cause outrage.

The European Court of Human Rights, in *Wingrove v United Kingdom*[8] upheld the right of the state to control blasphemous materials.

4 Public Order Act 1986, s 29K.
5 Obscene Publications Act 1959, s 1.
6 [1962] AC 220.
7 [1979] AC 617.
8 (1996) 24 EHRR 1.

Contempt of court

Conduct that is designed to 'obstruct, prejudice or abuse the administration of justice' is a contempt of court.[9] This may involve behaviour in court that disrupts proceedings. A contempt is also committed if a person disobeys a court order. The law is regulated by the Contempt of Court Act 1981.

It is an offence to 'interfere with the course of justice in particular legal proceedings, regardless of intent to do so' (section 1). Freedom of expression is protected by the provision that fair and accurate reports of legal proceedings, or discussions of general public interest are not to be treated as contempt.

The Official Secrets Acts 1911 and 1989

Under section 2 of the Official Secrets Act 1911 it was a criminal offence to disclose any official information without authorisation. The effect of section 2 was that all Crown servants – civil servants, members of the armed forces and police – were under a duty of non-disclosure in relation to any information they acquired. There was no defence of public interest.

High-profile prosecutions under section 2 led to its reform. Central to this was the case of *R v Ponting* (1985).[10] Clive Ponting was a senior civil servant at the Ministry of Defence. Concerned that the government was misleading Parliament over the sinking of an Argentinian ship by a British submarine during the Falklands War, Ponting passed information to an MP. Ponting argued that there was a public interest defence, but this the trial judge rejected. However, notwithstanding the clear breach of the Act, the jury refused to convict, leading to further calls for reform of the law.

The Official Secrets Act 1989 reformed the law. The 1989 Act provides that there are four categories of information that must not be disclosed:

- security and intelligence;
- defence;
- international relations; and
- criminal investigations.

The Act covers Crown servants and government contractors. Crown servants are defined as being a Minister of the Crown or members of the Scottish Executive, civil servants, members of naval, military or air force, the police. A government contractor is one who is not a Crown servant but who provides goods or services to Crown servants.[11]

The Act introduces the concept of 'damaging disclosure'. In relation to members of the security and intelligence services, it is a criminal offence to

9 Report of the Phillimore Committee on Contempt of Court, Cmnd 5794, 1974, p 2.
10 [1985] Crim LR 318.
11 Official Secrets Act 1989, s 12.

disclose any information without lawful authority. In relation to other Crown servants, however, the unauthorised disclosure will only be guilty of an offence if the disclosure is 'damaging'. The concept of damaging disclosure also applies in relation to defence, international relations and crime.[12]

The law of confidence

Under common law, if information is received in a situation where the recipient knows or ought to know that the information is confidential and therefore not to be disclosed to others, that confidentiality is protected by law. Any unauthorised disclosure is actionable.

Originally, actions for breach of confidence were mainly used to protect trade secrets. However, the law has expanded into many other areas, proceeding on a case-by-case basis. The disclosure of information may amount to a breach of confidence if the relationship is based on marriage or a contract of employment or potentially any situation involving a confidential relationship.

There are a number of defences to an action for breach of confidence, including:

Staleness: In *Attorney General v Jonathan Cape Ltd*[13] (1976), for example, it was held that the publication of a former Cabinet minister's diaries which disclosed – in breach of the convention – the substance of Cabinet discussions should not be restrained by injunction on the basis that the information was some ten years old and that no harm would come from its disclosure.

The material is already in the public domain: Where information is readily available, the courts may refuse to enforce a duty of confidence. This issue was central to whether an injunction to prevent the former MI5 officer Peter Wright's book, *Spycatcher*, should be continued. The book was freely available outside the UK and therefore in the public domain.

To correct false information: If it is necessary to breach a duty of confidence in order to correct some falsehood, that will be a defence to an action.

To reveal evidence of a crime: Breach of confidence may be excused if the defence of revealing criminal or fraudulent activities are made out.

12 In relation to crime the concept is complex and outside the scope of this work. See R Stone, *Textbook on Civil Liberties and Human Rights*, Oxford: OUP 2006, Chapter 8.

13 [1976] 1 QB 752.

Public interest: If information is revealed in breach of confidence, it is a defence to prove that its disclosure is in the public interest. For example, in *Lion Laboratories v Evans and Express Newspapers*[14] (1984) the newspaper revealed details of faulty breathalyser machines, which could have resulted in wrongful convictions for driving under the influence of alcohol. The matter was of public interest, which overrode any claim to confidentiality.

Privacy under the ECHR Article 8

The European Convention on Human Rights, Article 8, provides for a right to privacy in relation to one's private and family life, home and correspondence (see also Chapter 10). Article 8 provides:

> Everyone has the right to respect for his private and family life, his home and his correspondence.
>
> There shall be no interference by a public authority with the exercise of this right, except such as is in accordance with the law and is necessary in a democratic society in the interests of national security, public safety or the economic well-being of the country, for the prevention of disorder or crime, for the protection of health or morals, or for the protection of the rights and freedoms of others.

A summary of illustrative case law from the European Court of Human Rights may be considered under the following headings:

- respect for individual privacy, including private sexual life; and
- privacy of the family.

Respect for individual privacy

- In *Malone v United Kingdom* (1984) the Court ruled that the absence of statutory authority for intercepting an individual's communications was unclear and 'lacking the degree of protection to which citizens are entitled under the rule of law in a democratic society . . .'.[15]
- In *Khan v United Kingdom* (2000) covert surveillance by the police without statutory authority violated Article 8.[16]

14 [1984] 2 All ER 417.

15 See also *McLeod v United* Kingdom (1999); *Armstrong v United* Kingdom (2002); *Taylor-Satori v United Kingdom* (2002); *MG v United Kingdom* (2002). The government's response to *Malone* was to introduce the Interception of Communications Act 1985: see, further, Chapter 24.

16 See now Police Act 1997. See, also, *Wood v United Kingdom* (2004).

- In *Halford v United Kingdom* (1997) the Court ruled that it was unlawful to intercept an employee's telephone calls at work.
- In *Dudgeon v United Kingdom* (1982) the prohibition on homosexual conduct between adult males was ruled unlawful.[17]

Privacy of the family

- In *Hoffmann v Austria* (1994), the law denying a woman custody of her children on grounds of her religious belief was unlawful.[18]
- In *TP and KM v United Kingdom* (2001), the separation of a mother and daughter for nearly a year violated Article 8.[19]
- In *Buckley v United Kingdom* (1997), the Court ruled that there was no violation of Article 8 by the authorities denying a Gypsy the right to live on her own land without planning permission: the legal restriction pursued a legitimate aim and were proportionate to the aim pursued.[20]

The law of confidence and privacy

In recent years the law of confidence has been developing to protect the privacy of public figures. It should be noted at the outset that there has never been, under English law, a 'right to privacy'. Whether such a right is now established is questionable. In the absence of a legal *right to privacy* under domestic law, the law of confidence – now interpreted in light of the Human Rights Act 1998 – has proven central to extending the legal protection of aspects of privacy. Key factors in recent developments include the following:

- Section 6 of the Human Rights Act, which requires the courts, as a public body, to comply with Convention rights and thereby enables the courts to give horizontal effect to Convention rights;[21]
- Article 8 of the Convention: the right to respect for private and family life, home and correspondence;
- Article 10 of the Convention: the right to freedom of expression, which includes restrictions on that right expressed as follows:

17 Leading to the Homosexual Offences (Northern Ireland) Order 1982 reforming the law. See, also, *Lustig-Praen v United Kingdom* and *Smith and Grady v United Kingdom* (2000): the ban on homosexuals in the armed forces violated Article 8. See, also, *ADT v United Kingdom* (2000): the ban on consensual sexual acts between more than two men in private was unlawful.

18 (1994) 17 EHRR 293.

19 Compare *G v United Kingdom* (2000).

20 See also *Chapman v United Kingdom* (2001).

21 Meaning that private bodies are required to comply with the Convention: see, further, page 151ff.

> The exercise of these freedoms, since it carries with it duties and responsibilities, may be subject to such formalities, conditions, restrictions or penalties as are prescribed by law and are necessary in a democratic society . . . **for preventing disclosure of information received in confidence** . . .

- Section 12 of the Human Rights Act, which provides that where there is an application to a court to restrain in advance the publication of information, or prevent further publication of information to which confidentiality applies:

> (3) No relief [affecting the exercise of freedom of expression] is to be granted so as to restrain publication before trial unless the court is satisfied that the applicant is likely to establish that publication should not be allowed.

In *Campbell v MGN* (2004)[22] the House of Lords upheld the award of damages to the model Naomi Campbell. Balancing the 'right to privacy' against the right of the media to publish information, the House of Lords ruled that Ms Campbell's privacy had been infringed. The reporting of her attending a drug treatment clinic of itself did not invade her privacy, but the publication of photographs of Ms Campbell 'added greatly' to the intrusion on her private life.

Since that case, the law has been developing to extend the right to privacy of figures in the public eye. In *McKennitt v Ash* (2007),[23] *HRH Prince of Wales v Associated Newspapers Ltd* (2007)[24] and *Lord Browne of Madingley v Associated Newspapers Ltd* (2007),[25] the courts have extended the law of confidence in a manner that protects the Article 8 right to privacy – despite the intention of the government that the Human Rights Act should not be used as a vehicle for introducing a right to privacy into English law.

Summary

Freedom of expression is a fundamental constitutional right. Before incorporation of Convention rights under the Human Rights Act 1998, it was regulated by both common law and statute. Consistent with the traditional British approach to civil liberties, the scope of freedom of expression was defined by the restrictions placed on it – it was residual. Accordingly, to understand what freedom of expression entails, it has been necessary to

22 [2005] 1 WLR 3394.
23 [2007] 3 WLR 194.
24 [2007] 3 WLR 222.
25 [2007] 3 WLR 289.

examine all the restrictions. Although Parliament did not intend that the Act should be used to develop a right to privacy – by restricting the freedom of the press, for example, in relation to celebrities and public figures – the courts have been steadily developing the law of confidence in a manner that grants a right to privacy. The law in this area is still evolving.

Further reading

Amos, M, 'Can We Speak Freely Now? Freedom of Expression under the Human Rights Act' [2002] EHRLR 750.
Barendt, E, *Freedom of Speech* (2nd edn, 2005) OUP.
Edwards, S, 'On the Contemporary Application of the Obscene Publications Act 1959' [1998] Crim LR 843.
Jaconelli, J, 'Defences to speech crimes' [2007] EHRLR 27.
Miller, CJ, 'Some Problems of Contempt' [1992] Crim LR 107.
Morgan, J, 'Privacy in the House of Lords Again' [2004] 120 LQR 563.
Stone, R, *Textbook on Civil Liberties and Human Rights* (7th edn, 2008), Oxford: OUP.

? *SELF-ASSESSMENT QUESTIONS*

1. Explain what is meant by the phrase 'civil liberties'.
2. What is the distinction between civil liberties and rights?
3. List five different legal restrictions on freedom of expression.
4. Explain what is meant by 'contempt of court'.
5. Is there a right to privacy under English law?

SAMPLE EXAMINATION QUESTIONS

Critically assess the impact of the Human Rights Act 1998 on freedom of expression.

Chapter 12

Freedom of assembly and public order

CONTENTS

KEY WORDS AND PHRASES

Affray	Conduct giving rise to violence
Assembly	Two or more persons gathered in public
Harassment	Conduct causing alarm or distress
Procession	A body of persons moving along a route
Riot	Twelve or more persons acting violently

Introduction

Closely linked to freedom of expression, freedom of assembly and public order law relate to the right of individuals to gather together for the purpose of expressing their views. The right to political protest is extremely important to the democratic process, and represents the most direct and immediate way in which people can express their concerns. However, because demonstrations, whether in the form of processions or a static gathering, can cause inconvenience to the general public, public order law imposes conditions and restrictions on rights of assembly. What is important is whether the law strikes an appropriate balance between protecting the right to demonstrate with the more general right of society to public order. Article 11 of the European Convention on Human Rights provides:

> Everyone has the right to freedom of peaceful assembly and to freedom of association with others, including the right to form and to join trade unions for the protection of his interests.
>
> No restrictions shall be placed on the exercise of these rights other than such as are prescribed by law and are necessary in a democratic society in the interests of national security or public safety, for the prevention of disorder or crime, of the protection of health or morals or for the protection of the rights and freedoms of others. This article shall not prevent the imposition of lawful restrictions on the exercise of these rights by members of the armed forces, of the police or of the administration of the State.

Before considering the impact of Article 11 on this right, the domestic law needs to be explained.

Freedom of assembly

An individual is free to assemble with others to the extent that the law does not prohibit such assemblies or the assembly does not involve unlawful actions. Consistent with the traditional approach to civil liberties, the 'right' – or 'freedom' – is one that can only be understood when the legal restrictions on its exercise are understood.

The right to assembly on private land is restricted by the law relating to trespass – a person is civilly liable unless present with the consent of the owner of the property. The right to assemble on land to which the public have a right of access is controlled by local authority by-laws. In relation to particular public sites – such as Trafalgar Square and Parliament Square in London – there are statutory controls. As will be discussed below, assemblies and processions are regulated under the Public Order Act 1986.

Indirect restrictions on the right of assembly

Breach of the peace and obstructing the police

If the police reasonably believe that the words or actions of an individual or group will lead to a breach of the peace, the police may order that person or persons to move on and/or stop the conduct in question. Breach of the peace is now the only ground on which the police may arrest a person under common law. A constable may arrest a person who is causing a breach of the peace or who is acting in a manner that causes the officer to reasonably believe that a breach of the peace is about to occur (an 'apprehended' breach of the peace). Where there is no actual breach of the peace, the courts have stressed that the power of arrest should be exercised only where strictly necessary.

A breach of the peace was defined in *R v Howell* (1982)[1] as follows:

> . . . there is a breach of the peace whenever harm is actually done or is likely to be done to a person or in his presence his property or a person is in fear of being harmed through an assault, an affray, a riot, unlawful assembly or other disturbance.

If a person is acting lawfully and an actual or apprehended breach of the peace is caused by the violence of others, then the person acting lawfully is not liable for the breach of the peace: *Beatty v Gillbanks* (1882). However, in *Duncan v Jones* (1936)[2] the court took a less sympathetic view. The defendant intended to address a gathering on a street near a training centre for the

1 [1982] QB 416.
2 [1936] 1 KB 218.

unemployed. A police officer, fearing a repeat of a former disturbance at the centre which occurred on the same day as the defendant addressed a meeting at that site, ordered the defendant to move to a nearby street. She refused and was arrested for obstructing a police officer in the execution of his duty. Dismissing her appeal, the court ruled that there was a connection between the earlier meeting and the disturbance and that accordingly the police officer was entitled to reasonably apprehend a breach of the peace.

There will, in general, be a close connection between the conduct in question and the breach of the peace. Two cases that raise this issue are *Moss v McLachlan* (1985) and *R (Laporte) v Chief Constable of the Gloucestershire Constabulary* (2006).

In *Moss v McLachlan* the police intercepted striking miners who were going to support their fellow workers at Nottingham collieries. Those who refused to obey the order to turn around were arrested for obstructing a police officer in the execution of his duty.[3] Dismissing an appeal the court ruled that the fact that there was between one and a half and five miles between the spot at which they were stopped and the collieries did not mean that the police could not reasonably apprehend a breach of the peace.

A different result was reached in *Laporte*, which had the benefit of the Human Rights Act being in force. Some 120 protesters were travelling in three coaches to join a demonstration against the Iraq war at an air force base. On the orders of a Chief Superintendent the coaches were ordered to return to London without stopping. Laporte sought judicial review and the matter went to the House of Lords. The House of Lords ruled that there was no imminent breach of the peace. The action of the police in imprisoning the defendant on the coach for over two hours was disproportionate and amounted to a breach of Article 5, the right to liberty.

The European Court of Human Rights examined the rights of protesters in *Steel and others v United Kingdom* (1999).[4] Three situations were examined. In relation to Steel, the applicant was protesting at a grouse shoot, and walked in front of a member of the shoot to stop him firing. In the second situation, there was a protest against a motorway extension in which the

3 Under s 51(3) Police Act 1964, now s 89(2) Police Act 1996.
4 (1999) 28 EHRR 603.

protesters climbed trees and climbed on to a JCB digger. In the third situation, the applicants were holding banners and handing out leaflets outside a conference centre in London.

The Court of Human Rights ruled that the arrest of the third applicants was unlawful and violated the right to liberty. Their protest was entirely peaceful. The police's actions were not proportionate or necessary and therefore not justifiable under Article 10(2). The right to liberty of the other applicants, however, was not infringed – their conduct could have provoked violence in others and the arrest was therefore justified. In relation to freedom of expression (Article 10), the Court ruled in relation to the first two applicants that the arrests were designed to achieve a legitimate aim under Article 10(2) – namely the prevention of disorder and protecting the rights of others. The arrests were not disproportionate.

The power of the police to detain people in order to prevent the outbreak of violence and ensure their peaceful dispersal was considered by the House of Lords in *Austin v Commissioner of Police of the Metropolis* (2009).[5] On 1st May 2001 a crowd of demonstrators assembled in Oxford Circus, Central London. By the afternoon there were some 3,000 people assembled in Oxford Circus and thousands more in adjoining streets. Fearing violence, the police sealed off the area, detaining the demonstrators for seven hours. The stated objective of the police was solely to ensure that there was a controlled release of the crowd.

The claimant sought damages for false imprisonment and for breach of her right to liberty under Article 5 of the Convention. The House of Lords dismissed her appeal. Lord Hope pointed out that Article 5 makes no reference to restrictions on the right in the interests of public safety or the protection of public order. Nevertheless, measures taken in the interests of public safety were designed to protect people from violence. Provided that the action was taken in good faith and proportionate to the situation, the action was lawful.

Public order law

In order to balance the right of protesters to demonstrate and the right of the general public to a peaceful and safe environment, the law imposes controls on public protest. The Public Order Act 1986, as amended, is the relevant statute. The Act distinguishes between public processions and assemblies.

5 [2009] UKHL 5; [2009] 2 WLR 372.

Public processions

A procession is not defined in the Act. In *Flockhart v Robinson* (1950)[6] a procession was defined as being '. . . not a mere body of persons: it is a body of persons moving along a route'. To be governed by the Act a procession must be in a public place, defined as being any highway and any place to which the public has access (section 16).

Giving notice: section 11

Section 11 or the Public Order Act 1986 requires that written notice be given to the police by the organisers of a public procession which is intended:

- to demonstrate support or opposition to the views or actions of any person or body of persons;
- to publicise a cause or campaign; or
- to mark or commemorate an event, unless it is not reasonably practicable to give any advance notice of the processions.

The requirement of notice does not apply to processions which are 'commonly or customarily held' or to funeral processions (section 11(2). The House of Lords considered section 11(2) in *R (Kay) v Commissioner of Police of the Metropolis*,[7] ruling that a monthly mass cycle ride through London did not require notification to the police under section 11(1) of the Public Order Act 1986.

The cycle rides have been held on the last Friday evening of the month since 1994. There is no advance planning of the route. Lord Phillips of Worth Matravers stated that the mass cycle ride was 'a procession' which was 'commonly or customarily held' in the area. However, since those who took part knew where the ride would start, it was unlikely that there was any advance planning or organisation. Accordingly, it was difficult to see how section 11 'could have any application to it'.

Imposing conditions: section 12

If a senior police officer reasonably believes that the procession may result in 'serious public disorder, serious damage to property or serious disruption to the life of the community, or the purpose of the persons organising the procession is to intimidate others, he or she may impose such conditions as are necessary. These include conditions as to the route of the procession or prohibiting the procession from entering a specified public place'.

6 [1950] 2 KB 498.
7 [2008] UKHL 69; [2008] 1 WLR 2723.

Banning orders: section 13

If a senior police officer considers that the powers under section 12 are insufficient to prevent serious public disorder, s/he may apply to the local authority for a banning order lasting no longer than three months.

Public assemblies

Section 16 of the Public Order Act 1986 defines a public assembly as an assembly of two or more persons in a public place that is wholly or partly open to the air.

Imposing conditions: section 14

A senior officer of police may impose conditions on a public assembly on the same grounds as for a procession. Directions may be made as to the place at which it may be held, its maximum duration, or the maximum number of persons who may attend, for the purpose of preventing 'disorder, damage, disruption or intimidation'.

Trespassory assemblies

A trespassory assembly is one held on land to which the public has no right of access, or a limited right of access and likely to be held without the permission of the occupier of the land, or that the assembly is likely to exceed the limits of any permission given. If a senior officer of police reasonably believes that the assembly might result in the serious disruption of the life of the community, or significant damage to a building or monument of historical, architectural, archaeological or scientific importance, the officer may apply to the local authority for a banning order. An assembly for this purpose is defined as one of 20 or more persons (section 14A).

> *Director of Public Prosecutions v Jones* (1999)[8] upheld the right to peaceful assembly. An order had been granted under section 14A prohibiting the holding of a public assembly within a four-mile radius of Stonehenge. A group was heading for Stonehenge, on the public highway, and was within the four-mile radius. The House of Lords ruled, by a majority, that the public had the right to use the highway for reasonable and usual activities, including peaceful assembly.

8 [1999] 2 AC 240.

Regulating protest in Parliament Square

The Serious Organised Crime Act 2005, sections 132–138, provides for the regulation of demonstrations within a 'designated area' – namely Parliament Square and the immediate surrounding area. The Act requires that those who organise a demonstration must give written notice to the Metropolitan Police Commissioner. The Commissioner is under a duty to authorise the demonstration, but may impose conditions. This power was considered in *R (Haw) v Secretary of State for the Home Department* (2006).[9] Brian Haw had been demonstrating in Parliament Square since 2000. The issue for the court was whether the 2005 Act applied to existing demonstrations. At first instance the court held that the Act did not apply retrospectively. On appeal to the Court of Appeal, the Court ruled that Parliament had intended that the Act apply to all demonstrations within the designated area.

The Metropolitan Commissioner had imposed conditions on Haw's site. These were challenged. The High Court ruled that the conditions were void on the grounds that they lacked clarity and were unworkable. The Court also held that the Commissioner had the right to delegate the power to impose conditions.[10]

Public order offences

The 1986 Public Order Act replaced a number of common law offences.

Riot: section 1

A riot is defined as being where 12 or more persons who are present together use, or threaten to use, unlawful violence for a common purpose and that their conduct is such as would cause a person of 'reasonable firmness' to fear for his or her personal safety. A riot may take place in public or private. The mental element, the *mens rea* is that a person 'intends to use violence or is aware that his conduct may be violent'. The offence is triable by jury and on conviction carries a maximum term of imprisonment of ten years.

Violent disorder: section 2

The offence of violent disorder differs from riot in two principal ways. First, there need only be three people involved. Secondly, there need be no common purpose. The offence is triable by jury or summarily (before magistrates) and carries a term of imprisonment of up to five years if tried by jury and up to six months if tried summarily.

9 [2006] All ER (d) 94; [2006] 2 WLR 50.
10 *Director of Public Prosecutions v Haw* [2007] EWHC 1931.

Affray: section 3

A person is guilty of an affray if s/he uses or threatens to use unlawful violence towards another and his or her conduct is such as would cause a person of 'reasonable firmness' present at the scene fear for his or her personal safety.[11] The offence may take place in public or private. As with violent disorder, the offence is triable by jury or before magistrates. It carries a maximum prison term of three years if tried on indictment, or up to six months before the magistrates.

Causing harassment, alarm or distress: sections 4, 5

Designed to deal with hooliganism and rowdy behaviour in public, it is an offence to use threatening, abusive or insulting words or behaviour causing harassment, alarm or distress. The words or behaviour must be in the presence of a person who is likely to be alarmed, and so on, but there is no need to prove that a person present was actually harassed, alarmed or distressed.

Harassment: the Protection from Harassment Act 1997

It is a criminal offence to pursue a course of conduct that amounts to harassment. An individual may seek an injunction against a person who is harassing them.

Incitement to racial hatred

The Public Order Act 1986 provides penalties for public order offences that are motivated, wholly or partly, by racial hostility.

Racial hatred is defined in section 17 as meaning '. . . hatred against a group of persons defined by reference to colour, race, nationality (including citizenship) or ethnic or national origins.

It is an offence to use 'threatening, abusive or insulting words or behaviour' or to display any written material that is 'threatening, abusive or insulting' with the intention to stir up racial hatred or in a situation where racial hatred is likely to be stirred up. It is a defence to prove that there was no intention to stir up racial hatred.

It is also an offence to publish or distribute material which is threatening, abusive or insulting', if it is intended to stir up racial hatred or is likely to do so. Having such material or visual images or sounds in one's possession is also an offence.

11 A person of reasonable firmness does not need to be present: it is sufficient that s/he would fear for their personal safety if they were at the scene.

Incitement to religious hatred[12]

Religious hatred is defined in section 29A as meaning '. . . hatred against a group of persons defined by reference to religious belief or lack of religious belief'.

It is an offence to use 'threatening words or behaviour' or to display any written material that is threatening. It is also an offence to publish or distribute such material, or be in possession of such material. In each case there must be the intention to stir up religious hatred. Any person who presents or directs the public performance of a play that uses threatening words, with the intention of stirring up religious hatred commits an offence.

In order to protect freedom of expression, section 29J Public Order Act 1986 provides that:

> Nothing in this Part shall be read or given effect in a way which prohibits or restricts discussion, criticism or expressions of antipathy, dislike, ridicule, insult or abuse of particular religions or the beliefs or practices of their adherents, or of any other belief system of the beliefs or practices of its adherents, or proselytising or urging adherents of a different religion or belief system to cease practising their religion or belief system.

The Crime and Disorder Act 1998 provided for increased penalties to be imposed in relation to public order offences[13] that are motivated by racial or religious hatred. Racial or religious aggravation is defined under section 28 of the Crime and Disorder Act 1998 as follows:

(a) at the time of committing the offence, or immediately before or after doing so, the offender demonstrates towards the victim of the offence hostility based on the victim's membership (or presumed membership) of a racial or religious group; or
(b) the offence is motivated (wholly or partly) by hostility towards members of a racial or religious group based on their membership of that group.

In addition, a court may take into account 'racial aggravation' when sentencing.[14]

12 Section 29A–29G Public Order Act 1986; inserted by the Racial and Religious Hatred Act 2006.

13 Sections 4 and 5 Public Order Act 1986; ss 20 and 47 Offences Against the Person Act 1861; common assault, criminal damage and harassment under the Protection from Harassment Act 1997.

14 Crime and Disorder Act 1998, s 82.

Anti-social behaviour orders

The Crime and Disorder Act 1998 introduced anti-social behaviour orders (ASBOs). An anti-social behaviour order is designed to protect the community from bad behaviour rather than punishing an offender. It is prospective in that it seeks to regulate future behaviour.

An anti-social behaviour order is a civil order issued by a magistrates' court. A local authority, chief constable or housing trust may apply for an order. In addition, an ASBO may be issued at the conclusion of other civil proceedings in a county court or following conviction for a criminal offence.

The grounds on which an ASBO can be issued are set out in section 1 of the Crime and Disorder Act 1998:

> . . . that the person has acted in an anti-social manner, that is to say, in a manner that caused or was likely to cause harassment, alarm or distress to one or more persons not of the same household as himself; and that such an order is necessary to protect the relevant persons from further anti-social acts by him.

Breach of an ASBO is a criminal offence carrying a maximum sentence of five years' imprisonment.

The Crime and Disorder Act 1998 introduced child curfew schemes, which enable a local authority or chief officer of police to ban children from a specified area unless they are in the care of an adult. The 2003 Anti-Social Behaviour Act supplements this power with power to disperse groups and to return unsupervised young people to their homes. The power to return young people home is coercive: see *R (W) v Richmond upon Thames LBC* (2006).[15]

Summary

The law seeks to balance the rights of individuals to gather together in support of or in opposition to various causes with the rights of the general public to a peaceful and secure society. The domestic law must be read in light of Convention rights now incorporated under the Human Rights Act 1998. In addition to regulating processions and assemblies, the Public Order Act 1986, as amended, places a number of common-law offences on a statutory basis. The law also seeks to protect minority groups by criminalising incitement to racial or religious hatred and providing for increased penalties for offences that are motivated by racial or religious hatred.

15 [2006] EWCA Civ 458.

Further reading

Ashworth, A, 'Social Control and "Anti-Social Behaviour": the Subversion of Human Rights' (2004) 120 LQR.

Bonner, D and Stone, R, 'The Public Order Act 1986: Steps in the Wrong Direction' [1987] PL 202.

Fenwick, H and Phillipson, P, 'Public Protest, the Human Rights Act' [2000] PL 627.

Geddis, A, 'Free Speech Martyrs or Unreasonable Threats to Social Peace? "Insulting" expression and section 5 of the Public Order Act 1986' [2005] PL 853.

Loveland, I, 'Public Protest in Parliament Square' [2007] EHRLR 251.

Stone, R, *Textbook on Civil Liberties and Human Rights* (7th edn, 2008), Oxford: OUP.

SELF-ASSESSMENT QUESTIONS

1. Explain the concept of 'breach of the peace'.
2. Is the definition of breach of the peace sufficiently clear?
3. Outline the conditions that may be imposed on (a) public processions; (b) public assemblies.
4. Which Act of Parliament regulates demonstrations in the vicinity of Parliament?

SAMPLE EXAMINATION QUESTIONS

To what extent does the law relating to public order achieve an appropriate balance between the rights and freedoms of individuals to demonstrate and the rights of others to a peaceful, secure society.

Chapter 13

Judicial review of administrative action

CONTENTS

KEY WORDS AND PHRASES

Intra vires	Within the scope of the power granted
Justiciability/non-justiciability	A self-imposed restriction on the subject-matter the courts will review based on the need to preserve the separation of powers between the judiciary and executive
Natural justice	The common law requirements (often incorporated into statute) of procedural fairness, which includes the right to a fair hearing before an impartial court
Proportionality	The requirement that the action taken be no more than required to achieve the objective
Public law	Law that relates to all in society, as compared with private law, which regulates the relationship between two or more people (for example a contract, or marriage)
Sufficient interest	The term denoting a person who has a legitimate interest in the matter challenged and is deemed to have 'standing' to apply for judicial review
Ultra vires	Outside the scope of power granted

Introduction

Judicial review lies at the heart of administrative law. It is a procedure that is designed to test and ensure the legality of acts of those public bodies – ministers of the Crown, local authorities, National Health Service Trusts, universities, and so on – on which Parliament has conferred powers. The requirement that public bodies act according to law involves a number of issues, such as:

- whether the public body has correctly interpreted its powers granted by statute or common law;
- whether any discretion conferred by statute has been lawfully exercised;
- whether the decision-maker has complied with the requirements of natural justice (or fairness);
- whether the decision-maker has violated a person's human rights as protected under the Human Rights Act 1998;
- whether the decision-maker has acted in a manner proportionate to the objective.

Judicial review is a specialised process and should not be confused with rights of appeal. The differences between judicial review and an appeal are:

- whether or not an appeal is available is a matter of law and if available the individual has a right to pursue an appeal;
- by contrast there is no 'right' to judicial review: an application must be made and the court will decide whether the necessary criteria for review exist or not;
- where an appeal is available, the court will consider the verdict reached in the court below and if necessary overrule that verdict and substitute its own decision;
- by contrast with judicial review, the court is not concerned with the merits of the case but rather with the question of whether the procedure used to reach the decision was correct or not. The court will not substitute its own decision but will require the original decision-maker to reconsider the matter and decide the issue according to law;
- if an appeal is successful, there is a right to a remedy. By contrast in judicial review, there is no right to a remedy: it is discretionary.

From a constitutional standpoint, judicial review upholds both the will of Parliament and the rule of law by ensuring legality of those to whom power has been delegated. However, it is important that the judiciary does not interfere in decisions that are more appropriately taken by the democratically elected and accountable government. The judges use the concepts of justiciability and non-justiciability to decide where the boundary lies between the correct scope of the judicial function and areas best left to the executive.

Making an application for judicial review

The basis for judicial review lies in section 31 of the Supreme Court Act 1981 and the Civil Procedure Rules 1998. Combined, the law requires that the applicant must have a 'sufficient interest' in the matter to which the application relates and that the application must be made within three months of the decision against which review is sought, unless statute provides for a shorter period for challenge.

In addition to the requirements of standing and time limits, the matter must be one involving a public body and be a matter of public law.

Public bodies and public law

There is no strict definition of what constitutes a public body for the purposes of judicial review. It is not a matter simply of whether the body is owned by the State or is in private ownership. Nowadays, many functions for which the State is responsible are in fact undertaken by bodies that are privately owned. It is for the court to decide, on an application for judicial review, whether or not the body in question is a 'public body' for judicial review purposes. Again, it is necessary to look at some illustrative case law.

In *R v City Panel on Takeovers and Mergers ex parte Datafin Ltd*[1] the court ruled that although the City Panel had no statutory or other legal source of power, it was nevertheless subject to judicial review on the basis that if the Panel did not exist, its functions would have to have been undertaken by a government department.

Compare that case with *R v Disciplinary Committee of the Jockey Club ex parte Aga Khan*.[2] The Jockey Club disqualified a winning horse from a race for failing a dope case. On an application for judicial review of the decision, the Court ruled that the relationship between racehorse owners and the Club, and the powers of the Club, derived from an agreement between the parties. Accordingly it was a matter of private, not public law.[3]

Judicial review includes safeguards (the requirements of standing and time limits for example) for public bodies to prevent unjustified challenges to the administrative process. If an issue is governed by private law, then the aggrieved person should pursue a legal remedy in private law proceedings: not through judicial review. The case of *O'Reilly v Mackman*[4] illustrates what has become known as the 'exclusivity principle', by which public and private law are kept separate.

1 [1987] QB 815.

2 [1993] 1 WLR 909.

3 Note that the definition of public bodies for the purposes of the Human Rights Act 1998, unlike the position for judicial review, is laid down by statute. This may lead to differences between interpretations.

4 [1983] 2 AC 237.

The applicants for judicial review had taken part in a prison riot and the Board of Visitors, which had disciplinary powers, had imposed a penalty. The applicants tried to establish that the Board had acted contrary to the rules of natural justice. This they tried to do using the private law procedure, which does not require the leave of the court. The House of Lords ruled that it would be contrary to public policy to allow an applicant to evade the provisions of the judicial review procedure.

There may be cases that involve matters of both public and private law, and here the court has a discretion as to whether or not to grant an application for judicial review. A case that illustrates this point well is:

Wandsworth London Borough Council v Winder.[5] In this case, the House of Lords allowed a matter of public law (the lawfulness of the Council's decision) to be used as a defence to private law proceedings (for possession of property) commenced by the Council. Winder sought to argue in his defence that the decision of the Council to raise rents was void on the ground that it was unreasonable. The Court, citing *O'Reilly v Mackman*, recognised that the interests of good administration required protection from 'unmeritorious challenges' but that this had to be weighed against the rights of private citizens to protect themselves against unfounded claims. In this case, Winder had not initiated proceedings: he was merely trying to defend himself against the act of the Council.

The 'exclusivity principle' was also undermined in:

Roy v Kensington and Chelsea and Westminster Family Practitioner Committee.[6] The applicant sought to recover payment withheld by the Family Practitioner Committee (a public law body). The High Court ruled that it was a matter of public law and proceedings should be through judicial review. On appeal to the House of Lords, the Court ruled that where a litigant had a private law right in relation to a matter that involved a matter of public law, he was not to be denied a remedy in private law proceedings.[7]

5 [1985] AC 461.

6 [1992] 1 AC 624.

7 See also *Mercury Communications Ltd v Director General of Telecommunications* [1996] 1 WLR 48; *O'Rourke v Camden London Borough Council* [1997] 3 WLR 86; *Trustees of the Dennis Rye Pension Fund v Sheffield City Council* [1997] 4 All ER 747.

'Sufficient interest' or locus standi

Also referred to as 'standing' and in Latin *locus standi*, the requirement of sufficient interest is designed to ensure that individuals who have only a casual or passing interest in the matter do not interfere with the administrative process. As with the requirement of complying with time limits, sufficient interest is designed to strike a balance between ensuring that public bodies act lawfully and enabling those who are carrying out state functions to achieve their legitimate objectives without undue interference.

Individuals whose legal rights are adversely affected by a decision of a public body will generally be deemed to have sufficient interest. However, the courts recognise that there are also representative bodies and pressure groups that act on behalf of others, or act more generally in the public interest, and where this is the case the court may hold that the body in question has sufficient interest. However, there is no hard and fast rule and the court has discretion in the matter. It is necessary to look at some illustrative case law to see how the courts decide the issue.

Individual interests

In *Schmidt v Secretary of State for Home Affairs*[8] students who had been refused permission to remain once their permitted period of stay in the United Kingdom had expired had sufficient interest to challenge the decision of the Home Office which affected their personal liberty.

Representative groups acting on behalf of their members

In *R v Liverpool Corporation ex parte Liverpool Taxi Fleet Operators' Association*[9] the Association which represented taxi drivers had standing to apply for judicial review of the Corporation's decision to increase the available number of taxi licences without consulting the taxi drivers.

Similarly, in *Royal College of Nursing v Department of Health and Social Security*[10] the Royal College had sufficient interest to challenge the Department's circular relating to the role of nurses in abortions operations.

8 [1969] 2 Ch 149.
9 [1972] 2 QB 299.
10 [1981] AC 800.

Groups acting in the public interest

Here, in order to prevent too wide a scope for interference in the administrative process, the courts may be restrictive. Compare the following cases:

R v Secretary of State for the Environment ex parte Greenpeace Ltd (No 2).[11] The court ruled that Greenpeace had sufficient interest to challenge the decision of the Inspectorate of Pollution to allow the siting of a nuclear reprocessing plant at Sellafield. Greenpeace had over 400,000 supporters in the United Kingdom and it was in the interests of justice to allow the action on behalf of all those concerned with the decision.

By contrast, in *R v Secretary of State for the Environment ex parte Rose Theatre Trust Company Ltd*[12] the Court ruled that the company did not have sufficient interest to challenge a decision affecting the future of the Shakespeare's Globe Theatre site in London. The Company had thousands of supporters but there was no membership list as such.

Time limits

Under the Civil Procedure Rules 1998, an application for judicial review must be made within three months of the decision being challenged.[13] This rule does not apply where an Act of Parliament provides for a shorter time limit. A shorter time limit is applied, for example, in relation to planning matters as the following case illustrates:

Smith v East Elloe Rural District Council.[14] By statute, any challenge to a compulsory purchase order had, by statute, to be made within six weeks. The applicant sought, some six years later, to challenge the order on the basis that the clerk of the Council had acted in bad faith. The House of Lords ruled that the words of the statute were clear and there could be no exception to its application.[15]

11 [1994] 2 All ER 352.
12 [1990] 2 WLR 186.
13 Pt 54.5.
14 [1956] AC 736.
15 See also *R v Secretary of State for the Environment ex parte Ostler* [1957] 1 QB 574.

Ouster clauses

In order to protect the administrative process, Parliament may attempt to exclude any judicial review of decisions. It does this by inserting an 'ouster clause' in an Act of Parliament. This is problematic for the courts. On the one hand they are under a duty to respect Parliament's will, but on the other hand they have the duty to ensure that public bodies who have been entrusted with powers keep within the scope of those powers and comply with the rule of law.

A look at some case law illustrates the court's approach.

In *R v Medical Appeal Tribunal ex parte Gilmore* (1957)[16] the statute provided that 'the decision on any medical question by a medical appeal tribunal . . . is final'. Gilmore had lost his sight and applied for compensation under an accidental industrial injuries scheme. Rather than be assessed at 100 per cent disabled, the tribunal assessed his disability at 20 per cent – a misinterpretation of the law (an error of law). Could the court correct the error or was its jurisdiction ousted? Lord Denning stated that the word 'final' only meant 'without appeal'. It did not mean that the jurisdiction of judicial review was excluded. Accordingly 'certiorari (now known as a quashing order) can still issue for excess of jurisdiction or for error of law . . .'.

However, in *South East Asia Firebricks v Non-Metallic Mineral Products Manufacturing Employees' Union* (1981) an ouster clause was upheld by the courts. In this case, the Privy Council[17] distinguished between an error of law that was within jurisdiction and one that took the tribunal outside its jurisdiction. Here, the tribunal had applied its mind to the correct questions and any error was not so fundamental as to deprive it of jurisdiction. Accordingly, the ouster clause was respected.

In *Anisminic v Foreign Compensation Commission* (1969),[18] the House of Lords refused to have its jurisdiction ousted. Anisminic had property in Egypt, which was sequestered by the Egyptian authorities and subsequently sold to an Egyptian organisation – TEDO. There was a treaty that provided for the return of sequestered property, but this did not include the time period in which Anisminic's property was taken over. The Foreign Compensation

16 [1957] 1 QB 574.

17 The Judicial Committee of the Privy Council hears appeals from those Commonwealth countries that continue to accept its jurisdiction.

18 [1969] 2 AC 147.

Order 1962 provided that for compensation to be payable, both the applicant and the successor in title had to be British nationals. Anisminic did not qualify because TEDO was not a British organisation. The Foreign Compensation Act 1950 provided that the decision of the Foreign Compensation Commission (FCC) 'shall not be called into question in any court of law'.

Anisminic sought judicial review of the FCC's decision. The House of Lords ruled that its jurisdiction was not ousted and that the FCC's decision was null and void on the basis that it had misinterpreted the Foreign Compensation Order, and that the nationality of the successor in title was not a relevant consideration when the applicant was the original owner of the property. The FCC had acted outside its jurisdiction and the court – notwithstanding the ouster – was entitled to correct its error.

Anisminic raises difficult issues and demonstrates that the courts must be very careful not to have their jurisdiction ousted, even in the face of clear words in a statute. However, it is not always clear when a decision will be so 'bad' that the tribunal had no jurisdiction to make it (and the decision will be declared void) and when a decision is within jurisdiction and the courts will respect the ouster clause.[19]

Justiciability and non-justiciability

In order to avoid trespassing on matters that, for the sake of separation of powers, should be left to either the executive or Parliament to decide, the judges employ the concepts of *justiciability* and *non-justiciability*. 'Justiciability' means that a matter is regarded as suitable for review by the courts. By contract, 'non-justiciability' means that the judges regard the matter as one that should not be reviewed by the courts, but left to the executive or Parliament to determine. In *Council for Civil Service Unions v Minister for the Civil Service* (1985) the House of Lords examined the concept of justiciability, holding that matters such as the appointment of ministers, dissolution of Parliament, grant of honours, treaties and matters of national security were not appropriate subjects for review by the courts. Matters of public policy are also regarded as non-reviewable, particularly when the issue relates to economic policy such as the funding of local authorities. The concept of non-justiciability therefore restricts the scope of judicial review.

The grounds for judicial review

Two key concepts in judicial review are *intra* and *ultra vires*. In other words has the public body acted within the power granted by statute, or has it in some way acted unlawfully and outside its power? The bare concepts, however,

19 See also *Pearlman v Keepers and Governors of Harrow School* [1979] QB 56; *Re Racal Communication Ltd* [1981] AC 374.

do not reveal the many and varied ways in which bodies can act unlawfully. In *Council for Civil Service Unions v Minister for Civil Service* (the *GCHQ* case)[20] the House of Lords took the opportunity to rationalise the heading for judicial review, Lord Diplock stating that these were:

- illegality (has the decision-maker correctly interpreted the relevant law?);
- irrationality (is the decision so outrageous that no sensible person could have arrived at it? A standard derived from the case *Associated Provincial Picture Houses Ltd v Wednesbury Corporation*[21] and referred to as *Wednesbury* unreasonableness);
- procedural impropriety (has the decision-maker failed to observe the required procedural rules or failed to observe the rules of natural justice and/or fairness?).

Lord Diplock also recognised that there may be additions to these three principal grounds, most particularly that of proportionality, which is a well-established principle of law in many European countries. The three established broad headings each represent an umbrella term for more detailed failures on the part of administrators, some of which may overlap in any given situation. These may be summarised as follows:

Irrationality

- *Wednesbury* unreasonableness;
- failing to act proportionately, especially under the Human Rights Act 1998.

Illegality

- errors of law and/or fact;
- attaching onerous conditions;
- using powers for the wrong purpose;
- taking irrelevant factors into account;
- failing to take relevant factors into account;
- acting in bad faith;
- fettering discretion;
- unauthorised delegation of decision-making power;
- failure to act;
- failing to comply with Convention rights.

Procedural impropriety

- failing to comply with mandatory procedures;

20 [1985] AC 374.
21 [1948] 1 KB 223.

- breach of natural justice (the right to a fair hearing; rule against bias);
- breach of Article 6 of the European Convention on Human Rights;
- failing to respect legitimate expectations;
- failing to give reasons.

In order to understand each of these headings more clearly it is necessary to look at some illustrative case law.

Irrationality

Wednesbury unreasonableness

The term 'unreasonableness' is an umbrella term covering a multitude of administrative failures and is interchangeable with the term irrationality. Unreasonableness has been said to encompass bad faith, dishonesty, paying attention to irrelevant considerations, disregarding proper decision-making procedures.[22] Judges use various terms to express the same idea: 'arbitrary and capricious', 'frivolous or vexatious', 'acting perversely'. It must be stressed, therefore, that compartmentalisation of the grounds for judicial review can never be watertight: there are too many overlapping concepts.

The classic explanation of the term comes from *Associated Provincial Picture Houses Ltd v Wednesbury Corporation* (1948). In this case the local authority had the power to attach such conditions as it 'thought fit' to licences granted to open cinemas. In relation to a Sunday licence, the authority attached a condition that no children under the age of 15 could be admitted. Lord Greene MR stated that an authority could, even though it had considered the relevant matters, nevertheless:

> . . . come to a conclusion so unreasonable that no reasonable authority could ever have come to it.

Failing to act proportionately

Proportionality is a key concept in European law – whether the law of the European Union or that of the European Court of Human Rights. It has gradually entered into judicial thought in the UK and today is a commonplace requirement. It does not, however, represent a distinct heading for judicial review, although Lord Diplock in the *GCHQ* case (1985) speculated that it might become one in the future.

The basic idea of proportionality is that decision-makers must do only as much as is necessary to achieve a particular objective, and no more. In everyday language, the phrase 'using a sledgehammer to crack a nut' illustrates what is not proportionate.

22 By Lord Greene MR in the *Wednesbury Corporation* case discussed below.

Where either EU law or the Human Rights Act 1998 is under consideration, proportionality will play an important role. Proportionality has, however, long been an aspect of reasonableness or otherwise of decision-making. For example, as long ago as 1976, Lord Denning MR in *Barnsley Metropolitan Borough Council ex parte Hook* quashed a decision to revoke a stallholder's licence because he had urinated in public, on the ground that the penalty – the loss of the licence – was disproportionate to the 'offence'.

Proportionality was also relevant in *R v Chief Constable of Sussex ex parte International Trader's Ferry Ltd* (1999).[23] The decision of the police to restrict the number of police officers available to prevent demonstrators from obstructing exporters was challenged. In the House of Lords, Lord Slynn stated that when answering the question whether appropriate measures had been taken, the correct approach was to ask whether the steps were proportionate to what was required. Proportionality is thus another way of expressing what is reasonable in the circumstances.

The Human Rights Act 1998, which incorporates European Convention on Human Rights Articles into domestic law, brings the concepts of proportionality and necessity to the forefront. The majority of Convention rights are qualified – that is to say, they are not absolute, but limited by restrictions (for example, in the interests of public safety, or national security) that are 'necessary' in a democratic society. These limitations require the courts to examine the decision-making process to determine whether the action taken was the least likely to undermine the Convention right. In other words, was the action taken both 'necessary and proportionate'?

A case illustrating this new approach is that of *R (Daly) v Secretary of State for the Home Department* (2001).[24] The Home Office had a policy of requiring prisoners to leave their cells so that prison officers could conduct searches, which included scrutinising privileged legal correspondence. The House of Lords ruled the practice unlawful: it was neither necessary nor proportionate.

Proportionality was also at issue in *A v Secretary of State for the Home Department* (2004).[25] In this case, the indefinite imprisonment of foreign terrorist suspects[26] was held to violate their right to liberty (Article 5, ECHR). It was also discriminatory (breaching Article 14 ECHR), insofar as British terrorist suspects were not subject to indefinite imprisonment. The issue of proportionality arose in relation to the government's decision to derogate from Article 5. Derogation is only permitted in a situation that amounts to 'a time or war or other public emergency threatening the life of the nation'. Moreover, the measures taken must be no more 'than strictly required' to deal with the situation.[27] The majority of judges in the House of Lords held

23 [1997] 2 AC 418.
24 [2001] 2 AC 532.
25 [2004] UKHL 56; [2005] 2 AC 68.
26 Under s 23 of the Anti-terrorism, Crime and Security Act 2001.
27 Article 15, European Convention on Human Rights.

that the power contained in section 23 was not 'strictly required', that is, proportionate, to deal with the situation.

The question that now arises is whether or not the doctrines of necessity and proportionality will apply throughout judicial review, and whether they will replace the concept of 'reasonableness', which has applied for so long.

Illegality

Using powers for the wrong purpose

Attorney General v Fulham Corporation (1921).[28] The local authority was empowered to establish washhouses for the use of its residents. Instead it decided to open a commercial laundry. That decision was *ultra vires*.

Westminster Corporation v London and Northern Western Railway Company (1905).[29] The authority had the statutory power to provide public conveniences. It decided to build these midway between two entrances to a new subway. On a challenge to the legality of this decision, the court ruled that provided that the primary purpose for which the power was granted had been achieved, an incidental or complementary objective did not take the authority outside its powers.

R v Secretary of State for Foreign and Commonwealth Affairs ex parte World Development Movement (1995).[30] By statute the Secretary of State had the power to authorise payments to another country only for the purpose of promoting its economic development. The provision of monies for the development of a dam in Malaysia, regarded as economically unsound, did not promote the country's economy and was unlawful.

Relevant and irrelevant considerations

Roberts v Hopwood (1925).[31] The local authority had the statutory power to pay its employees 'as it thought fit'. The council decided to pay

28 [1921] 1 Ch 440.
29 [1905] AC 426.
30 [1995] 1 All ER 611.
31 [1925] AC 725.

men and women equally and to pay them more than the national average. This was unlawful. The council had a duty to its local taxpayers and its decision was in conflict with that.

A case showing the overlap between using powers for the wrong purpose and irrelevant considerations is *R v Somerset County Council ex parte Fewings* (1995).[32] The local authority decided to ban stag hunting on land which it owned and which it had power to regulate under statute. The court ruled that the ban was motivated by the moral objection of the councillors to stag hunting – that was not a legitimate consideration and the decision was unlawful.

In *Wheeler v Leicester City Council* (1985)[33] political motivations also rendered a decision unlawful. The council disapproved of South Africa's then-policy of apartheid and wanted to stop local sportsmen from visiting South Africa. An English rugby team was due to visit South Africa. The team was to include three local players. The council threatened to ban the local club from using its sportsground for a 12-month period. The House of Lords ruled that a political policy could not provide the lawful basis on which to deprive the local club from engaging in its lawful activities.

Onerous conditions

Hall & Co Ltd v Shoreham-by-Sea Urban District Council (1964).[34] The council granted planning permission for a development, subject to the condition that the developer build an access road running the full length of the development. The condition was unlawful: the council was in effect requiring a private company to provide a road for public use without compensation.

Similar considerations applied in *R v Hillingdon London Borough Council ex parte Royco Homes Ltd* (1974). In this case the condition attached to planning permission was that accommodation had to be provided for those on the Council's waiting list for public housing, and that for a

32 [1995] 1 All ER 513; [1995] 3 All ER 20, CA.
33 [1985] AC 1054.
34 [1964] 1 WLR 240.

ten-year period the properties would be occupied by those subject to security of tenure under housing legislation. The conditions were unlawful.

More recently, in *Director of Public Prosecutions v Haw* 2007[35] conditions imposed on a demonstration outside Parliament were held to be *ultra vires* on the ground that they were unclear and unworkable.

Acting in bad faith

Acting in bad faith will usually be linked to some other failure in the administrative process. In essence it means acting with an improper motive or unreasonably.

Unauthorised delegation

Where an Act of Parliament confers decision-making powers to a particular office-holder, it may – depending on the seriousness of the matter in question – be unlawful for that power to be sub-delegated to another. Not all delegations will be unlawful. The courts are prepared to accept, for example, that a minister is not required to personally take every decision for which he is responsible. Two early cases illustrate what is, and what is not, lawful.

In *Carltona v Works Commissioners* (1943)[36] wartime regulations gave the Commissioners the power to requisition property. Carltona's property was requisitioned, the order being signed, for and on behalf of the Commissioners, by a senior civil servant. Accepting the legality of this delegation, Lord Greene MR stated that:

> It cannot be supposed that the particular statutory provision meant that in every case the minister in person should direct his mind to the matter. Constitutionally, the decision of such an officer is the decision of the minister; the minister is responsible to Parliament. If the minister delegated to a junior official then he would have to answer to Parliament. . . .

35 [2007] EWHC 1931; Times LR 11 September.
36 [1943] 2 All ER 560.

By contrast, the delegation in the following case was unlawful.

In *Barnard v National Dock Labour Board* (1953)[37] disciplinary powers had been delegated by statute to the London Dock Board. These were sub-delegated to a port manager. The delegation was *ultra vires*: the powers were intended to be exercised by the Labour Board and must be exercised by the Board.[38]

Fettering discretion

This heading for judicial review entails considering whether an administrative body actually exercised the powers it has, or whether because of some policy it has adopted, it has in effect failed to exercise its powers as required.

For example, in *H Lavender & Sons Ltd v Minister of Housing and Local Government* (1970)[39] the applicant had applied for planning permission to extract sand and gravel from high-grade agricultural land. Being refused, he appealed to the Minister of Housing and Local Government. The Minister rejected his appeal, having been persuaded by the Minister of Agriculture that the land should be preserved for agricultural purposes. The Court ruled that the Minister had acted unlawfully by fettering his discretion: his decision was based solely on another minister's objection. In reality, the decision was that of the Minister of Agriculture and he had no power to make such decisions.

Adopting a rigid policy, which in effect means that the merits of an application will not be considered at all, is also unlawful.

In *Stringer v Minister of Housing and Local Government* (1970)[40] the Court ruled that it was lawful to have a policy, provided that the policy did not result in his failing to take into account relevant issues in each application for planning permission.

In *R v Chief Constable of North Wales Police ex parte AB* (1997)[41] the court upheld the right of the police to have a policy of disclosing to local residents the existence of a paedophile in their neighbourhood. The police had given careful consideration to the particular case and so had not fettered their discretion.

37 [1953] 2 QB 18.

38 See also *R v Talbot Borough Council ex parte Jones* [1988] 2 All ER 207.

39 [1970] 1 WLR 1231. Compare *British Oxygen Co v Board of Trade* [1971] AC 610. See, also, *R v Port of London Authority ex parte Kynoch* [1919] 1 KB 176.

40 [1970] 1 WLR 1281.

41 [1997] 3 WLR 724.

However, in *R v Secretary of State for the Home Department ex parte Simms* (1999)[42] the House of Lords ruled that the Home Office policy of not allowing prisoners to be interviewed by journalists, on the basis that publicity would undermine prison control and discipline was unlawful. The applicants had been convicted of murder but continued to plead their innocence. They had been refused permission to appeal against conviction. They wanted to pursue their claim to justice through the press. The House of Lords ruled that the ban was disproportionate, undermined the rights of prisoners and was unlawful.

Failure to act

If a public body is given power to take action, and simply fails to act at all, that will be unlawful.

For example, in *R v Secretary of State for the Environment ex parte Norwich City Council* (1982)[43] the Council had the duty to sell council houses to tenants at a discounted rate. If the Council failed to act, the Minister could step in and exercise their powers. However, if the Minister failed to step in, the court would oblige him or her to exercise the statutory power.

Procedural impropriety

This third category for judicial review (on Lord Diplock's classification) focuses on whether or not certain procedural requirements have been satisfied. These may be related to a particular procedure to be followed, for example the requirement of consultation in planning matters. Or it may relate to a failure to comply with the common law rules of natural justice or fairness, which the courts will insist should apply in the administrative process.

If a decision-maker ignores a mandatory procedure, the decision will be void.

In *Bradbury v Enfield London Borough Council* (1967)[44] the Education Act 1944 provided that if a local education authority intended to establish new schools or cease to maintain existing schools, notice must

42 [2000] 2 AC 115.
43 [1982] QB 808.
44 [1967] 1 WLR 1311.

be given to the Minister following which public notices must be published in order to allow interested parties to comment. The Council breached the requirement of notice. The Council argued that if they were required to comply with the requirement educational chaos would follow. The court had little sympathy. Lord Denning was clear: '. . . if a local authority does not fulfil the requirements of the law, this court will see that it does fulfil them.'

If, however, an authority fails to comply with an essential procedural requirement but the end result is nevertheless fair, the court may uphold the decision.

In *Berkeley v Secretary of State for the Environment* (2000), the Minister was required to issue an 'environmental statement' in relation to planning permission. He failed to do so. The Court of Appeal ruled that this did not invalidate the decision. The Secretary of State had appointed an inspector and a public hearing had been held at which the environmental impact of the development had been considered. The procedures were sufficiently thorough and effective to enable the inspector to make a sound decision on the matter.

Breach of natural justice or fairness

The rules of natural justice have been developed by the judges to ensure that those who have decision-making powers are obliged to act fairly towards those affected by their decisions. Nowadays, many of the requirements of natural justice are contained in statute. Most prominent of all is the Human Rights Act 1998, which enshrines the right to fair trial (Article 6). Natural justice is, however, a far wider concept than the right to fair trial. There are two basic rules to natural justice, namely:

1. the rule against bias: *nemo iudex in causa sua*; and
2. the right to a fair hearing: *audi alteram partem*.

It should be noted, however, that the requirements of natural justice do not automatically apply to each and every case – different situations will give rise to different requirements. The rules of natural justice are flexible: they are not and should not be rigid. As Lord Bridge explained in *Lloyd v McMahon* (1987):[45]

45 [1987] AC 625; [1987] 2 WLR 821.

> . . . the so called rules of natural justice are not engraved on tablets of stone. To use the phrase which better expresses the underlying concept, what the requirements of fairness demand when any body, domestic, administrative or judicial, has to make a decision which will affect the rights of individuals depends on the character of the decision making body, the kind of question it has to make and the statutory or other framework in which it operates.

The rule against bias

Financial bias

The requirement that a decision-maker acts without bias is a fundamental principle of law. It is reflected in Article 6 of the European Convention, which states that a person is entitled to a fair trial before an 'independent and impartial tribunal established by law'. Bias may take several forms. It may be that the decision-maker has a personal interest – financial or other – in the outcome of a case. If that is so, it may reasonably be thought that the decision-maker is biased. There is no need to establish that the decision-maker is actually biased: it is sufficient if a reasonable person looking at the situation would consider that s/he is likely to be biased. A good example of this is seen in the case of *Dimes v Grand Junction Canal Ltd* (1852).[46]

> In *Dimes* Lord Cottenham LC held shares in the canal company which was involved in litigation. The House of Lords set aside the decision in which he participated, not because he was actually biased but because it was crucial that no one should suspect that he was biased. Accordingly, the mere existence of a financial interest will be sufficient to disqualify a judge from adjudication.

Financial bias was also at issue in the following cases:

> *R v Sussex Justices ex parte McCarthy* (1924).[47] In this case a magistrates' clerk had retired with the magistrates when they were making their decision on a charge of dangerous driving. McCarthy later

46 (1852) 3 HL Cas. 759.
47 [1924] 1 KB 256.

discovered that the clerk was a solicitor who had represented the person who was suing McCarthy for damages. It was held that the magistrates had not sought the clerk's advice, nor had he offered any. Nevertheless, McCarthy's conviction was set aside on the basis of the possibility of bias.

Metropolitan Properties Ltd v Lannon (1969). A property company challenged the decision of a rent assessment committee on the basis that Lannon, a member of the committee, had given legal advice to tenants of a close business associate of the property company. On the question of bias, Lord Denning MR stated that:

> . . . the court looks to the impression which would be given to other people. Even if he was as impartial as he could be, nevertheless, if right minded persons would think that, in the circumstances, there was a real likelihood of bias on his part, then he should not sit. And, if he does sit, his decision cannot stand. . . .

Bromley London Borough Council v Greater London Council (1983).[48] The case concerned the Greater London Council's transport policy which required that all London boroughs contribute to its cost. On the issue of bias, it was held that the fact that all the judges in the Court of Appeal were both taxpayers and users of public transport did not disqualify them from hearing the case.

Other forms of bias

Judges, like everyone else, may show bias in relation to race, sex, politics, background, association and opinions: the forms of possible bias are almost limitless. However, what is crucial is that when adjudicating judges must be completely impartial in relation to the parties before them, and the issue being judged. If a judge cannot meet this requirement s/he should stand down from the case ('recuse' themselves). The most high-profile case of recent years is that of *R v Bow Street Metropolitan and Stipendiary Magistrate ex parte Pinochet Ugarte* (1999).

48 [1983] 1 AC 768; [1982] 2 WLR 62.

Spain was seeking the extradition of the former Chilean head of state, General Pinochet, in order to put him on trial for atrocities carried out during his time as President. Pinochet was on a private visit to Britain at the time. The issue went to the House of Lords. One of the judges, Lord Hoffmann, had links with Amnesty International, the charitable pressure group. Amnesty had been allowed to give evidence to the court. The participation of Lord Hoffmann in the case was challenged by Pinochet's lawyers. The decision was set aside and a rehearing held in front of a new bench of seven judges.

Uncertainty in the test for bias

In *R v Gough* (1993),[49] two different tests for bias were put before the court for consideration. The first was whether a fair, a reasonable and fair-minded person sitting in the court and knowing all the relevant facts would have had a reasonable suspicion that a fair trial of the defendant was not possible: the 'reasonable suspicion' test.

The second was whether there was a real danger or real likelihood that the trial was not fair on the grounds of bias: the 'real likelihood' test. The House of Lords ruled that the correct test was whether there was a real likelihood, in the sense of a real possibility, of bias.

The test for bias was reconsidered in *Porter v Magill*.[50]

It was alleged that the Leader of Westminster Council had adopted a policy of selling certain properties to tenants in the hope that they would vote Conservative in a forthcoming election. The district auditor, Mr Magill, was accused of bias in that he had investigated the allegations and had prejudged the issue. The test for bias came under fresh scrutiny – not least because different approaches were taken to it in the English and Scottish courts and in the Court of Human Rights.

Lord Hope stated that the test for bias should be phrased in the following manner:

> The question is whether the fair-minded and informed observer, having considered the facts, would conclude that there was a real possibility that the tribunal was biased.

49 [1993] 2 All ER 724.
50 [2002] 2 AC 357.

The right to a fair hearing

In addition to impartiality on the part of the decision-maker, fairness requires a number of other considerations, such as:

- the right to be given notice of a hearing;
- the right to be given indications of any adverse evidence;
- the right to be given an opportunity to respond to the evidence;
- the right to an oral hearing;
- the right to legal representation at a hearing;
- the right to question witnesses.

These requirements reflect the requirements of Article 6 of the Convention on Human Rights, now enforceable in the domestic courts under the Human Rights Act 1998. Whether any or all of the above aspects of fair trial are required will depend on the facts of the case. As with Article 6, the courts are concerned with the overall fairness of the proceedings, and an individual defect may not have the effect of rendering proceedings unfair overall. The courts will be very reluctant to find a trial unfair where the individual defect made no difference to the outcome of the proceedings, or where a procedural defect could be remedied on appeal.

Where an individual's rights are at stake, the court will set a high standard of procedural fairness.

For example in *Ridge v Baldwin* (1964)[51] a Chief Constable had been suspended from duty following a charge of conspiracy to obstruct the course of justice. Despite being cleared of any wrongdoing, Ridge was dismissed. He was not given the opportunity to attend and address the meeting which decided on his dismissal. He applied for, and was granted, a declaration that his dismissal was unlawful on the grounds of a breach of natural justice.

The concept of legitimate expectations

Fairness underlies the concept of legitimate expectations. A legitimate expectation will be created in the mind of a person affected by a decision where a decision-maker – by words or actions – leads him or her to believe that certain procedures will be followed, or certain assurances adhered to. Where such an expectation is created, the law will ensure that the expectations are realised and not ignored. The concept of legitimate expectations is primarily designed to ensure that the correct procedures are followed. However, as will be seen

51 [1964] AC 40.

from the *Coughlan* case discussed below, it can also lead to a decision-maker being required to honour an undertaking that involves a matter of substance and not mere procedure.

In *R v Liverpool Corporation ex parte Liverpool Taxi Fleet Operators' Association* (1972),[52] the local authority had given undertakings to the taxi drivers that their licences would not be revoked without prior consultation. When the authority acted in breach of this undertaking, the court ruled that it had a duty to comply with its commitment to consultation.

Assurances were given in the case of *Attorney General for Hong Kong v Ng Yuen Shiu* (1983).[53] The Director of Immigration had given a public undertaking that illegal immigrants would not be deported without first being interviewed. Ng Yuen Shiu, an illegal immigrant, was detained and an order made for his deportation. The Privy Council ruled that while there was no general right to a hearing, nevertheless a legitimate expectation had been created in the mind of the immigrant and accordingly fairness demanded that the deportation order be quashed (set aside).

In *R v North and East Devon Health Authority ex parte Coughlan*,[54] Ms Coughlan was living in a care home. She had been assured by the predecessor to the health authority that her home was hers for life. The Health Authority decided to close the home and to transfer her to the care of the local authority. The Court of Appeal ruled that the assurance given created a legitimate expectation which the court would protect. Moreover, closing the home would represent a breach of Article 8 of the European Convention on Human Rights (the right to respect for private and family life).

Remedies

The granting of a remedy is within the discretion of the court and even where a case is made out, the court may refuse a remedy if there has been an unjustified delay in bringing proceedings, the applicant has acted

52 [1972] 2 QB 299.
53 [1983] 2 AC 629.
54 [1999] LGR 703.

unreasonably or where the cost of a remedy would be damaging to the administrative process.

A quashing order (formerly known as certiorari)

A quashing order is one that sets aside as a nullity the original decision. If only a part of a decision is unlawful, that part may be severed from the good and the quashing order granted only in relation to the bad part.

A prohibiting order (formerly known as prohibition)

This order prevents a body from making a decision that would be capable of being set aside by a quashing order. It is therefore protective in nature and prevents a public body from acting unlawfully in the future.

Mandatory order (formerly known as mandamus)

This order is one that compels an authority to act. It would not be a suitable order where a body has a wide discretion as to how to act. A mandatory order prevents a body from failing to act.

Declarations

A declaration is a statement of the legal position of the parties to proceedings. Accordingly it is not strictly a 'remedy'. Although lacking coercive force, public bodies will respond to declarations.

Injunctions

Injunctions may be positive or negative, temporary or permanent and may be used to prevent a body from acting unlawfully.

Damages

An applicant for judicial review may be granted damages in conjunction with one of the other remedies. They may only be awarded if they would have been recoverable under private law proceedings.

Default powers

An Act of Parliament may confer on a minister the power to act where a decision-making body fails to comply with its duties. If a minister has default powers and fails to use them, this failure may also be remedied by judicial review.

Summary

Judicial review is a process by which individuals or representative groups with a sufficient interest in the matter may challenge the legality of actions and decisions made by public bodies. In order to protect the administrative process from unmeritorious challenges, there are procedural requirements and time limits for bringing an action.

Regulated by the Supreme Court Act 1981, the Civil Procedure Rules 1998, and the common law rules of natural justice, constitutionally judicial review upholds both the supremacy of Parliament (by ensuring that Parliament's intention is upheld) and the rule of law (by keeping public bodies within the law). Judicial review also reflects the separation of powers insofar as the courts have developed the concepts of justiciability and non-justiciability to establish the appropriate allocation of supervisory power between the judges and the executive.

Judicial review focuses on the procedure used to reach a decision. Whereas under appeal proceedings, the merits of the case are re-examined and a new decision reached, in judicial review the court is solely concerned with whether the correct procedure has been used. If it has not, the decision can be set aside and the decision-maker required to retake the decision according to law. The court is not substituting its decision for that of the decision-maker.

The grounds on which an application for judicial review may be made are judge-made and subject to development. The influence of European law is being felt in judicial review, with concepts such as that of proportionality, which supplements the traditional grounds and is increasingly being used to evaluate the legality of administrative action.

Further reading

Cane, P, 'Accountability and the Public/Private Distinction', in N Bamforth and P Leyland (eds), *Public Law in a Multi-Layered Constitution*, 2003, Oxford: Hart Publishing.

Cane, P, *Introduction to Administrative Law* (4th edn, 2004), Oxford: Clarendon Press, Chapter 3.

Craig, P, 'Competing Models of Judicial Review' [1999] PL 428.

Craig, P, 'The Common Law, Shared Power and Judicial Review' (2004), 24 OJLS 129.

Craig, P, 'Judicial Review, Appeal and Factual Error' [2004] PL 788.

Fordham, M, 'Judicial Review: the new rules' [2001] PL 4.

Jowell, J, 'Of *vires* and Vacuums: the Constitutional Context of Judicial Review', [1999] PL 448.

Jowell, J, 'Beyond the Rule of Law: Towards Constitutional Judicial Review', [2000] PL 671.

Le Sueur, A, 'Three Strikes and it's out? The UK government strategy to oust judicial review from immigration and asylum decision-making' [2004] PL 225.

Lever, A, 'Is Judicial Review Undemocratic?' [2007] PL 280.

Oliver, D, 'Public Law Procedures and Remedies – Do we need them?' [2002] PL 91.

Rivers, J, 'Proportionality and the Variable Intensity of Review' [2006] CLJ 174.
Steele, I, 'Substantive Legitimate Expectations: Striking the Right Balance' (2005) 121 LQR 300.
Woolf, Lord, 'The Rule of Law and a Change in the Constitution' [2004] CLJ 317.

SELF-ASSESSMENT QUESTIONS

1. Which statute regulates the jurisdiction for judicial review?
2. Write a brief definition of the phrases 'intra vires' and 'ultra vires'.
3. Name the three principal headings that represent grounds for judicial review.
4. Several subheadings fall under these three principal headings, list at least four.
5. Write a brief sentence defining the word 'proportionality'.
6. List the remedies that are available under judicial review.

SAMPLE EXAMINATION QUESTIONS

1. Judicial review of administrative action does little to protect the rights of the individual against the power of the state.'

   Do you agree?
2. 'In making sense of the inconsistencies in the application of the rules of natural justice, it should never be forgotten that natural justice is not intended to be a precise and uniform code of procedure.' (de Smith)

   Discuss.

Chapter 14

Ombudsmen

CONTENTS

KEY WORDS AND PHRASES

Maladministration	Not defined in statute. Neglect, delay, incompetence, arbitrariness and so on
MP filter	The requirement that complaints initially go to a Member of Parliament
Ombudsman	Swedish, meaning a representative of the people

Introduction

The word 'ombudsman' is Swedish and means a representative of the people. In Sweden the office of Justitieombudsman was established in 1809. Since that time, but mostly during the mid-twentieth century, countries throughout the world adopted some form of office of ombudsman.

In 1959 the British section of the International Commission of Jurists, JUSTICE, established an inquiry into grievances against the administration of government. The existing mechanisms for the handling of complaints against government departments were found to be inadequate. If a person complained to the department, the department would handle the complaint. If a Member of Parliament (MP) was approached to look into the matter, s/he had no powers to compel the department to disclose information or to put the matter right. The JUSTICE report, *The Citizen and the Administration*, 1961, advocated setting up an additional avenue for the redress of grievances, modelled on the same lines as the Swedish Ombudsman.

In 1967, the Parliamentary Commissioner Act was passed. Since that time there have been several other similar offices introduced in the public sector. Furthermore, in the commercial sector, similar offices have been introduced. The existing scheme for Commissioners for Administration in the governmental sector is as follows:

Parliamentary Commissioner for Administration	1967
Parliamentary Commissioner for Administration and Commissioner for Complaints (Northern Ireland)	1969
Health Services Commissioners, England, Wales and Scotland	1972
Local Government Commissioners: England and Wales	1974
Local Government Commissioner: Scotland	1975
Legal Services Commissioner	1990
Scottish Parliamentary Commissioner	1998
Welsh Administration Ombudsman	1998
Public Services Ombudsman for Wales	2005

In addition, a European Union Ombudsman was introduced in 1992.

The Parliamentary Commissioner for Administration

Appointment

The Parliamentary Commissioner (PCA) is appointed by the Crown on the advice of the government, following consultation with the Chairman of the House of Commons' Select Committee on the Parliamentary Commissioner for Administration. The post is held 'during good health and behaviour' and is effectively until retirement. The office of Parliamentary Commissioner and Health Service Commissioner is held by the same person, usually a former senior civil servant.

The constitutional position of the PCA

The Commissioner investigates government administration and reports to Parliament. He or she has the equivalent powers of a High Court judge and it is an offence to obstruct the investigations of the Commissioner.

The aims and objectives of the Parliamentary and Health Service Ombudsman

The purpose of the office, according to the Commissioner's 2003–2004 Business Plan, is to:

- consider and resolve complaints impartially and promptly and to achieve appropriate redress of grievances;
- to report the results to complainants, MPs and the bodies complained about; and
- to promote improvements in public services by feeding back the lessons learned from casework to policy makers and providers.

The complaints procedure

Complaints must be made in writing and made to the citizen's MP. This requirement enables the MP to attempt to investigate the matter, and resolve it if possible. However, if that is not possible, the MP may forward the matter to the PCA for investigation and report.

The 'MP filter' is not something that applies in many other countries and has been the source of complaint by successive PCAs.

The basis for the complaint, under section 5(1) of the 1967 Act, is that a person 'claims to have sustained injustice in consequence of maladministration'.

The meaning of 'maladministration'

Maladministration is not defined in the Act. In debate in Parliament the Minister responsible for introducing the Bill, Richard Crossman, described maladministration as including 'bias, neglect, inattention, delay, incompetence, ineptitude, perversity, turpitude, arbitrariness and so on'.

Maladministration is a more limited concept than that employed in other jurisdictions. In Denmark, for example, the ombudsman may examine 'mistakes' and 'unreasonable decisions', and in Norway the ombudsman can investigate decisions that are 'clearly unreasonable'. In the UK, being tied to the concept of maladministration, the PCA is not concerned with the merits of any decision taken, nor the fairness or otherwise of the rules governing any situation, but rather with the manner in which the rules have been applied.

Jurisdiction

Schedule 2 of the Parliamentary Commissioner Act 1967 sets out those departments subject to the PCA's jurisdiction. The Parliamentary and Health Service Commissioners Act 1987 extended the Commissioner's jurisdiction to cover some non-departmental bodies. The complete list of bodies within the Commissioner's jurisdiction is now in Schedule 1 to the 1987 Act, as amended by the 1994 Parliamentary Commissioner Act.

Matters that are excluded from the Commissioner's jurisdiction include:

- the work of the police;
- nationalised industries;
- Cabinet office and Prime Minister's Office;
- the Parole Board;
- Bank of England;
- Criminal Injuries Compensation Board;
- Government commercial and contractual transactions.

The Commissioner may not investigate any matter where the complainant has a right of appeal or to review by the courts.

Other excluded matters, set out in Schedule 3 to the Parliamentary Commissioner Act 1967, include:

- matters relating to the government's relations with foreign governments;
- matters relating to the administration of overseas territories;
- matters relating to extradition;
- matters relating to national security;
- the exercise of the prerogative of mercy;

- matters relating to the employment of the armed forces and other offices under the Crown;
- the grant of honours.

The Commissioner's discretion

Where a matter falls within the PCA's jurisdiction, the Commissioner has discretion as to whether to accept the complaint. Because of this broad discretion, the prospect of having the Commissioner successfully judicially reviewed is slim.

Investigation and report

The 1967 Act confers strong powers on the Commissioner. He or she has the same power as a court of law in respect of access to documents and the examination of witnesses. Under section 10, where the Commission accepts jurisdiction and investigates a complaint, a report of the findings is sent to the complainant and the principal officer of the department concerned. If the matter has not been remedied, or is unlikely to be, s/he may lay a special report before each House of Parliament. The Commissioner produces an Annual Report, which is laid before Parliament.

The Commissioner has no power to grant a remedy or to grant compensation. He or she does, however, make recommendations as to the appropriate remedy and the level of suitable compensation.

The select committee

The Commissioner is aided by a select committee, which considers the annual and special reports of the Parliamentary and Health Service Commissioner. The committee takes evidence from government departments and health authorities on matters arising from reports in order to ensure that all reasonable effects are made to tighten up procedures, prevent the repetition of faults and provide any appropriate remedy. The committee is able to exert pressure on government to comply with the recommendations of the Commissioner.

The volume of complaints

In 2005–2006 the Parliamentary and Health Service Ombudsman handled 14,510 enquiries. In 2006 to 2007, the number of cases accepted for investigation and concluded by the Parliamentary Commissioner was 1,363 and by the Health Commissioner – 1,139.

Reform of the office of Parliamentary Commissioner

The requirement that citizens must first send their complaint to their MP is a restriction that does not apply elsewhere. The filter also does not apply in relation to the Health Service Ombudsman. However, when the Select Committee on the Parliamentary and Health Service Ombudsman looked into the matter in the 1990s, it concluded – as did a majority of MPs surveyed – that the advantages outweighed the disadvantages. The Committee was against restricting the ability of MPs to deal with complaints of their constituents.

The Health Service Commissioner

The Health Service Act 1977 provides that the Commissioner may investigate regional, district and special health authorities, the Mental Health Commission, Dental Practice Board and National Health Service Trusts.

The Health Service Commissioner has jurisdiction to investigate any matter relating to an alleged failure to provide a service and any other action taken on behalf of the body in question – a far broader power than that covered by 'maladministration'. A complaint, however, must be one that involves injustice or hardship suffered as a result of the failure or other action.

Individuals have the right of direct access to the Commissioner.

Commissioners for Northern Ireland, Scotland and Wales

Northern Ireland, Scotland and Wales each have a Parliamentary Commissioner for Administration with similar powers and functions as the English Parliamentary Commissioner.

Local Government Commissioners

The Local Government Act 1974 established Commissioners for Local Administration for England and Wales. The Scottish system was established under the Local Government (Scotland) Act 1975.[1] Commissioners are appointed by the Crown and hold office 'during good behaviour'.

Commissioners have jurisdiction to investigate any complaint of maladministration or failure in service provision by council committees, their members and officers of the council. Police authorities, water boards, development corporations and those bodies with whom the council has partnership

1 See now s 91 Scotland Act 1998.

agreements for the provision of services are also within the Commissioners' jurisdiction.

Since 1989 the public has had a right of direct access to the Commissioners.

Further reading

Abraham, A, 'The Ombudsman as Part of the UK Constitution: A Contested Role?' (2007) 61.1 Parliamentary Affairs, 601.
McMurtie, SN, 'The Waiting Game – The Parliamentary Commissioner's Response to Delay in Administrative Procedures' [1997] PL 159.
Millett, Lord, 'The Right to Good Administration in Europe' [2002] PL 309.

SELF-ASSESSMENT QUESTIONS

1. List three examples of 'maladministration'.
2. What is meant by the 'MP filter'?
3. Is the Parliamentary Commissioner obliged to investigate a complaint?
4. What remedies can the Parliamentary Commissioner grant?
5. To which body is the Parliamentary Commissioner accountable?

SAMPLE EXAMINATION QUESTIONS

Compare and contrast the strengths and weaknesses of seeking a remedy under proceedings for judicial review and through the Parliamentary Commissioner for Administration.

Chapter 15

A very brief history

CONTENTS

Introduction

The majority of constitutions around the world are in written form and their origins can be traced to a specific date in history. The United Kingdom's Constitution, by contrast, is one that has never been rationally constructed and formally written down, but has gradually evolved over the centuries. To study public law successfully, it is not essential to have an in-depth knowledge of constitutional history, but having an appreciation of some of the issues and the most important periods of development does make the contemporary Constitution and its different elements easier to understand.

The UK today comprises the four nations of England, Northern Ireland, Scotland and Wales. It was not always that way. It was Henry VIII (reigned 1509–1547) who claimed the island of Ireland as his own. It was to remain united with England until 1922 when the island was divided – six counties in the north remaining united with England while the south became the independent Republic of Ireland. Scotland was united with England through the Acts of Union 1706/07,[1] which created Great Britain. Wales on the other

1 The difference in dates being explained by the two countries using different calendar years.

hand was conquered in the twelfth century and has been united with England since that time.

Early origins: 1066–1500

As every schoolchild is supposed to know, at the Battle of Hastings in 1066, the Norman King, William, beat the English King Harold and claimed the English Crown. William set about unifying the differing areas of England (any union with Ireland, Scotland and Wales lay far in the future). He also undertook a nationwide survey of the land and property: the *Domesday Book*, a clear record of where wealth and influence lay.

It was in the reign of Henry II (1154–1189) that a legal system common to all of England developed. The King installed a system of courts staffed by the King's judges, with the task of establishing common procedures and a law common to all: the English common law.

From these early days of a united England, kings and queens held near absolute power. That power supposedly derived from God, the 'divine right of Kings'. In order to keep their power, however, kings and queens, were dependent upon their supporters who not only provided financial support but also men to fight in support of the King. It was a two-way relationship: in exchange for support the king or queen granted land and titles – the origins of the contemporary honours system.

In the reign of King John (1199–1216), discontent with the system of taxation and complaints about the criminal justice system administered by the Crown led to the first formal limitation of royal power: *Magna Carta* 1215. *Magna Carta* was an agreement between the aristocracy and the Crown. It established the right to jury trial, thereby ensuring that a citizen's liberty could only be removed by a legal process rather than by the arbitrary exercise of royal power. Furthermore, *Magna Carta* proclaimed that the King was accountable to law, laying the foundation for the idea of government under – rather than over – law.

The king's loyal supporters and advisers made up the House of Lords, the earliest of the two chambers of Parliament to be established. Gradually it became the practice for the king to summon representatives of the common people to advise him: it was in the thirteenth century that the House of Commons came into being. By Edward III's reign (1327–1377) members of the House of Commons were elected to represent local areas. The system was far from democratic. It was not the 'ordinary' men and women who voted but rather those who owned property (it was to be the twentieth century before the right to vote was fully extended to all men and women, irrespective of property).

1500–1700

In the reign of Henry VIII (1509–1547), a situation arose which was to have a profound consequence for the future. England at the time was a Roman Catholic country, its religious head being the Pope in Rome. Henry VIII had first married his deceased brother's widow, Catherine of Aragon. Catherine gave Henry a daughter, later Queen Mary, but not a male heir. Henry turned his attentions to Ann Boleyn. The Roman Catholic Church did not recognise divorce and marriages could only be formally set aside by a decree of nullity issued by the Church. Henry sought an annulment, claiming that his first marriage was not valid on account of Catherine being his deceased brother's widow. The Pope refused Henry's request. Determined to get his way, Henry declared that England would no longer follow the Catholic Church, but rather establish its own church, the head of which would be the King. And so the Church of England came into being. Henry's marriage to Catherine was annulled and Henry married Ann.[2]

The break with Rome ushered in a period of severe religious repression. Mary Tudor, Henry's daughter by Catherine of Aragon (reigned 1553–1558), was an ardent Roman Catholic. She married the Catholic heir to the Spanish throne, Philip, and was intent on re-establishing Catholicism in England. Elizabeth I (reigned 1558–1603), Henry VIII's daughter by Anne Boleyn, by contrast, firmly established the Church of England. The political situation at home was complicated by the fact that England was now a Protestant country while her sometime allies (sometime enemies) to the south – France, Italy and Spain – remained Catholic.[3] Nevertheless, Elizabeth I's long reign was characterised by religious tolerance and a flourishing of the arts. Furthermore, England was now established as an international power. The Tudor era ended with Elizabeth's death in 1603, the crown being assumed by James VI of Scotland who assumed the title of James I of England, thereby uniting the two countries under a common crown.[4]

James' reign was characterised by a shortage of money. When Parliament denied him funds he resorted to issuing proclamations to achieve his objective, thereby making law without Parliament's consent. When a judge had the impertinence to challenge the King's use of the prerogative to make new law, the King dismissed the judge – Coke CJ.[5]

The reign of Charles I (1625–1649) was also one marked by tensions between the Crown and Parliament. Charles I was autocratic and made full use of his royal powers. When Parliament displeased him, he dismissed it and

2 Ann Boleyn was beheaded and Henry would go on to marry Jane Seymour, Anne of Cleves, Catherine Howard and Catherine Parr.

3 The Protestant Reformation took hold in Northern Europe and also in Scotland.

4 James succeeded under the terms of the Treaty of Berwick, 1586, agreed by Elizabeth and James.

5 See the *Case of Proclamations* (1610) 12 Co Rep 74; 2 St Tr 723.

assumed the power to rule under the prerogative. This abuse of power was, however, to lead to civil war, which first broke out in 1641. Charles I was tried for treason and executed in 1649. England was now under military rule. Oliver Cromwell declared himself Protector of England. The monarchy was abolished, as was the House of Lords and the Church of England.

Under Cromwell, Britain became a republic. A period of puritanical rule commenced, with music, dancing and all forms of entertainment banned and acts of immorality met with harsh punishment. In 1653 Cromwell drafted a written constitution – the Commonwealth Constitution – for England, Scotland and Ireland, but it was never to come into being. By the end of the 1650s England had had enough of military rule. Following Oliver Cromwell's death and the inability of his son to assert the same authority as his father, the monarchy was restored.

While civil war raged in England, Charles I's heir was in France. His return to England as Charles II (reigned 1660–1685), not only restored the monarchy, but also ushered in a period in which culture, science and the arts flourished and international trade expanded. During this period also, the seeds of what would later become the two main political parties – Conservative and Liberal (although going by different names) – were sown.

When Charles II died he was succeeded by his brother James II (reigned 1685–1688). Although Charles II was suspected of remaining sympathetic to Roman Catholicism, he gave little outward sign of it. James II, however, was blatantly Catholic, appointing Catholics to public posts and the army, and suspending laws that penalized Catholics. He sought complete religious toleration and issued Declarations of Indulgence to secure that end. Concern grew that James and Mary would produce a male heir to the throne who would return England to the Catholic Church and, indeed, in 1688 a son was born. Having lost the support of those he relied on, James fled the country. While James had been abusing his position and using powers to reintroduce Catholics to public life, negotiations had been entered into with James's Protestant son-in-law, William of Orange, with the intent that William and his wife Mary should seize the throne. With James fleeing, their arrival was peaceful.

Kings and queens were no longer to enjoy the wide-ranging powers of the past. William (reigned 1689–1702) and Mary assumed the throne under the conditions provided for in the *Bill of Rights* 1689. The right to suspend Parliament's laws, the right to raise taxation without Parliament's consent and the right to raise and keep an army without Parliament's consent were abolished. Article 9 of the *Bill of Rights* provided absolute protection for freedom of speech in parliamentary proceedings – a protection that remains today. The right for Parliament to meet regularly was asserted. The right to trial by jury, first provided for by *Magna Carta* was reaffirmed. However, while the *Bill of Rights* restricted some of the powers of the Crown, it left many prerogative powers in tact. Moreover, it did not address the succession to the Crown or the position of the judges: it was to be 1701 before those issues were tackled under the Act of Settlement.

1700–1901

The Act of Settlement provided that succession to the throne should be restricted to Protestant heirs and, moreover, that no heir to the throne could marry a Roman Catholic.[6] The Act of Settlement also protected the independence of judges by providing that senior judges could only be removed from office by a successful address to both Houses of Parliament.[7]

William and Mary were succeeded by Queen Anne (reigned 1702–1714) – the younger daughter of James II. It was during Anne's reign that the union between England and Scotland was secured. Although united with England under the same Crown (from the reign of James I), Scotland retained its own sovereign law-making Parliament. Under the Acts of Union of England and Scotland, both the English and Scottish Parliaments were effectively abolished, giving rise to the single Parliament of Great Britain.

When Queen Anne died in 1714 the Crown passed from the House of Stuart to the House of Hanover – to George I – the son of Anne's named (but now deceased) successor. By this time Britain was established as a world military power with a large army and expanding navy. Maintaining Britain's international power was expensive and the King required Parliament's and the people's support. George I (reigned 1714–1727), however, was not a popular King. His English was poor and he had little interest in England. George appointed a 'first minister' – Sir Robert Walpole – who served for over 20 years – in effect the first Prime Minister of Britain.

The emergence of the Cabinet – the innermost circle of contemporary central government – came in the reign of George II (1727–1760).[8] Society was also undergoing change. While the majority of the population remained involved in agriculture, new production techniques led to industrial expansion. Allied to that came greater urbanisation and the development of the road system. In 1760, George III came to the throne (reigned until 1820). Britain's empire was growing: under the Treaty of Paris Britain acquired Canada, parts of southeastern America and islands of the Caribbean from the French. However, unrest in the North American colonies was on the increase. In 1765, under the Stamp Act, the British imposed direct taxation on the colonies for the first time. The sentiment of 'no taxation without representation' fuelled revolt and the government abolished the Act. Import duties on goods continued to be levied, as did rebellion, which culminated in

6 A restriction that still remains in place.

7 See, now, the Supreme Court Act 1981. Also, see, the Constitutional Reform Act 2005.

8 Note that local government predated central government by some centuries. Today the system is entirely statutory.

the Boston Tea Party of 1773 in which 342 chests of tea were dumped in the sea. Full-scale revolution started in 1775, and the Congress of 13 colonies formally passed the Declaration of Independence on 4 July 1776. War with Britain escalated, ending in 1783 with the British acceptance of American independence and the signing of the Treaty of Paris in 1783.

In 1789 the French revolution swept away centuries of aristocratic rule. In 1793 France declared war on Britain and Holland and conflict in Europe was to endure until 1815. The French revolution and years of war brought change. While Britain now had a vast empire, at home there was economic depression and mass unemployment. Amidst the hardship came demands for political reform and universal male suffrage. Reform came in 1832. The Representation of the People Act 1832 reformed constituencies and extended the conditions that qualified adult males to vote and introduced a register of voters. The right to vote was confined to those with property: men without property and women were still not entitled to vote. By this time the Industrial Revolution was moving apace. Cities were developing around the centres of industrial production. Workers organised into unions to press for better conditions.[9] Economic and industrial change forced the government into a massive extension of legal regulation into such areas as health, factories, housing and employment.

By the time Victoria came to the throne in 1837 (reigned until 1901), the Constitution was much changed. The office of Prime Minister, and the Cabinet were now established as the executive. Over the eighteenth century, two distinctive political parties (Tories and Whigs) had become established, each offering voters political choice. The House of Commons had acquired greater legitimacy due to the reformed electoral system. The role of the monarch had also changed. No longer exercising autocratic power, the Crown was perceived as being above politics. As the political journalist Walter Bagehot expressed it, she had the 'right to be consulted, the right to encourage and the right to warn'.[10] The monarchy had been transformed into a 'constitutional monarchy'. In George III's reign (1760–1820) the Civil List had been introduced. This agreement between Parliament and the Crown, provided for the public finding of the official work of the monarch in exchange for the surrender of much of the hereditary revenues of the Crown.[11]

Constitutional conventions had developed alongside the evolution of the executive, which was now perceived to be accountable to Parliament. While the Crown retained the formal power to summon and dissolve Parliament, the convention had developed that Parliament would be dissolved only at the request of the Prime Minister. The Crown also retained the formal right to

9 A former ban on unionisation was repealed in 1824.

10 *The English Constitution*, (1867), 1993 London: Fontana.

11 See the Civil List Acts 1952, 1972 and 1975. The Queen first became liable to income tax on her private income in 1993.

reject a Bill when it had passed through both the House of Commons and House of Lords. However, the convention had developed that the Crown would grant the necessary Royal Assent (without which a Bill cannot become law) to a Bill that had duly passed both Houses. No formal legal rules existed regarding the choice of Prime Minister or in which House of Parliament s/he should sit. However, by convention, the Crown appointed the leader of that political party which won the majority of seats in a general election and could command a majority in the House of Commons.[12] In the early nineteenth century, the Duke of Wellington (Prime Minister 1828–1830) commented that it would be more appropriate for the Prime Minister to sit in the House of Commons – the elected House – rather than the Lords. The last Prime Minister to sit in the House of Lords was Lord Salisbury (1886–1892) and it is now a firm convention (but not law) that the Prime Minister is a member of the Commons.

It was towards the end of the nineteenth century that the origins of today's Labour Party are found, coming into being with the objective of providing representation in Parliament for ordinary working men and women.[13] Whereas Members of Parliament had hitherto regarded their parliamentary work as public service for which no payment was made, for those who were to become representatives of the working class, sponsorship was needed to help meet the costs, not only of standing for Parliament, but also to enable them to carry out their parliamentary duties. It was in 1911 that salaries first became payable to members of the House of Commons.[14]

1902–present

Victoria died in 1901, to be succeeded by Edward VII (1901–1910). It was in this decade that a protracted struggle took place between the House of Commons and House of Lords over their respective legislative powers. As the Commons grew in democratic legitimacy, so the convention became established that the House of Lords would give way to the Commons over matters of national finance.[15] However, the Liberal government's budget proposals were controversial and the House of Lords, in breach of convention, rejected them. A general election later, and a threat by the King (now George V) to create enough new peers to force the legislation through, the House of Lords

12 A personal decision had to be made when there was no obvious candidate. This ended only in the 1960s, when the major parties introduced their own system of electing their leader.

13 The right to vote having been considerably extended by the Reform Act 1867. Women did not get the right to vote until 1928.

14 Members of the House of Lords are not salaried. They receive a daily allowance for attendance.

15 There is a further convention that requires that the Lords give way to legislation that gives effect to a government's policies which were put to the electorate at a general election on the ground that the electorate had 'mandated' the policy(ies).

gave way. The Parliament Act 1911 was enacted to avoid future conflicts, setting a strict timetable in which the Lords could reject a proposal and allowing the Commons to seek the Royal Assent without the Lords agreement at the end of the specified period, thereby ensuring the ultimate legislative supremacy of the Commons.[16]

That decade also saw a battle over the future status of Ireland, which had become united with England, Scotland and Wales under the Act of Union 1800. The nineteenth century had brought economic disaster to Ireland and thousands emigrated. In addition, there was discrimination in the provision of education and in property rights against the majority of the population, who were Roman Catholics. Dissatisfaction with British rule turned to violence and the demand for home rule grew. However, one of the obstacles to home rule lay in the significant minority of Protestants who had settled in Ireland over the centuries and who vehemently rejected any idea of being ruled by an independent Irish state. The solution lay in separating a part of Ireland off from the rest. As the situation worsened and Civil War looked imminent, the First World War (1914–1918) erupted, postponing any settlement over Ireland.

In 1920 the Government of Ireland Act was passed, partitioning the country, with six of the northern counties being separated from the remainder. In 1921 an Anglo-Irish Treaty was signed, giving the Irish Free State (southern Ireland) the right to self-governance within the British Commonwealth. The Constitution of the Irish Free State was published in 1937, declaring independence from Britain. It was not to be until 1949 that the United Kingdom formally accepted Irish independence.

Electoral reform continued with women finally being given the right to vote in 1928. Meanwhile, the pressure on Parliament's time and energy had led to a massive growth in delegated, or secondary, legislation. This in turn gave rise to increased legal challenges by way of applications for judicial review to test whether the powers conferred by Parliament had been correctly interpreted and applied by those bodies on which they were conferred.

The Second World War, 1939–1945, tore Britain and Europe apart, with millions of people killed or displaced and economies ruined. But out of this devastation came two developments of profound constitutional importance. The first was the founding of the Council of Europe in 1949 with the express objective of improving the protection of civil rights and freedoms on a European-wide basis. Britain played a key role in drafting the European Convention on Human Rights, which came into being under the auspices of the Council of Europe. However, the idea of allowing citizens to apply to a court outside the UK for the protection of their rights was something that the

16 The 1911 Act was amended by the Parliament Act 1949, which reduced the permitted period of delay by the Lords.

government was not prepared to allow. That right only came into being in the 1960s. Nevertheless, the case law from the Court of Human Rights in Strasbourg has had a major influence, not only in findings against the British government for having breached citizens rights, but also in promoting the idea that a Bill of Rights that could be enforced before the local courts should be introduced. That was not to happen until the Human Rights Act 1998.

The second European development was the signing of treaties that would lead, ultimately, to the introduction of the European Union (EU). Initially, the objective was to ensure that the raw materials of war – coal, steel and atomic energy – should be placed beyond the control of nation states and regulated by 'supranational organisation'. Towards this end the European Coal and Steel Community (ECSC) and the Atomic Energy Community (Euratom) were introduced in treaties of 1951 and 1957. The next development was economic: the desire to create a tariff-free trading block that would make Europe more competitive on the world stage and also raise standards of living within its Member States. This was achieved, with six original members, in 1957, under the Treaty of Rome. Britain again stood aloof, only to have her first application for membership blocked by the French government. It was 1972 before Britain signed the Treaty of Rome and Community law entered into domestic law under the European Communities Act 1972, with effect from January 1973. The three Communities were subsequently merged and nowadays the European Community represents the largest component of the EU, which was introduced in 1992 and now has 27 Member States.

By 1996 a Conservative government had been in power for 18 years. The Labour Party, then under the leadership of Tony Blair, pledged significant constitutional reform if elected to office. The general election of 1997 brought in a Labour government with a majority of 179 seats in the House of Commons. Among the promised reforms were reform of the still unelected House of Lords, reform of electoral law, the introduction of a Human Rights Act, devolution of power to the nations of Scotland and Wales and redevolution of power to Northern Ireland. In addition, there was to be established a London-wide form of government and London Mayor. Devolution was the first reform to be effected.[17] In relation to the House of Lords, the government decided on a two-stage process. First, would be the removal of all the hereditary peers, to be followed by reform aimed to increase the democratic legitimacy of the House. The House of Lords Act 1999 managed to remove all but 92 hereditary peers. In 2009, further reform is still awaited.

On the electoral front, a Commission was established to consider the voting system used for general elections. In the event, the Report proposed a

17 See the Scotland Act 1998, Government of Wales Act 1998, Northern Ireland Act 1998, Greater London Authority Act 1999. Note that devolution to Northern Ireland was suspended due to breaches of the terms of the peace settlement between the various parties. A redevolution of power once again occurred in 2007.

'mixed system' – retaining the present system but adding to it an element of proportional representation. No further action has been taken. Legal regulation of political parties, however, has been increased. The Political Parties, Elections and Referendums Act 2000 introduced an Electoral Commission with the task of overseeing the democratic process. Political parties are now required to register all financial donations to the Party in order to achieve greater transparency in the political process. Furthermore, there is now a fixed limit to the amount of money that can be spent by the political parties at a general election.[18]

The Human Rights Act 1998 makes the majority of European Convention Rights enforceable before the local courts. It is now unlawful for any public authority to act in contravention of Convention rights, unless an Act of Parliament makes it impossible for them to act otherwise. Carefully drafted, the Act ensures that Parliament's supremacy is maintained and that the separation of powers between the judiciary and Parliament is preserved by ensuring that judges cannot challenge the validity of an Act of Parliament, but rather declare that the Act is incompatible with Convention rights.

It was in part the European Convention on Human Rights that brought about reform of the ancient office of Lord Chancellor. The Lord Chancellor formerly held positions in each of the three major institutions of the state. He sat as Speaker of the House of Lords. He was a political appointment with a seat in Cabinet. He was also head of the judiciary, with powers of appointment. Challenges in the courts questioned this breach of separation of powers. The end result was the Constitutional Reform Act 2005, which provides for most of the Lord Chancellor's functions in relation to the judges to be transferred to the Lord Chief Justice. The office of Lord Chancellor remains, but the Chancellor will no longer act as Speaker of the House of Lords and need no longer be a member of that House. The first Lord Chancellor following reform was a member of the House of Commons and held the office of Lord Chancellor in conjunction with the newly established office of Secretary of State for Justice.

The Constitutional Reform Act 2005 also provides for a new Supreme Court to be established. Currently, the highest domestic court is the Appellate Committee of the House of Lords. The judges in the House of Lords, the Laws Lords,[19] are appointed under the Appellate Jurisdiction Act 1856 and in addition to acting as judges, are also members of the House of Lords, sitting as legislators. This comes to an end in 2009 with the establishment of the Supreme Court. The judges are to be known as Justices of the Supreme Court

18 There have been strict legal controls over individual candidate's expenditure during an election campaign for a long time, but until the recent Act no control over national party expenditure.

19 Technically, Lords of Appeal in Ordinary.

and will no longer be entitled to participate in the legislative work of the House of Lords, although retired Justices will be permitted to sit.

The future

In 2007 the government published its latest proposals for constitutional reform. In *The Governance of Britain*[20] the government proposed to surrender or limit a number of its prerogative powers to parliamentary control. The most important of these include: the power to deploy troops abroad; request the dissolution of and recall of Parliament; ratify treaties; decide the rules governing entitlement to passports; and the granting of pardons. The government also proposes to increase parliamentary scrutiny of some public appointments and to review the role of the Attorney General, develop further reforms for the House of Lords, and regulation of the Civil Service. The Draft Constitutional Renewal Bill sets out proposals to implement the Government's Green Paper, *The Governance of Britain.* At the time of publication of *Understanding Public Law,* the consultation process between the government and interested bodies was continuing.

Also before Parliament at the time of publication is the Political Parties and Elections Bill 2007–08 to 2008–09. This Bill aims to strengthen the regulatory powers of the Electoral Commission. It will also amend the definition of 'election expenses' and 'candidate' in the Representation of the People Act 1983 to take into account spending on elections prior to the dissolution of Parliament. The Bill will impose further requirements on political parties and donors to clarify the source of donations. It will also amend the Representation of the People Act to provide a more flexible system for adding to the register of electors.

Finally, there is the Draft Equality Bill which is expected to be passed in 2010. This will overhaul the law relating to equality and discrimination, bringing together the existing laws, from the Race Relations Acts of the 1960s to the 2005 Disability Discrimination Act and more than 100 statutory instruments.

The government also proposes to open a national debate on 'British values' and citizenship and to consider introducing a British Bill of Rights and Duties to supplement the Human Rights Act and to consider whether to introduce a written constitution. It is recognised by the government that this is a process that will require an extended period of consultation and debate.

20 Cm 7170. www.official-documents.gov.uk/document/cm71/7170/7170.pdf.

Index